MASS MEDIA WRITING

Telling a Good Story Well

John P. McHale

Illinois State University

Kendall Hunt
publishing company

Cover image © Shutterstock, Inc.

Kendall Hunt
publishing company

www.kendallhunt.com
Send all inquiries to:
4050 Westmark Drive
Dubuque, IA 52004-1840

Copyright © 2011 by John P. McHale

ISBN 978-0-7575-9481-6

Kendall Hunt Publishing Company has the exclusive rights to reproduce this work,
to prepare derivative works from this work, to publicly distribute this work,
to publicly perform this work and to publicly display this work.

All rights reserved. No part of this publication may be reproduced,
stored in a retrieval system, or transmitted, in any form or by any
means, electronic, mechanical, photocopying, recording, or otherwise,
without the prior written permission of the copyright owner.

Printed in the United States of America
10 9 8 7 6 5 4 3 2 1

This book is dedicated to Maggie, Woody, and my students.

May we always challenge ourselves to become better.

MASS MEDIA WRITING:

TELLING A GOOD STORY WELL

Preface……………………………………………………………vii

About the Author………………………………………………..xii

1) Telling a Good Story……………………………………....1
2) Theoretical Consideration of Mass Media Writing…………..9
3) The Writing Process……………………………………….23
4) Writer's Toolbox…………………………………………..39
5) Style: Telling It Well………………………………………49
6) Inverted Pyramid………………………………………... 67
7) Ethics and Mass Media Writing…………………………... 75
8) Feature Print Writing……………………………………... 87
9) Legal Issues in Mass Media Writing …………………….97
10) Broadcast Media Writing………………………………... 101
11) Radio News……………………………………………... 113
12) Telling a Visual Story……………………………...................121
13) Scripting the Visual……………………………………... 129
14) Television News………………………………………… 145
15) Advertising……………………………………………... 157
16) Public Relations and Story……………………………... 167
17) Television Entertainment…………………………………179
18) Documentary…………………………………………… 185
19) Feature Film Writing……………………………………... 197
20) Social Media……………………………………………. 211

Appendix………………………………………………… 221

Bibliography……………………………………………… 289

Index……………………………………………………… 291

PREFACE

Mass Media Writing: Telling a Good Story Well is designed to be the basic textbook material for an introductory or survey course on mass media writing. The primary intended audience for *Mass Media Writing: Telling a Good Story Well* is college students majoring in mass media or communication. This particularly includes college freshman or sophomores in Communication, Journalism, or Mass Media who are preparing for more intensive study of a particular area of mass media writing and production. It is, in addition, appropriate for a much wider range of students. The contents could be valuable to the aspiring high school mass media writer to the college seniors or graduate students whose program of study never focused on writing for mass media. *Mass Media Writing: Telling a Good Story Well* could also be useful for students on other disciplines who need an education on mass media message design to augment their primary fields.

There are several possible markets for *Mass Media Writing: Telling a Good Story Well* other than the college or university writing students. High schools with media writing programs are another possible market. In addition, universities and colleges in other nations could use *Mass Media Writing: Telling a Good Story Well* to prepare students for media careers by acquainting them with international mass media standards. Finally, media practitioners who are challenged by the market realities of convergence could use this book to respond to those career demands.

The industry trend of convergence has greatly influenced *Mass Media Writing: Telling a Good Story Well*. Due to technological advances and the consolidation of media ownership, media writers/practitioners are called upon to produce in a variety of contexts. Media employees are asked to do work in media forms other than their primary field. The radio reporter may be asked to take a video camera to an event to gather footage for the television station owned by the same entity. The television reporter may be asked to prepare a story for the station's web page. The writing approach espoused in this book begins to prepare future practitioners for such challenges. This book uniquely addresses convergence. In addition, schools seeking to prepare students for the realities of the job market can no longer afford to focus on one type of mass media communication and exclude coverage of others. To do so ignores the competitive realities of the evolving mass media workplace.

PURPOSE

Mass Media Writing: Telling a Good Story Well is designed for use in an introductory survey course on writing for mass media. It exposes students to the various mass media forms they may encounter later in their programs of study and/or in their future careers. Specifically, this text will equip students to engage in the preparation and presentation of various mass media communication writing formats. Through inclusion of examples, professional stories and explication of industry standards, students will develop the writing skills necessary to professionally succeed in a variety of media writing contexts. Another important goal is to acclimate students to the demands of writing for a living. Toward this end, practitioners emphasize the balance between accuracy, deadlines, and clarity. Finally, an important function of *Telling a Good Story Well* is to help students develop a critical understanding of quality print, radio, television, public relations, Internet, documentary, television program and dramatic feature film writing. Critical disposition will be useful to students whether or not they pursue mass media writing as a career. The text will emphasize one of the most important functions of the study of communication: educating students to be critical consumers of mass media.

This is one of the few books students will read that will be useful even if they decide, after they leave school, that they are going to live in their parents' basement for the rest of their life, eating potato chips and watching reruns of *Jersey Shore*. This book is going to benefit students because it will help them learn to develop the ability to critically analyze mass media. When they are asked, "What are you watching?" these students will no longer be able to answer, "I'm watching TV." The follow-up question, "What's on?" will not be answered with, "A show." Rather than allow mass media to wash over their passive consciousness, and not critically analyze it, students will be encouraged as they use this text to ask questions like, "What is the message they're trying to convey to me? How are they trying to persuade me? How are they going to get me to do what they want me to do?"

This book will help students critically analyze questions of this nature. Students will be encouraged to critically analyze: *Is this a good story? Why does this movie work and why does it not work? Why is the film "Land of the Lost" so crappy? How is the use of editing trying to persuade me of something? How are they trying to use my psychological weaknesses to sell me crap I don't need?* Students will be challenged to break down dramatic and structural elements and identify why a mass media message is successful or not. In sum, this book is going to help students become more critical consumers of mass media as well as help students become better writers. After reading this book, I hope that students will never look at mass media the same.

A second purpose of this book is to help students develop writing skills sufficient to write for print, radio, television, or film. This book will help students learn the fundamental principles of good writing. Then students will develop the ability to apply those principles to various areas of mass media writing. Good writing is good writing, no matter what the particular medium. This book will help students adapt good writing skills (their proverbial toolbox) to be able to write for a variety of mass media forms.

A third purpose of this book is to acclimate the student to the demands of writing for a living. Toward this end, a course that employs this book will push students to face seemingly incessant and fast-approaching deadlines and meet standards of professional rigor. Those who teach writing for mass media will demand rigor. Teaching about writing for mass media is about imparting a commitment to high standards and commitment to quality. Students who have been taught writing for mass media with the model presented in this book have moved from the university classroom to attain jobs at large public relations firms, MTV, CNN, Fox Broadcasting, Jim Henson Productions, major film studios and have become professionals who manage network affiliate newsrooms. Students taught under this model later report that they were grateful for expectations of professional rigor in the classroom. Those expectations helped them succeed in the professional realm. Students who study writing for mass media should be prepared to write constantly and under much pressure. That is how it will be in the work world.

The paradigm articulated throughout this book poses a guiding question: "What would your boss say?" Undergraduate students sometimes fail to understand the expectations that await them in the real world. If a mass media writer does not perform well in the professional world, it does not just translate into a C- grade. Writers who do not meet professional expectations put their employment security at risk. These writers may be fired. Their reputation may be irreparably damaged, and they may be unable to get hired again in that particular field. Students may resent this rigor in the middle of a course that uses this paradigm. The student may develop temporary animosity toward this author as they rise to the challenge presented in this book. However, when students succeed in such a class, they will look back at the experience with gratitude. Their supervisors will recognize that they are prepared to work like professionals. Employers will be able to rely upon these graduates to write, and rewrite, until that copy is professional. Thus, using this book will help acclimate students to writing for a living.

Approach

One of the unique features of this book is the emphasis on a dramatic approach to mass media writing. This text contends that quality storytelling is important in all areas of mass media writing; thus, the organizing principle is that students should consider using the principles of drama as a foundation for all mass media writing. Another feature that clearly sets this text apart from other mass media writing texts is its comprehensive scope. Rather than choosing news over other mass media communication forms, this book focuses on news, as well as promotional and entertainment communication.

Organization of the Text

This text will move from basic writing principles to print writing, then to writing for electronic media including radio, television, and the web. It will conclude with chapters on documentaries, television programs, and feature films. Each chapter is organized around the main theme of the book.

This book is an introduction to the variety of mass communication media students may encounter in their careers. Students will engage in preparation and presentation of various mass communication formats.

In this text, generally the subject will be the mass media writer. Often, because the book is written for and to the aspiring writer, "you" will be used to refer to readers.

ACKNOWLEDGEMENTS

Many people helped with the preparation of this manuscript. Amber Dzierzynski, editorial assistant, was very helpful in transcribing lectures that provided a base from which this manuscript was prepared. Benjamin Slack, Adam Kastor, and Brian Seay were also very helpful in the early preparation stages. These students suffered through early version of these chapters, pushing me to improve them. Derick Downey also provided essential editing assistance and formatting. This book could not have been completed without the help of students in the Illinois State School of Communication. Scott Richardson, Xavier Jackson, and students enrolled in Mass Media Writing and Teaching Mass Media Writing were very helpful in providing suggestions and feedback.

Illinois State University granted me a sabbatical for completion of this book. School of Communication Director Larry Long and Assistant Director Steve Hunt were consistently supportive of the work. The faculty in the School of Communication offered much encouragement, especially Tom Lamonica and Joe Blaney.

I am grateful for the help of the professionals at Kendall Hunt Publishing Company, particularly Philip France, Jr. and Charmayne McMurray.

I would not have been able to write this without the opportunities afforded by many people. The University of Missouri-Columbia Communication Department gave me the opportunity to begin my teaching career in mass media writing. I owe Michael Porter, Michael Kramer, Pam Benoit, Bill Benoit, and Jon Hess thanks for that opportunity. Pamela McElroy Bonanno provided encouragement and delectable sustenance. Marc Svenson heard about this book too much and always supported. Woody and Maggie were always there with hugs, smiles, and encouragement. I also owe thanks to teachers who taught me to write as well as I can, including Jeri Krieger and Richard Lanigan. Dr. Kimberley P. McHale was with me through much growth. Michael and Helen McHale gave the love and support that made this possible. I will always be indebted to Anthony Alioto for kicking me out of his office and telling me to go get my union card: my PhD. Tony also gave me of example as a teacher with a commitment to share his ideas in print. Ultimate thanks to the Divine Spirit in us all.

ABOUT THE AUTHOR

John Patrick McHale is an Associate Professor in the School of Communication at Illinois State University. He has earned a bachelor's degree in Political Science and a master's degree in Communication from Southern Illinois University, a bachelor's degree in History from Columbia College, a master's in Political Science and a Ph.D. in Communication from University of Missouri at Columbia, and earned Professional Certification in Film Production from New York University. McHale has published a number of books, chapters, and journal articles, including *Communicating for Change: Strategies of Social and Political Advocates (2004; Rowman & Littlefield)*. McHale has also written, produced, and directed a number of films, including the awarding winning *Picture This: The Fight to Save Joe*, which was an important catalytic factor in Joe Amrine's release from Missouri death row in 2005. McHale has taught at a number of institutions, including University of Missouri, Southern Illinois University at Carbondale, Yale, Princeton, Stanford, and Northwestern. McHale is also the recipient of several awards, including received the FYI Walter Cronkite Civic Engagement Leadership award at the United Nations in New York in 2006.

CHAPTER 1:
TELLING A GOOD STORY

When "60 Minutes" producer Don Hewitt explained the secret of "60 Minutes'" success, he wrote, "It's four words every child knows: Tell me a story," (CBS, 1999). (http://cbs2.com/entertainment/don.hewitt.dead.2.1134964.html)

Mass media writing is telling a good story *well*. Discussion of good stories begins with consideration of drama. In this book, I offer a "dramaturgical" approach to writing for mass media. Dramaturgical means incorporating a story in what we communicate in mass media. Regardless of the form of mass media we find ourselves writing in, telling a good story is the best way to connect with an audience.

Print media will be the first medium discussed in this book. We will start with straight news and then move to feature writing. It is essential that we tell a good *story*. Storytelling is also critical for radio writing. The book will then shift to visual mass media, television news, commercials, television drama, documentaries, and feature films.

Thus, in this chapter we will discuss the necessity of the mass media writer to tell a good story. We will describe a model of drama, structural considerations, and the role of a mass media writer as a storyteller. Above all, the mass media writer must think like a dramatist.

DRAMATIC MODEL

From the dawn of time, people have enjoyed and learned from a good story. We are either hard-wired to like a good story, or we learn to like them. The importance of stories to human communication is most likely a combination of both.

Storytelling is an intrinsic aspect of being human. It is an essential form of communication. When the first speaking, pre-historic, Cro-Magnon man came back to the cave with an antelope over his shoulder, his fellows inquired with a series of guttural grunts, "Wow, where'd you get the antelope?" He probably told them a good story. He told them about him being hungry, then the aim of getting some food for his family and the rest of the tribe. Then he talked about the complications, the trials, and tribulations: the weather was bad, his spear was dull, and he had to chase the antelope through the brush. But even in that story, there is a climax. He said, "I got the antelope! And I brought it back to the tribe, and now we're all going to eat." The essence of dramatic theory would likely have been present in such a story.

Our conception of drama was first articulated by the Greeks. Basic dramatic concepts can be found in Greek plays like *Antigone* and *Oedipus Rex* by writers such as Sophocles and Euripides. The Greeks suggested the best way to communicate is to tell a good story. Our conception of drama has been honed through the history of civilization through stories shared orally, in theaters, in television writing, and in films.

Effective television commercials often communicate a good story. For instance, some of the home alarm system advertisements portray a dramatic scenario. The commercial features a family at their home. There is a father, a mother, and a young child or two. The father drives off for work that day and the mother and the children are left alone. All of a sudden, we have a big dramatic question: Is the house *really* protected? Suddenly a nefarious-looking thug kicks in the front door and there is a big scare! The mother frantically runs upstairs with the children. The mother locks the door and the telephone rings. On the other end of the telephone a professionally uniformed official says: "This is an Acme Home Security System representative. Are you safe?" The mother replies that they are safe. The representative confidently says he is sending security personnel to the home. You have a dramatic question. The woman in the spot has a will, want, or desire: to be safe. That need provides the basis for the dramatic question. The home security corporation, at the climax, becomes the hero and is going to keep her safe. Even in television advertising, a good story is an effective form of communication.

PROTAGONIST

It is necessary to abstractly consider the elements of a good story. It is helpful to consider the dramatic model. First of all, in drama, you have a protagonist. A **protagonist** is a character who has a goal and they *take actions that move the story forward*. This is the person that makes decisions and that acts in the drama. The protagonist is a main character who, because of their choices that are the result of their will or want, actively moves the drama forward. This may also be a group of people.

WILL/WANT

The protagonist is motivated throughout the drama by a **will/want**, which is what the protagonist desires to achieve and their will and potential ability to make such a thing occur. Sometimes there is explicit will or want and sometimes it is more implicit. The will/want often manifests as a conflict. The overall will or want is what the main character is trying to achieve, whether it be external or subconscious. The flaws in the protagonist often contribute to the conflict. That leads to the dramatic question, which is, "Will they achieve it?"

Dramatic Model

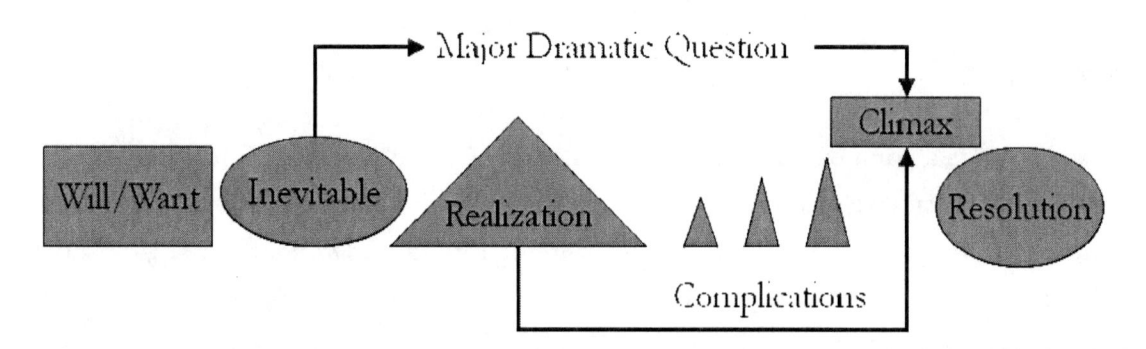

The Lord of the Rings trilogy is an excellent example of an effective story. In *The Lord of the Rings*, Frodo Baggins, a hobbit from the Shire in Middle Earth, is the person who is acting (protagonist), and has a desire: to destroy the ring. Destruction of the ring is his will or want. This leads to the dramatic question: "Will Frodo make it to Mount Doom and destroy the ring?"

REALIZATION

Usually this is a little more subtle, but the **realization** is the point at which the main character realizes what they have to do. It becomes very clear to Frodo that he must destroy the ring. And then Frodo, the protagonist, realizes that he has a quest. Frodo accepts a major will or want. There is a dramatic question that Frodo's actions will answer. There is usually a point in the story when the main character realizes what their goal is and what they have to do to achieve it. What is Frodo going to have to do to destroy the ring? Frodo will have to travel a long way and face many enormous challenges. The moment of his dramatic realization is when Frodo accepts those challenges.

COMPLICATIONS

A series of complications are another major component of an effective story. **Complications** are roadblocks to achieving the will or want. Anybody or anything that can impede the achievement of the will or want is an obstacle or complication. Some stories focus on internal complications, where the main character struggles against himself or herself. The best drama has both internal and external complications. These complications tend to progress, or get more severe, as the plot develops. Thus, the progressive character of complications entails elements of rising action.

CLIMAX

There is a point of climax toward the end of effective drama. **Climax** is the point at which the tension related to the dramatic question is most acute. In *The Lord of the Rings,* this is the point where Frodo makes it to Mount Doom. Even after he reaches the place at which the ring can be destroyed, Frodo, once again, has to fight with Gollum. Gollum bites his finger off, but Frodo gets the ring back. Frodo has the ring, and he is ready to throw it in, but the audience can see that the power of the ring starts to take Frodo over. The dramatic question, most poignant here, is, "Will he do it?" The climax is where the dramatic question is answered. Is Dorothy going to make it home to Kansas? Or does Andy Dufresne, in the *Shawshank Redemption*, get out of prison? If so, how does he do it?

RESOLUTION

Finally, effective stories have a **resolution**. Resolution, or denouement, is the point at which things go back to stasis, albeit sometimes changed. Action falls, and some sort of stasis resumes. For example, in *Wizard of Oz*, Dorothy is in her bed in Kansas. In *The Lord of the Rings*, Frodo and Sam are hanging out in the Green Dragon tavern. In *Shawshank Redemption*, Andy Dufresne, meets Red on a tranquil coast beach in Mexico. Peace returns to the situation.

A good story is constructed with this kind of structure in mind, whether the story is from the ancient Greeks or the most recent multiplex blockbuster.

Another excellent example of a quality story is *The Wizard of Oz.* Consider Dorothy, the protagonist. What does she want? She wants to go over the rainbow. Then when she gets to Oz, she realizes that rather than staying over the rainbow, she would really like to go back to Kansas. Dorothy grows. She also faces several complications; the wicked witch who wants the slippers, the wizard who can help her, but who throws a giant complication in the way when he says, "I'll help you, but only if you get the broomstick of the Wicked Witch." There are flying attack monkeys and then the giant, ominous hourglass. Dorothy must overcome several frightening complications until she throws the water on the witch. And then, the balloon leaves without her! It turns out that she can still get home by clicking her heels. Why did the Good Witch not tell her that from the beginning? Because if she did, THERE WOULD HAVE BEEN NO STORY! Imagine if the witch had said, "Just click your heels three times, and you'll go home." There would have been no need for the film *The Wizard of Oz.* Effective drama requires complications to be an engaging good story.

The key thing is that the effective mass media writer needs to think as a dramatist. The writer will serve their company well. They will be able to write effective and engaging mass media messages if they can think like a dramatist.

Mass media is ubiquitous, and a mass media writer should to think about story when they consume mass media. Good stories, be they found in television, film, or news, utilize the dramatic principles in this model. Aspiring writers will watch mass media differently. They will be able to critically analyze stories and say, "Is there a major dramatic question based on a will or want? Did the complications increase in severity as the plot goes along?" The aspiring writer will notice these things because they are going to become critical consumers of mass media. The developing dramatist should watch for the features of effective or ineffective storytelling in the television and film content they watch. They should look for good stories and seek to understand how they work. Aspiring mass media writers should also critically consume bad examples to know what does not work. As writers attempt to stand on the shoulders of giants, they need to study stories the giants wrote that worked and why these seminal stories worked.

STRUCTURAL CONSIDERATIONS

Not only do we want to talk generally about dramatic principles, but in addition, we are going to talk about the four structural considerations that should always be present when you write.

UNITY

Structural considerations are important when writing for mass media, whether it is TV, radio, film, or news. The first consideration is unity. **Unity** is whether or not everything is related. Sometimes, it is a little disconcerting when the pieces do not fit together. Do all the pieces add to the general message of the mass media piece? If so, that is unity. Extraneous elements in a story decrease unity.

VARIETY

A second structural consideration when writing for mass media is variety. **Variety** is change or alternation in story or program elements. Variety can also be found in incorporation of differing story lines. To use variety in writing a TV commercial, the writer could choose different shots and different angles to keep people interested. If it is TV comedy, every two minutes or so, the writers could change the scene, the characters, or the subject that is being discussed. Television viewers have many program choices as the number of television channels has expanded into the triple digits. If television writers cannot keep viewers interested, viewers are going to change the channel.

PACE

The third consideration is pace. **Pace** is the speed at which the plot moves along. A media message should not be too slow or too rushed. Pace is how quickly the mass media presentation unfolds. And the key is that it's appropriate for the message. Think of Jimmy John's sandwich commercials; they are fast to communicate the idea that Jimmy John's is astonishingly fast. On the opposite end of the pace spectrum there are Corona beer television advertisements. These are slow paced, showing the one shot with the bottle and often slow camera movement. Why would the pace of the Corona television advertisement be slow? Corona beer helps relax us, like we are just hanging out on the beach.

CLIMAX

The final structural consideration is a climax. **Climax** is the point at which the dramatic tension is the greatest. Whatever we write, we want to have a climax. In *The Lord of the Rings*, it is where Gollum has the ring, and he falls in the lava, leaving the ring to dissolve in the lava of Mount Doom.

MASS MEDIA WRITER AS A STORYTELLER

Telling a story is about principles, not rules, as Robert McKee has suggested. There are no strict rules, but rather effective storytelling principles. Saying the protagonist always has to be the good guy would be an example of a rule. That is mostly the case, but when writers break the mold and cut what is standard, the outcome can be good. Dramatic form is like classical musical theory in jazz: artists learn the basics, and then mess with the basics to make something new. We have all seen predictable cookie cutter movies where we know everything that's going to happen. That is not a good story. The writer is not going to surprise us and, thus, not satisfy our desire for engaging drama. The writers are following strict formulas without breaking the rules in service of the principles. Why would audience members want to pay admission to a feature film for an unsatisfying cinematic experience?

Effective storytelling is about eternal universal forms, not formulas, again from McKee. When I think of universal forms, I think of Darth Vader. He is dressed in black. He is an evil guy. These are universal forms, not formulas. There are archetypes; some things about good versus evil are universal. We are interested in the stories about good versus evil. But we should not say, "Well, this is how it happened in that movie, so that is what I am going to do in my story." Dramatists must seek to utilize universal forms and archetypes instead of just using what has worked before. And notice I said "archetypes," not "stereotypes." *Unforgiven* (directed by Clint Eastwood) won the Oscar for Best Picture because it worked against the stereotypes. Sometimes in order to be good, the good guy has to be really bad.

Mass media writing is hard work. There are no shortcuts. **A writer needs to know at least twice the information about their subject than will actually end up in the story**, whether the story be for television, news, radio, whatever. A writer needs to do research. Writing is about making choices, especially choices about inclusion and exclusion. Writers have to be thorough to make good story choices. When a writer takes shortcuts on a plot, the audience can tell. The *Transformers* films are big, expensive, special effects–driven fireworks displays and have gaping plot holes in their plots. We see that frequently in Hollywood films. In many multiplex films, there is no depth to the characters. The characters are often one-dimensional because the writer has taken shortcuts in character development.

In today's culture, we get explosions and special effects in place of a good story and characters. Any tool can be good or bad, and when I talk about *The Wizard of Oz*, and the use of color to show you she's in Kansas or she's in Oz was just great, and that was only possible because of special effects. The special effects, working with the story, really had an impact on me. As long as there is CGI, then we do not need to know about the story these days.

The reality is that writing is hard. To be a successful mass media writer requires much work. Quality writers master the art of storytelling, not second-guess the market place, according to McKee. Quality writers do not want movies that are simplistically based on what has worked before. Great writers craft stories that mean something to us, and that have some truth we think we can communicate to our audience.

In this chapter we have discussed the necessity of the mass media writer to tell a good story. We discussed a model of drama, structural considerations, and the role of a mass media writer as a storyteller. The mass media writer must think like a dramatist.

CHAPTER 2: THEORETICAL CONSIDERATION OF MASS MEDIA WRITING

The central focus of this book is teaching students how to write a good story well. In previous chapters we have discussed the importance of story and the decline of story. This chapter will delve into the structural considerations that must be employed when writing a good story. It is imperative that we take a mass media approach and teach students that writing for the mass media involves following a **communication process**. As writers we need to think on a theoretical level when writing stories. To do this, we must identify:

- **the actual message**
- **potential interference**
- **the necessary channel (or channels) in which the message is sent**
- **the sender (media writer)**
- **the context in which the media writer functions**
- **the audience (receiver)**
- **anticipated feedback**

To help students better understand this process, the **Transactional Model of Communication** must be introduced.

The Transactional Model is helpful because it recognizes communication as a dynamic, two-way process. In this model the sender is also a receiver. There is a message delivered and feedback offered by the receiver in response to that message. At this point, the receiver is now also a sender and vice versa. This model of communication provides a better structure for writers working toward becoming strong communicators in mass media. Students must understand that they are not communicating *at* their audience, but instead participating in an interactive dialogue.

Transactional Model of Communication

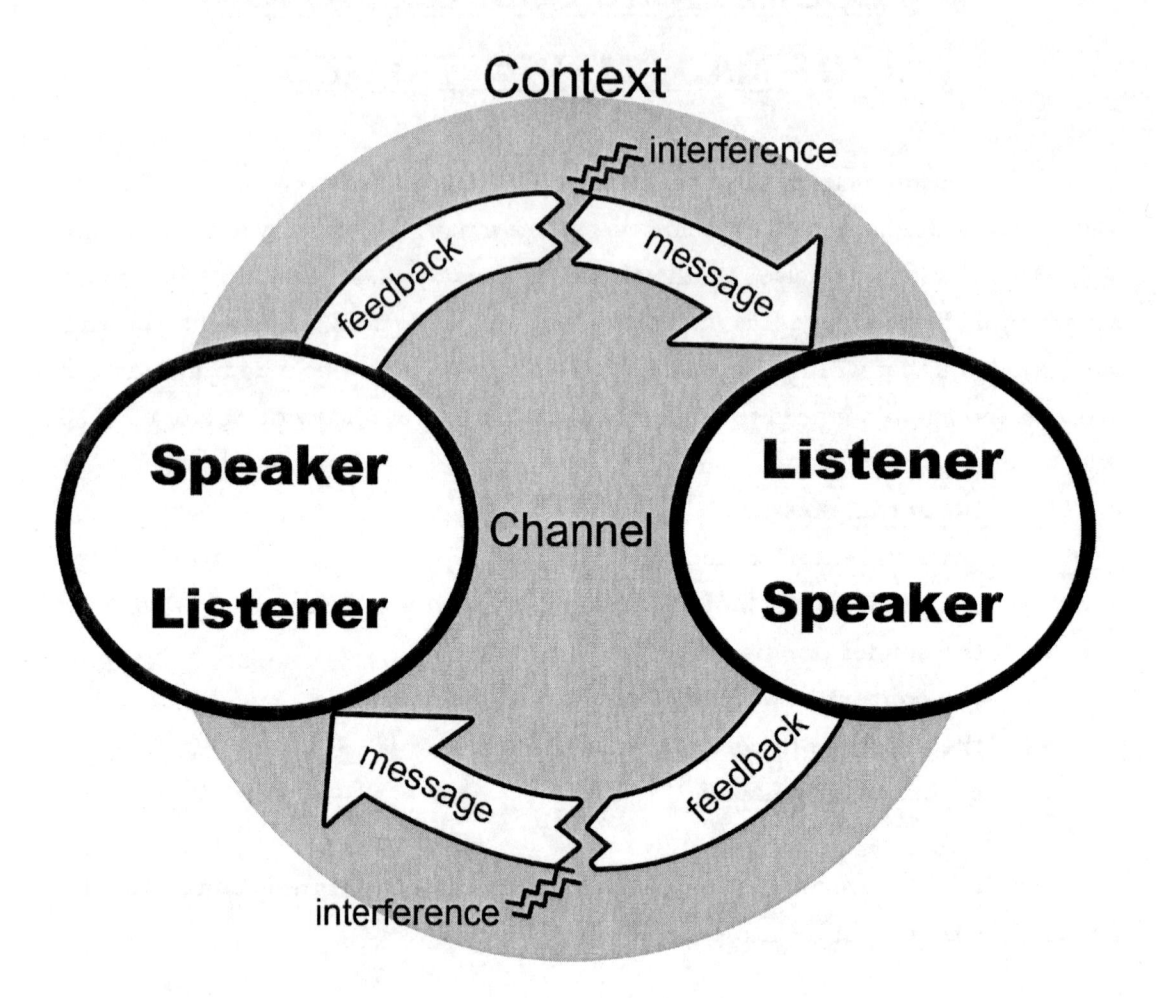

[Diagram: Two overlapping circles labeled "Speaker/Listener" (left) and "Listener/Speaker" (right) within a larger circle labeled "Context." Arrows labeled "message" and "feedback" connect the two, with "interference" marked on both message arrows. "Channel" is labeled in the center.]

Remember, we are taking a theoretical approach to writing for mass media. We discussed the types of messages and structural considerations that must be employed when writing them, which was the first theoretical element. Now we will move on to a discussion regarding interference.

INTERFERENCE

Interference is noise or any other element that affects the clarity of a message. Interference can be internal, like a television news anchor with a headache or bad nerves, or it could be external, like bad reception or background noise. Mass media is ubiquitous because it happens everywhere at once. This ubiquity is an everyday occurrence. I get texts as I am in my car listening to NPR, as I am seeing billboards advertising Miller Lite. I turn on my computer and I am getting messages from six different news sources. Our world is becoming increasingly exposed to media gluttony—media competing with media for your attention. A well-crafted media message is the best way to cut through that din.

The mass media writer wants their intended message to be as close as possible to the actual message, and clarity decreases interference. If the writing is not clear, it leaves the audience guessing what they are supposed to get out of the message. Lack of clarity can be a source of interference in many ways. For instance, interference can come from a **diffused message**. If one part of the message is unclear, but the rest of the message has clarity, the reader might get distracted by the confusing part and miss the remainder of the message. What's worse, the audience may stop reading the message all together.

Piquing the interest of our audience through use of **strategic ambiguity** can be a useful tool, but we need to be clear about that curiosity. As mentioned earlier, ambiguity is not necessarily a lack of clarity because it still takes consideration and a strategic use of signs. For example, newspaper headlines often only give a small piece of the story, which often begs the reader to read more. This ambiguity is strategic because it is utilized as a tool to clearly intrigue you to the point where you decide to buy the paper or magazine. I hate to admit it, but today I saw an US magazine and the headline read: "OctoMom speaks: 'Mistakes were made.'" The cover blurb caught my interest because it strategically made the story sound like her whole life was one dramatic mistake after another. In actuality, the story did not disclose that reality as alarming as my reading of the headline indicated.

A third form of interference is **bad writing**. A mistake or awkward sentence in an article may immediately pull the audience's attention away from the message as a whole. Recently, I read a movie review in a local paper and the very last line of the article was, "Only the future will tell if"... The sentence did not have any punctuation or signal that it continued elsewhere. I looked through the entire paper to find the rest of the story and eventually assumed it was a layout error. I began to think about what that last sentence could be and I wondered if the writer had somehow botched the deadline he had in column inches. Suddenly, I was not even thinking about the movie. At that point I was more focused on the mistake than the message. All of these errors occur in a situation where the intended message is not close to the actual message because we are distracted. This distraction is a product of interference, and it can negatively impact your story.

CHANNEL

The next theoretical concept is the consideration of the **channel**. Newspapers, radio, television, the web, cable, and film all come to mind when we think of the different channels in mass media. Fractionalization of audiences, which means that mass media audiences are getting more and more specific (not smaller), occurs as a result of media convergence. We now have massive specialized audiences as a result of having so many media options. In the past there were only three large networks that offered television programming. Today we are offered hundreds of channels, each with a specific theme or subject. The takeaway here is that the television audiences have grown exponentially throughout the years, but the number of viewers on each channel at any given time has decreased at the same time. Like most media today, television is growing but becoming more specialized.

SENDER

Sender, the next theoretical element, is the writer of mass media. It is important to understand that writing is a part-time occupation, and for this reason it is equally important to never tell students what they *cannot* do. When educators or advisors tell you what you *can* do, in a way they are also telling you what you *cannot* do. I believe that the students who take Media Writing go on to do great things in their careers. Many students of media writing eventually work for major media companies and organizations such as CNN, Jim Henson Productions, or MTV. If a student has a dream to achieve great things in mass media and the will and desire to perfect his or her craft, the sky is the limit. Quentin Tarantino is an excellent example of this theory. Tarantino was working in a video rental store when he wrote *Reservoir Dogs.* All day he would suggest movies to customers, talk about movies with his friends, and watch movies on the job. When he went home, he would sit down and pound out these crazy scenes that swam around in his head all day. He had a will and a desire to make it to where he is today, and if he can do it, any writer can do it. When Oliver Stone wrote *Platoon*, he was driving a taxi in New York City. The Academy recognized *Platoon* as Best Picture in the mid-80s. Aspiring writers who dedicate themselves to honing their craft will write quality mass media messages. A writer must dream and work toward those dreams. Far be it for us to tell them what they cannot do.

The reality of being a mass media writer is that it is often a part-time job. Writing can be secondary as a career reality. Often times, you have a salesperson-writer who writes sales proposals as well as mass media messages for advertising—acting as a conduit between client and creative services. Account executives develop relationships with clients and assist in creating a mass media message. In the news there is often a researcher-writer who researches news items and then writes them to be read by the announcer or anchor. Likewise, a reporter will likely write some, if not most, of their own messages as well. In entertainment, the producer often facilitates the production team and writes some copy for the film or show, and works closely with the writing staff. The publicist-writer works with an organization looking to get media coverage, and in the mean time writes press releases and media kits for the group or company. The teacher-writer may be an interactive writer writing scripts to instructional videos. I once met a man who made interactive training process videos for FedEx employees. The proprietor of a business has to work with writers to communicate messages about their business to the masses. Public relations professionals may work for a corporation or for an agency, and in that case, help shape the client's image as well as writing press releases and fact sheets.

It would be a dream to write 24 hours a day, but like most people, I have to fulfill other requirements of my job (teaching) to be able to write. Writing is a part-time career. This is important to understand when considering the writer as a sender in the theoretical approach.

AUDIENCE

The audience or receiver of a message must always be considered when writing for the mass media. It is very important to first identify the **target audience** of a particular mass media message, so when we begin writing we are thinking of whom we want to reach with every sentence. Considering the target audience has two particular implications.

First, we must consider which symbols to use to reach that particular audience. Second, the channel used to reach this audience must be identified. If writing a message to sell pens, you will not advertise on a program like *South Park*. An educational program would suit the product better. The channel will influence the message. **When we are thinking about the specific audience, we want to know the following:**

- **What is their age?**
- **What is their income level?**
- **What is their education level?**
- **What is their gender?**

Ultimately, we want to craft a mass media message that speaks to a specific target audience.

When considering a mass media audience, we also want to think about *why* that particular audience should listen to the message. Again, it is important to remember that mass media is ubiquitous; if our audience is not engaged, they will change the channel. The best way to do this is through a good story. Even if it is a radio story, we need to involve the audience in an emotional way or stir up their curiosity. This may involve a message that articulates the will or want and answers the dramatic question. One of the ways we can get our audience to listen is to introduce some drama into the mix. Another way to grab our audience's attention is through **news values**. News values are an explanation of why the audience should care about a particular story. Is the news geographically close to them? Does it have impact? Good stories are important but being cognizant of news values is also very important. The message must explain why the information is valuable. It is also important to begin a mass media message with a bang. In an inverted pyramid print news story, it is the lead sentence. In a feature film, it is a tease that leads to the dramatic question. *CSI* uses this strategy to its advantage by beginning with a dead body in a crazy situation. Immediately, the audience is attentive to the story.

FEEDBACK

The last element of communication, theoretically, is **feedback**. Feedback is when the receiver sends information to the sender. This is why the Transactional Model of Communication is effective; it allows the sender and receiver to switch roles during feedback. Often feedback is in other communication forms. It may be verbal or it may be nonverbal. Mass media does not traditionally have the face-to-face interaction element, and typically, feedback has been judged in mass media by ratings (how many people watch the show). Sales are an indirect form of feedback. If an advertising company sees an increase in sales in their product after issuing a mass media message, then that is a form of audience feedback. There is more feedback in newer mass media forms. On the web, I can respond to articles and blogs by commenting directly to the message. I can email editors or publishers or writers and give them feedback on their mass media messages. The web often allows the sender to track, per clicks, where their audience searches and what articles or images they chose to view.

PURPOSES OF COMMUNICATION

Why do we tell the story? Why do we communicate to the masses? It is important for the mass media writer to determine the purpose of a story before he or she begins. The first thing to consider is the message itself.

Every mass media message includes one of three purposes:
- **to inform**
- **to persuade**
- **to entertain**

The message with an **informative purpose** is to impart information on the audience. When considering an informative message, it is imperative to think about news values. Why is this message important to the audience?

The second possible message intent is **to persuade**. In persuasion, a sender seeks to change the receiver in terms of attitudes, beliefs, or behaviors. In terms of a mass media message, this could be persuading the audience to purchase a particular product. In other cases, persuasion can be used to get the audience to think about an issue or to consider a new idea. For example, let's say we want the audience to consider that redemption is best sought through self-sacrifice. This message could be esoteric because it is a complex ideal. In future sections, the use of specific appeals in mass media messages will be discussed such as an intense burglar alarm commercial that persuades by appealing to fear. Other persuasive messages may appeal to safety, such as a cellular phone commercial involving a teenage girl whose car breaks down and yet she is safe because she has a cell phone that enables her to contact her father. This particular message appeals to an audience of parents.

Mass media is a business that is ultimately selling an audience to an advertiser. A television network does everything in its power to get as many viewers as possible so it can offer the attention of millions of viewers to advertising agencies. Simply put, your attention is being sold to major advertising companies by the minute. Promotional messages that incorporate the phrase "Stay tuned" can also be a persuasive function used to convince audiences to consume more mass media. Any messages that appear to be informative also have a persuasive function. If I say, "It's raining outside," could it be assumed that I'm suggesting you should use your umbrella? On one level, it seems as though I am informing you that it is in fact raining outside, but on another level I may be suggesting that you should wait to leave, or that you should consider using a coat. This illustrates the idea that even messages to inform or entertain have a **sermonic function**, or underlying persuasive intention. All mass media communication has this sermonic function, according to Weaver (1985). Walters (1994) suggests that mass media, even when it informs or entertains us, still involves a persuasive intent. We are persuaded to stay in our seats and leave the remote untouched so we will watch the advertisements.

The third possible intent of a message is **to entertain**. Of course, there is overlap between these functions. As writers, we want to entertain, and thus, there will be an underlying sermonic function we want to keep our eye on. When it comes to keeping attention, *Seinfeld* offers a great example because there is always a "kicker" in the end credits. I would never miss the commercials between the end of each episode and the credits because I wanted to see that anticipated "kicker." Sometimes the funniest part of the show occurred in that final moment during the credits. Perhaps Kramer would spout out a hilarious one-liner that syncs up the entire episode. I would faithfully stay tuned for that one line. Ultimately the writers and producers of the show are persuading you to watch those commercials so you don't miss the final humorous moment.

MESSAGE TYPES

When considering the purpose of a mass media message, it is important to understand various message types. The first type is **intended message**. What is the meaning I want to impart to the listener? What is the idea I intend to convey to them? Often times the intended message is very different from the **actual message**, or the message that the audience processes and understands. For example, imagine you run into a friend and say, "I'm so sorry your husband cheated on you," but your friend does not know that her husband is being unfaithful. My intended message—"I'm so sorry for your husband's behavior"—does not reflect the actual message she received— "Your husband is cheating on you." I like to define the actual message as the message heard by the audience. Even if you really did have concern for your friend, and your intention was to express your apologies, your friend may still interpret your message as a ploy to upset her marriage.

The basic idea is that we choose to communicate in a certain way (intended message), but our audience might take a different meaning from the message (actual message). I argue that good writing decreases the difference between the intended message and the actual message. When both messages are similar, it is the result of good writing. Likewise, it is important to think of the **residual message**, or the message you take away from the interaction and are thinking of ten minutes later. The residual message is what the audience will remember and is therefore incredibly important (i.e., McDonald's slogan: "I'm lovin' it.").

THEORETICAL COMMUNICATION

All of these ideas about the communication process go back to encoding and decoding a message on a theoretical level. **Encoding** is choosing the signs that will evoke a certain response in your consciousness. As a communicator in mass media, I choose to utilize symbols (utterances, words presented with font, pictures, music, etc.) that I hope will impart a message to my audience. Encoding is choosing which words to use, the order to put them it, the images to use, and computer-generated graphics to incorporate. This process allows me to effectively communicate the meaning I am trying to impart. **Decoding** is the process by which the receiver takes the signs and attributes conscious meaning to them. Meaning is constituted through these signs. We are the product of a culmination of socialized influences: education, religion, our parents, our peers. Such socialized influences shape how we look at and feel about the world. In decoding, as I take the signs offered, they interact with my consciousness and the culmination of socialized influences in my life. Ultimately, we want to use signs that evoke a certain meaning to the consciousness of our audience. If we think about this as writers, we realize the importance of certain details in our messages.

Let us break this concept down. The University of Missouri has testing rooms where individual words are displayed with pictures on a screen and a second-to-second meter measures the audience's reactions to the images. Researchers scrutinize every word and image displayed on the screen to determine which set evokes a desired meaning. From there, the researchers would break down results by demographic to determine which demographic was most affected by each word. The test is then edited and run again to get the best impact out of each part of the message.

Consider the term "estate tax." Somewhere in the process, "estate tax" became better known as "death tax." By changing the word "estate" to "death," a new meaning is evoked in the consciousness of the receiver. As writers, the concept of successfully encoding and decoding a message begs us to scrutinize each and every utterance used, and to be completely cognizant of our audience and their interpretation of our message.

CHARACTERISTICS OF GOOD WRITING

When considering message and formulation, it does not matter what type of mass media form you are writing. **Effective, strong mass media has four characteristics to consider:**
- Is it clear?
- Is it concise?
- Is it correct?
- Is it complete?

The most important consideration when writing for mass media is clarity. **Clarity** reduces the difference between the intended message and the actual message, so that the message I hope to get across is clearly interpreted by the receiver as I intended. This is the essence of clarity.

When it comes to being **concise**, I will quote Strunk and White: "Every word should tell." As writers we must be concise; there should not be excess, unnecessary signs offered to the audience. The message should be to the point in as few possible words. Here, I also suggest that it should have parsimony. It is elegant for a mathematician to take an equation and put it in the fewest possible terms. There is elegance in parsimony; praise comes when communication is in its most concise terms. In terms of mass media, every word costs money. You want to be concise so that you can fit it into the spot that you paid for.

The third characteristic that all mass media messages must have is to be **correct**. Wrong names, wrong time, and wrong place will undoubtedly anger the audience and negatively impact the credibility of the message. When I was teaching at Stanford, one of my fellow professors read that Michael Moore was coming to town. The story informed us that Moore was giving a speech at the Ladies' Flower Auxiliary, an event many of us did not know or care about. Regardless, we found it exciting that Michael Moore was scheduled to talk on our campus. The professor sent me the article illustrated with a picture of the documentary filmmaker Michael Moore. From a mass media perspective, we thought it would be a good idea for Michael Moore to come and speak to the political communication class we were teaching. He enthusiastically called the paper to obtain Moore's contact info and eventually got a hold of him. The professor told Moore that he could not wait for him to come and discuss politics and film to our students. Moore's response was unexpected. When inquired to speak to the class, Moore said, "Politics? Film? I don't think I'm the same Michael Moore that you're thinking I am. I'm a botanist; I developed a new type of flower." Suffice it to say, it was a very embarrassing situation. It was embarrassing for the botanist Michael Moore, who felt dismissed when we no longer wanted him to speak to our class, it was embarrassing to the paper that ran the story, and it was especially embarrassing to the writer of the article.

This example effectively illustrates the need to conduct thorough research to ensure our stories are always correct. The reporters received the information and just ran with it without doing a proper fact check. I would venture to say that the reporter does not work for that paper anymore. It hurts the reporter, it hurts the newspaper, and more significantly it hurts journalism as a whole. Situations like this make us look untrustworthy as writers and reporters in mass media.

The fourth consideration for effective mass media messages is they are **complete**. If you are writing a piece about an upcoming theatrical production but you do not include the time of the show, you have ruined the point of the story. When we are writing for mass media, we must be clear, concise, correct, and complete. As writers we can always find a place for strategic ambiguity, but it is important to note that this strategy is not the same as writing a story that lacks clarity. For example, the final episode of *The Sopranos* ended ambiguously. However, it was not unclear. The audience could clearly see that Tony was sitting at the dining room table and clearly recognize the blackout that occurred. Just because ambiguity is present does not mean a message is unclear. However, when using ambiguity in our writing, we must be just as strategic as we would if we were intending to be clear.

CONVERGENCE

Another element of mass media theory that is important to the writer is **convergence**. Convergence means that several modes of communication may be used together to impart mass media messages to the audience. When I am watching NFL, I can be online on NFL.com and I can get texts from my bookie about how much money I owe on a previous game. This is an example of how an individual can access a message from several channels simultaneously. This example of convergence indicates that smaller numbers of corporations own more of the available communication outlets (i.e., radio stations, television stations, newspapers and corollary internet web sites). Many **conglomerates** own several TV stations, Internet sites, radio stations, and newspapers. Under a single organization you can have numerous mass media forms. This is also known as **consolidated ownership**.

So what does this mean for writers of mass media? For starters, we are going to be assigned additional tasks on the job; tasks we are not used to completing. For example, I took my son and daughter to see presidential candidate John McCain speak, and while we were there a cameraman asked if I minded him taking a short video of us. I responded that I did not mind at all and asked which station he was reporting for. He said, *USA Today*. This was perplexing because *USA Today* is a newspaper. Why was he taking video for a newspaper? He explained, "Now we post video on the web as well as still photos." Functionally, this means that this reporter is capturing video, audio, photo, and writing for print. That is convergence. Today newspapers and other employers ask their employees to do more work for the same amount of money. In our unique approach, we teach that good writing is good writing no matter what form. In addition, this course teaches the students to write in mass media formats. A common question journalism students might hear in the interview now is, "Do you have experience writing for the web?" This is what will separate our students from the rest, as they will be prepared for convergence. Even with the production of a short video bit for the web, we want to make sure students apply the principles of the dramatic model—it should have a **mini climax** and **mini complications**. Such assignments should not just be random shots with information. The best video clips tell a story, no matter the length or purpose.

STRUCTURAL CONSIDERATIONS

As writers it is important to understand that every mass media message needs to be written with a set of **structural considerations** in mind:
- **Unity**
- **Variety**
- **Pace**
- **Climax**

Every time we sit down to write we must be cognizant of these structural considerations.

The first characteristic to consider is **unity**, which ensures that all pieces of a story hang together as some kind of cohesive whole. Sections and paragraphs that do not fit with rest of the story should not be used because they can confuse the reader and ultimately muddy the entire message. By taking unity into consideration, the whole of the story will equal something greater than the sum of its parts.

The second consideration is **variety**. Variety is changing up a story as it's told. This could be changes in scene, music, or characters. A great example of variety is used in Seinfeld when the bass line begins playing and the shot changes from Jerry's apartment to the coffee shop. In mass media television, the shot usually changes every 1.5 to 3 minutes. Why? For variety! In print media, variety can be employed by changing the speakers or individuals being quoted. Variety keeps the story fresh and interesting. The audience wants change to evoke stimulation. If you are teaching, you might want to move around the classroom to incorporate variety and keep the students engaged.

Pace is another important structural consideration. It involves how fast or how slow the mass media message unfolds. When considering pace, it is important to talk about different paces for different mass media messages. Jimmy John's commercials offer a great example for pace because the shots are quick and the dialogue is fast. This element of pace is employed because Jimmy John's offers speedy service—you order it, you get it fast. Now compare Jimmy John's to a Corona ad. Ah...that single shot of two people together sitting on the beach. We want a slower pace for Corona because we're trying to associate a feeling with a product. Corona is a beverage we enjoy while relaxing, so the pace for the ad is slow and relaxed. Sometimes variety in pace is good, too. In good television drama, for example, some scenes may unfold very quickly, like a montage. Other times the scenes happen very slowly. For instance, if a character has a deep and powerful realization, typically the pace will slow down significantly to accentuate the moment.

The final structural consideration is **climax**. It is very important to understand that, no matter what message you are writing, climax must ***always*** be considered. Sometimes in mass media a climax is unnecessary, but we should always consider it. In print writing, movies, and television drama, the climax is the point at which the major dramatic question of the story is answered. It is the point at which the tension relating to the dramatic question is most acute; the point at which that vital question is answered.

No matter what realm of mass media we are writing for, we must be **clear, correct, concise,** and **complete**, and we also have to consider **unity, variety, pace,** and **climax**. Good writing is good writing no matter what the format; these writing considerations are the same for any form of writing for mass media.

Overall, **quality writing is quality writing**. No matter the form—web, print, radio, TV, film—quality writing is quality writing. Good writing is concise, clear, correct, and complete. By taking a theoretical approach and analyzing sender, receiver, context, channel, and feedback, the writer can create effective mass media messages. When you consider the elements of theoretical communication, you can reduce the difference between the intended message and the actual message by increasing clarity. It all comes back to telling a good story *well*.

CHAPTER 3:
THE WRITING PROCESS

As the writer thinks about beginning to write and their proverbial toolbox, it is important that they be mindful of the steps of the writing process. Whenever a writer sits down for their first assignment, there are several stages of the process a writer needs to be especially mindful of as the writer grows. These stages include preparing to write, formulating the story concept, research, planning, listing planning, drafting, and sharing. The writer can produce a quality mass media piece if they thoughtfully execute these stages of the writing process.

PREPARING TO WRITE

When preparing to write, we need to consider several elements. The first of these is research, which I like to think of as a treasure hunt. We also need to consider concept formulation, research methods, and information gathering.

The writer is always part of a team. Whether you are a radio writer, working with someone on-air, or you are a reporter, working with a publisher and an editor, you will be working as a writer who is part of a team. Always remember that mass media production is a collaborative effort. Hopefully, in this process, the whole is greater than the sum of the individual parts contributed to it. Suffice it to say every time you see a piece of mass media, it is the result of a collaborative effort from many people. Be cognizant of this and know that you will be working with other people, and being clear to the people you are working with. This is a theme we have talked about throughout. How can you be clear?

As you prepare to write, please know that there will be pressure. Time is money in mass media. There are deadlines, and they are unmoving. Deadlines are set so that the work can go on-air or go to press. We talked about accuracy, and being correct. There are issues of originality, creativity, and job success. All of those things are important, but also know that you will be under great pressure while putting them together. Preparing to write the story first can help this process go more smoothly.

Concept Formulation

When preparing to write, the first consideration in the writing process is **concept formulation**. This occurs before we even research, and here, we are thinking about what we have to do. When we talk about concept formulation, we want to think about our approach, which is the dramaturgical approach. The key question here is: What is my story? What is the dramatic thing I am trying to tell them? It might be a sports story in print. It may be a radio story about a strike at a grocery store. It could be a television story about the invasion of gnats we have had lately. Whatever the media is, we want a *story*. We want to highlight the dramatic elements.

We need to think about our **angle**. Point of view, hook, slant, or angle is not the same as our editorial position. For instance, if I tell a story about the bugs outside, I can tell it from the point of view of a grounds keeper, or a student trying to get to class, or a teacher who tried to ride their bike through them. I could talk from the scientific position and interview biologists who study bugs. Whose point of view we tell the story from is our angle. Again, this is not the same as an editorial opinion.

Then, if we are writing a longer-length dramatic piece, such as a documentary or feature film, thinking about our idea, we are going to think about our concept formulation. Here, we are thinking about the story that we are going to develop. This could be for a commercial, or a documentary, or a news story; you get a concept, an idea, and you describe the idea you want to develop. What if an old dude decided to kick some gangster butt? That was the concept formula behind *Gran Torino*. Or what if some goofy employee of ADM decided to blow the whistle? This is *The* Informant. Usually, this is a "What if..." sort of concept.

Then, after we have a concept formula, we develop a treatment. A **treatment** is a point-by-point description of the story, the plot, the commercial, or the series of commercials part of a campaign. We will talk more about this later, but developing a treatment is usually what is used to do the actual writing of the piece.

Research

Research is preparation to make choices. The writer is going to make choices about what to include and what not to include. Unless the writer does research and is able to pick and choose information, the chance of the writer producing excellent work is slight. The first step for the writer, then, is to find information on their assignment topic.

It is important to think strategically about concept and formula when preparing to write a story. This leads into our next idea in preparing to write, which is **research strategies**. Writing is about making choices, as stated previously. In order to make choices, the writer needs to know more than is minimally necessary to complete a writing project so they can make choices of inclusion and exclusion. As the writer is thinking about their research, the first thing that they need to do is identify their needs. What are they trying to write? Is it primarily informative, persuasive, or entertaining? The writer needs to determine the format of communication so that the writer knows what they need when researching. The writer determines their objectives. What is the writer trying to get across here? Then, the writer thinks about what the design will be. What is the organizational sequence the writer is going to use? Last, the writer thinks about the actual writing. How are they going to tell the story? All of these factors affect the writer's research.

Research is like a treasure hunt. I used to debate competitively as a student, and a key part of debating is finding those key pieces of evidence that were going to make the other team fail when it came time to argue a point. I like finding those pieces of evidence. It is like finding treasure. If you decide to become a reporter, research skills will serve you well, and there is a lot of satisfaction in finding exactly the right quote or statistic or story.

For example, I have been working on a film about Illinois State University students who fought in the Civil War. I was down in the basement archives of the library researching and I found some information that gave me an interesting story piece. My research revealed that ISU students volunteered to go help the Union during the Civil War. The research source explained that they were taken to Missouri, and Captain Ulysses Grant commanded them. The students were in a group that was fighting Missouri confederate forces near Ironton, Missouri, and the Union troops were getting beaten because they did not have artillery, but the enemy did. One soldier-student, whom they nicknamed "Moose," became angry that his comrades were being hurt and decided to do something about it. Moose sprinted toward the rebel position, and the other Union soldiers, in a confused reaction, followed Moose. Moose breached enemy lines first, grabbed control of a cannon, turned it around, and began firing it on the enemy's own line. It completely changed the course of the battle. The battle was noteworthy because it was the first battle that Ulysses Grant won and it was the first Union victory west of the Mississippi River. The battle changed the momentum of the conflict in Missouri, an important strategic state in the geography of the Civil War. The victory at Ironton began the Union push that ended with Union forces taking control of parts of the Missouri River. This incident is an entertaining story. This also illustrates how research can reveal entertaining episodes.

It was finding a treasure to find that true story. I did much research. Finally, I came across that story, and it became a key incident in the screenplay. I could see Matt Damon and Ben Affleck playing that scene in my movie...the drama is there. Payoff in research is like finding a piece of gold, but a writer can only find it through much research.

McKee talks extensively about research methods. McKee says that there are three major research methods you can use when preparing to reach your audience. You can use research by memory, research by imagination, or research by fact. **Research by memory** is when you ask yourself questions about experiences in your life. How can this inform your mass media? In the film *Dazed and Confused,* (a film about high school students in Texas in the late 1970s) for example, the writer had to have some experience of living that way. The writer used memories of being that way in high school. The second thing McKee suggests is **research by imagination**. This is thinking about things that *could* happen. This works particularly well when a writer is crafting drama. What will happen if something else happens? The writer must use their imagination. Finally, the writer can **research by fact**. This is researching what really happened to get data for the story. In news writing particularly, this is researching hard facts for the writer's story, or research based on real facts. This is also used in dramatic writing.

The first step in this process is **information gathering**. Remember, the library is often forgotten, but it is a good place to conduct research. You know the library, right? That big building at the end of the quad? Libraries are great places to start for researching; they have books, government documents, journals, magazines, newspapers, films, music, art, tons of stuff. Yes, they also have the Internet, but do not forget the value of those print sources. Subject librarians are also really good; they usually know where to find subject information across sections of the library, and they can help you get the information you need. I also want to stress the use of government documents available in a library. They have copies of the law, copies of general hearings, census reports, etc. A particularly useful resource in the library is *The Reader's Digest of Periodic Literature.* This guide indexes magazine articles on various topics. Books can also be useful to the mass media writer. Reference materials can give basic information on various topics.

I think I mentioned that the reference library is God's gift to all of us. The reference library can really help you find facts and information. Go to the reference desk and ask the librarians for help; they are really gifted at what they do. I also talked about government documents. Those references can be very useful.

Online Research

Online research can be tremendously useful. A writer can find a lot of information on the web these days. The web is particularly useful when the writer scrutinizes the source. Internet databases such as Lexus-Nexus can be an excellent resource.

Online research is one of the benefits of living in the twenty-first century. There are many great sources you can get online. The web is a rich resource for government documents. If you want a speech by the President, you can get the transcript at the Rose Garden Online at the White House web site ten minutes before he gives that speech. Government documents are published now, and the web offers lots of access to this information. Another great source on the web is periodicals. Personally, when I go to my office and get online, the *New York Times* home page is what comes up. I can get just about any magazine or newspaper online. Finally, organizational web sites are a wonderful source. If I am doing a piece on Nike, I can go to their web site and get press releases and breaking news right from the organizational source.

Pitfalls of Online Research

There are pitfalls to researching online. First, you have to be careful of false or biased info. Let me say that each source has its own **slant** on issues. There is going to be slant wherever you go to get any information. When talking about slant, it is important to remember that it is not presenting the idea that constitutes "slant." It is which ideas we choose and how we organize them that can create slant. I can pick and choose; I can make a decision for myself, and that is what is great about America. Credibility is another huge pitfall in online research. For some reason, I think of Michael Jackson. I remember when he got arrested the second time, there were a bunch of rumors that all of this child pornography had been found at the scene, and CNN online published that information. Now, that turned out to be false; it was a rumor. CNN online did not clear it up very well. With the web, and with the 24-hour news cycle, everyone wants to be the first source to break a story. Here, CNN did not really check their information in their rush to be the first person to break the story. People may rush to judgments, and therefore, people rush to publish rumors instead of facts. It can be hard to verify information on the web, and it may be difficult to verify the source. How can we deal with these pitfalls of web research? Use advanced search engines or platforms that allow you to go to pre-screened sources. Using multiple sources is really the key here; you need to double-check your facts. Just because you find information online does not mean it is good. Old information also can be found online, but you need to be careful that you are scrutinizing the date as well as the author of these sources.

Research through Observation

The next type of research you might do is **observation**. The writer can watch something, be there, and act as a witness. First of all, "seeing," is not enough. A writer needs to double-check what they believe they saw when they are observing. The idea of a **Rashomon Effect** is helpful here. It comes from Kurosawa's 1955 film *Rashomon*, where characters are shown from multiple perspectives. A good example would be if I look at the desk in the front of the classroom. I may see a computer, a phone, a notebook. But Ben, my assistant, sitting *behind* that same desk, may see something quite different. He sees my phone, my keys, a pack of cigarettes, etc. Ben sees the desk differently than me. It is not that we are looking at different desks, but rather we are seeing the same desk from different views. This is the Rashomon Effect. When I observe, I have a situational perspective that effects what I see. Therefore, observation is not always enough. The writer needs to understand what lies behind their perception.

General observation is very beneficial. It offers you information on what was *actually* there at the time. That having been said, it is important to note that **observation changes action**. Elsewhere in this book we discussed quantum physics and Heisenberg's uncertainty principle. This idea means that simply being observed or measured changes the subject. In our case, people act differently when they are in front of a camera. To that extent, a reporter taking notes may influence the information. If the former Vice President thought that he was not being watched, imagine what he would have said instead of just, "go fuck yourself," on the senate floor that day...he probably would have shot the guy. People act differently when they are being watched.

As the aspiring writer thinks about observation, one possible approach is **participant observation**. Participant observation gives the writer inside information about an event. This is the difference between **etic knowledge**, which gives us information from the *outside*, and the idea of emic knowledge. **Emic knowledge** is the idea that when a person lives through an event, they are going to see it differently than the outside observer. It is kind of like embedded truths. It is one thing for a reporter to be on the outside looking at our trials and tribulations, talking about us fighting the enemy, but when that reporter is traveling with the convoy, day in and day out, they start to get a type of knowledge about it. If I hang out with the troops, I will have an insider's view. Paul Schrader, the writer of *Taxi Driver*, drove a cab for six months to try and understand what Travis Bickle, his main character, may have felt. There are other examples of this as well, but if you really want to know something when writing about it, you might want to try and *live* it. Hunter S. Thompson, the author of *Hell's Angels: A Strange and Terrible Saga*, was a gonzo journalist. Thompson wanted to get inside and know what it is to be in Hell's Angels, so what did he do? He became a member of Hell's Angels and started doing copious amounts of drugs. Nothing like a man on an ether binge....

If you are writing a screenplay, this is particularly important. I think about Nora Ephron talking about writers who come out of film school; they know nothing about *life*. All they know about is film school. So, when they get out, they turn around and write a movie about *being in film school*. If you are going to write about something, it may be incredibly beneficial to live through it so that you know about it.

In terms of observation and non-verbal communication, non-verbal communication gives depth to a story. A writer should not just observe the words; observe the non-verbal communication that goes with it. Sarcasm is a good example of this; it does not translate without some other form of accompaniment than just the words.

It is also important to note the relationship between observation and perspective. For example, the BBC, which is just left of center, and Fox News, which is to the right-of-center, can use the same set of facts and deliver a completely different story. The coverage of Hurricane Katrina in a major weekly news magazine is a case in point. The differences in captions under photographs were repugnant. The magazine featured a photograph of people of color carrying bottled water out of a grocery store, and the caption under the photograph read, "Looters pillage local grocery store." Five pages later, they had white people carrying DVD players and electronics out of a Walmart, and the caption read, "Survivors gather supplies." The difference between the captions was arguable unethical writing. Perspectives (biases) influence reporting, and writers, editors, and producers have a responsibility to be fair and balanced, not just *say* they are fair and balanced. This should be influenced by the goal of accuracy as well. A writer should strive to be correct and accurate in their observations.

Interviewing

Interviewing is also like a treasure hunt. There are certain challenges in interviewing. We are going to discuss these challenges, as well as pre-interviewing research, writing the questions, conducting the interview, selecting and using quotes, giving attribution to these quotes, and then also talk briefly about sound bites.

Interviews are valuable research opportunities. A writer can go to experts in the field. For instance, at a university, there are many experts (professors) on a variety of topics. These are easily accessible resources for a writer. If a writer was crafting a piece on a band, they could go to a music professor and conduct an interview about popular music. It is always a good idea for a writer to gather as much information as they can (see Appendix).

Interviewing is a challenge. A writer has deadlines; these get more acute as the writer moves through their career. Deadlines are everything in journalism. Imagine when you have to have a story done every day. Imagine having two or three stories you have to get in to the station by 5 P.M. This happens all the time in the mass media field. Writing is about choices of inclusion and exclusion. When you are thinking about interviews, it is the same thing. You have to think about which people to interview and which quotes to use from them.

The purpose of an interview is to gather information. If a writer wants facts about the situation, they can talk to the people that were there to get first-hand information. The second thing a writer can do with interviews is collect actualities for broadcasting. **Actualities** are sound bites. These are little pieces that are actual bits of sound from your interviews. For example, if the broadcaster is talking about the governor, and then it cuts to a clip of the actual governor speaking, that is an actuality or a sound bite. In radio, you would just hear the governor's voice. In a television broadcast the audience would see a video clip of him speaking. In television, there is a type of show called interview programming. This is a specific type of television broadcast in which an interview serves as the entire piece. Charlie Rose is an example of interview programming. Oprah also does this frequently.

Doing **interview pre-research** is important. In order to make choices of inclusion and exclusion, we need to know enough about the topic we are interviewing someone on. First, I will do some library, online, or observation research, then, I will ask questions about the topic. You do not want to go into an interview knowing nothing about them. For example, if you interview someone, you would do research before you call the subject, then call them to ask informed general questions before you sit down with them.

In terms of getting the interview, the first thing we must consider is *who* we are going to interview. Who could you interview? First, experts or professionals in the field are an option. If we are writing a piece about the stimulus package, we could interview economists or financial advisors. People who are directly affected by the story are also good interview subjects. In the case of the stimulus package piece, we could talk to people whose financial portfolios are being affected by the changes. Other great interview sources are those subjects who were there when the story happened. As a reporter, we are sharing our second-hand knowledge; we want someone who was there at the time.

Setting up the interview is the next step. This includes conducting the interview where the interview is comfortable for the interviewee. We are also going to discuss exactly where and when we are going to meet. Their setting of choice is often the best place. You might mention if you are going to use any recording devices, such as audio or video. Let me just say that if someone sits down with you, and they *see* that there is a recording device in front of them, they would have a hard time in court defending that you should not have been filming; it is almost an **implied consent**. For example, in the recent comedy *Borat*, several male college students were portrayed poorly in a certain scene in an RV. They tried to sue the film-makers on the grounds that they did not know the footage would be used in a major motion picture. They lost the lawsuit because the camera was *clearly* visible at the time Sacha Baron Cohen was filming them. Yes, they came off looking pretty bad, but they could see that they were being filmed. You should always ask consent to your interview subjects, but just keep that in mind. Some people know this, which is why their boss or organization will make you get prior clearance for recording in any way before the interview begins.

When sitting down to write your questions, the first thing a writer can do is write down all the subject areas they want to know more about. This is a wish list, of sorts. What kind of answers would the writer want? Then, create questions that will try to capture those. You want to get the basic information like the news elements, but then you also want to get some opinions. These can provide tones and colors for a piece. You want some prediction or forecasting. You might want to ask quantifying questions as well.

When conducting the interview, be punctual and respectful. As you start, you want to make them comfortable with some small talk. A writer should get to know the interviewee. Then the writer should begin asking the questions. Start with the easy questions first. Sometimes the writer will have some tough questions to ask. You want to get some sound bites and basic information from the interviewee first, just in case you offend them and they decide to end the interview. Therefore, start with easy, agreeable questions and work your way toward the tough information you really want. Do not start with, "Do you still molest kids?"

In terms of **off-the-record information**: *it does not exist.* Tell them that. If someone says, "I want to say this 'off-the-record,'" stop them. Say, "There cannot be any of that." You are a reporter. If you are there, it is not off-the-record. During the interview, it just does not exist. Think of the consequences of your questions.

In terms of recording, I recommend you do something to remember the information your interviewee is giving you. A voice or audio recorder is always a good idea because it is less invasive than a camera and usually less expensive. Always ask before you start recording. If you do not want to record, you can also take notes. I recommend you take notes even if you are recording just in case something happens to your file. For you public relations people, who will be giving the interview very frequently to reporters in the mass media, let me offer you a tip: speak as slow as you see the person who is interviewing you is writing. You can control the flow of what they are writing down. Make sure they get the quotes *you* want.

Remember that as an interviewee you have the power. The interview is over when you say it is over. Just because you agree to meet with someone does not mean you have to give them any information. You can control what information they get and how they get it. You might want to go in with some talking points. This is particularly useful in public relations work. The interview is over when you have gotten out your three talking points. You do not have to answer anything else. You can just say, "This interview is over, have a good day." If they are under a deadline, they are going to publish what you gave them.

After the interview, be polite. There is an issue here of whether you give them approval or not. Sometimes, the reporter will send a copy of the piece to the subject to double-check the accuracy of their quotes, and that can be good. We might possibly want to let them review the story, but that would be over and above courtesy. However, never give the right to edit your piece to your interviewee. That is just not their right. Whether or not you even give them the right to read it is up to you, but it is NOT the professional common practice to do so. If you are doing a public relations piece, you might want to double-check at least their quotes with them.

Using Quotations from an Interview

We are talking about the treasure hunt again when we are looking for interview questions and actualities that we can use to augment the story. Thus, we will next discuss using quotes in a story. There are several reasons for using quotes. The first is because we want to use colorful language that gives the piece character. The writer will also want to get exactly what the interviewee said. We want to get their exact mood. Remember again that quotes need to be accurate. "Yes" or "no" is not a quote. Watch for redundancies. Do not use a quote to say what you just wrote in the introduction of the quote or the story itself.

One thing to mention here is correcting the grammar of your speaker. We want to be lenient a little bit here. If you are going to correct their grammar, there are a couple ways to do it. First, I would recommend using an indirect quotation. The second thing we can do is include the incorrect grammar but then to identify, in brackets, "sic."

[Sic] indicates that we know it is wrong, but that is how they said it. It is a judgment call. Many times, I will take out the "um's" and "uh's" that appear in my quotations. If it detracts from the message, then remove it. If their bad grammar impedes clarity, then we might decide to go with clarity and correct it. Just to be by the book, however, it is often easiest to make it an indirect quotation.

Sometimes, however, we might want to embarrass them, or to show that they did not use the English Language correctly because it completes part of the piece we are writing. I think of former President George W. Bush saying, "Fool me once shame on you....fool me twice.....you can't fool me no more." To some extent, you might want to show that he actually misspoke that saying that way instead of correcting him.

When it comes to considerations in using quotes, the first is that you do not have to use every quote you get. You are going to be making choices and include the quotes that will help your story and exclude the ones that will not. To that extent, what you need to do is get more quotes than you actually need. This way, you are able to make choices about what to select for inclusion. Variety in quotes is a good thing. Whether this is in the language that they use or incorporating multiple speakers, variety is important. If the writer wants to get eyewitness accounts, they may also want to get several different sources for our quotes. Always use AP style when using quotes.

Also, when in doubt, leave it out. If the style or the language is mangled or unclear, or there is any reason to not use it, leave it out. It is better to be smart and concise than to add something that detracts from the clarity of the message. Work on your tape or digital recording skills. It is important to have these so you can always have what your interviewee actually said.

PLANNING

The second step a writer can take in crafting a story is evaluating and planning. Here, a writer is going to ponder on the notes and resources they have collected. During this stage the writer will be making more choices: *What information do I need? What do not I need? What do I have information on? Do I need more on other things? Do I need to go back and do more research? How can I narrow my topic (depth verse breadth)?*

LISTING

Another step in the writing process is listing. This is when a writer decides what information they are going to use in a story. This is an imaginative variation where the writer is brainstorming and setting up the ideas that they want to communicate. Those could become the main paragraphs or main ideas of the story. There is an element of prioritization when a writer is making lists. If a writer is writing for straight news, they may choose to use an inverted pyramid organizational sequence. In this case, the writer is going to think about organization so that readers start with the most important thing and move to the least important thing. Or, the writer might want to tell a dramatic story. In this case, the author could use some chronology and highlight the dramatic elements. Thus, when the writer lists and revises such lists, they choose appropriate information and an organization scheme.

DRAFTING

At this point in the writing process, the writer should **write the draft as they would say it.** The important thing here is for the writer to get their ideas down on paper. With computer technology now, after the initial draft, the writer is going to edit, and edit, and edit, and edit. Thus, at this stage, it is important for the writer to get some ideas down on paper (or on the hard drive). One approach to starting a story is for the writer to get it out on the keyboard as they would tell the story orally. At this stage the writer has an intuitive sense of how the language works grammatically. University students are supposed to be the educated elite; they should know grammar. Thus, the writer of the draft should just sit down and let the words come out naturally. The writer can type an initial draft as they would say it.

Then, the writer gets to the first stage of re-writing. Redundancy will help me reinforce this point. The writer would look at this rough draft and scrutinize it. The writer must edit it and shift its elements around to make sure that they are sticking to the suitable design they have chosen. The writer should try to fix any potential problems in the initial draft. Then the writer can print the working draft. At this point, the writer should read the copy and mark it up. The writer should make sure they are choosing the best word, and triple-check for any grammar problems. Note any mistakes or areas that could be improved. Using a red pen and marking the copy can be helpful at this stage. The writer can then go back onto the computer, access a soft copy, make those changes on the computer, save, and print. Repeat this stage of the process several times. There is utility in the presence of a physical paper copy at this point. The tactile presence demands the writer's attention and presents a challenge: where can I find mistakes or places where changes will improve the piece? Again, the goal is to find several places for improvement at each pass. The goal, then, is not to decide that the piece is good enough, but to identify changes that will make it better. I would suggest that it is probably the third or fourth version that you use for the next step.

As always, when we write, we need to be considerate of the editing process. Here, we need to write, revise, rewrite, revise, rewrite, and revise. Your employers will appreciate your dedication to excellence in writing if you revise and rewrite. Go to the computer, make the revisions, print it up, read it, make the changes, print it out again, read it, make changes, print it again, etc. Am I being redundant here? Good!

When you re-read your story, make sure that you read it out loud and think about structure. Is the most important thing coming first? If not, move it up to the first graph. Continue to reexamine your structure. You are also checking for accuracy. Make sure every name is spelled right and every word is chosen well. Make sure you are using clear language. If you have two independent clauses, break them up. Also, watch for excess language. Concision requires we get rid of extra words. Think of Strunk and White—"every word should tell." For example, if you have "very important," get rid of the "very." The real-world boss expects these choices to be made.

The next step is sharing. We need other writers to read our material. When you print it up, have your roommate read it. Make appropriate changes, and then have the person you go to the movies with read it. Make appropriate changes, and print another copy. Take it home to your mom and have her read it. Make appropriate changes, and print another copy. Have a classmate do it in exchange for the same from you. Offer to buy lunch for a friend if they will read it. Then, after all that, take it to somewhere like the University Writing Center. Most universities offer services where writing tutors are paid with tuition and fees to read student writing and offer suggestions. Students will be well advised to utilize these services whenever offered, considering the students are paying for such services already. Your readers do not have to know whether or not your radio story format is correct, you just need someone to go over the copy and check for sentence structure and word choice and grammar.

A writer should pick and choose which suggestions to incorporate into subsequent versions depending on how much the writer trusts the writing ability of those who review the story. If a similar comment comes from more than one reader, a writer may decide to consider the suggestion more seriously. Ultimately, the writer is looking for the opinion of a reader that is similar to those who will read the work once it is published or produced.

For instance, a co-author and I seek a publisher for a non-fiction manuscript working about the papacy of the Roman Catholic Church. We have been working on it for several years. It has gone through many revisions and is very different from the first drafts. I have a co-author, but we have gotten many people to read it (colleagues, friends, priests, representatives from publishing companies, reviewers for academic conferences, even unfortunate family members ☺) and revise it, and it has not even gotten to an editor or a publisher yet.

No matter the professional level of a writer, the best product results from numerous revisions. I have had the opportunity to write a voice-over for Danny Glover who narrated a documentary that I produced and directed. The script went through at least 50 versions before I spent the thousands of dollars, picked up Glover in a limo, and took him to the studio. I needed to make sure it was the very best it could be, and that necessitated many revisions. I had to write it, re-write it, and then share it with the assistant director. Then, when I got his comments back, I took it, and made the changes and printed it up again and gave it to the second assistant director, and then I made those changes. Then I took it to a colleague in my university department to read and offer suggestions. I made those changes and then I put in a scratch VO, which is a version that would not be included in the final film, and then we had hundreds of students watch it. We took their suggestions to revise it again.

Print writers work with editors and publishers, and part of their job is to get paid to tell the writer how their writing can be improved. Editors are invaluable friends for the writer. When a writer gets comments back that say "you really should say more about this," it is probably in your best interest to go back and say more about that. Writers *need* editors, and we need to go through this process of sharing and revisions in order to make good writing. During this sharing process, it is important that the writer does not tie their ego to the piece. What is the most important thing? Clarity! Even a very good writer should not sit down, spit out a page, and assume it cannot be improved. The fundamental question is: *How can I more clearly communicate my ideas to my audience?*

Then, the final stage is polishing. Yopp and McAdams suggest that we need word-by-word perfection. In the final stages, a writer is rigorously scrutinizing their work. The attitude of, "No, he doesn't know me. I wrote for my high school newspaper. I'm a great writer. I can crank this out the night before," will get a student a "D," or maybe a, "C," if they are lucky. Does the student want to earn a "B?" You need revise and re-write. In the real world, slack is not accepted. Revise and re-write, over and over. Everything you turn in should go through at least five rewrites. I once read in a business magazine that most copy had to go through nine revisions before it is accepted in this business publication. Welcome to the real world. That is how we make our writing clear. I want us to aware that to become a good writer, you have to be committed to bouncing it off other people.

The writer of *The Boondock Saints* just sat down and thought, "Well, I do not know how this is going to come together or how to say it, but I'm just going to put it out there." He did not have final drafts, and when it came time for casting, Brad Pitt was considering the lead role of one of the brothers, but the script he got was not a final version. When they sat down to do readings, the magic was not there. If he had sat down and revised and rewrote and edited, then that film could have been so much more. At last, you want to give your piece the once-over. If you work with this process, you will do great things in your career. This is the first step in writing excellence.

In this chapter, we have discussed the stages of the mass media writing process. These stages include preparing to write, formulating the story concept, research, planning, listing planning, drafting, and sharing. The writer can produce a quality mass media piece if they thoughtfully execute these stages of the writing process.

CHAPTER 4:
THE WRITER'S TOOLBOX

Vocabulary and grammar are essential tools for the mass media writer. If every writer were metaphorically equipped with a toolbox full of the elements that enable writing, vocabulary (words) would be in the top drawer of the toolbox. Grammar, the rules for putting words together into sentences, would be in the second drawer.

THE ELEMENTS OF STYLE
by WILLIAM STRUNK Jr. and E. B. WHITE

The Elements of Style by William Strunk Jr. and E. B. White, a classic book on compositional style, has much to say about basic composition and grammar. The following is a foreword written by Stephen King for his book *On Writing*:

> This is a short book because most books about writing are filled with bullshit. Fiction writers, present company included, don't understand very much about what they do—not why it works when it's good, not why it doesn't when it's bad. I figured the shorter the book, the less the bullshit.
>
> One notable exception to the bullshit rule is *The Elements of Style*, by William Strunk Jr. and E. B. White. There is little or no detectable bullshit in that book. (Of course it's short; at eighty-five pages it's much shorter than this one.) I'll tell you right now that every aspiring writer should read *The Elements of Style*. Rule 17 in the chapter titled Principles of Composition is "Omit needless words." I will try to do that here.

The Elements of Style can help a writer develop a great foundational starting point when it comes to compositional style. When I start writing a book or an academic article, I find that reading through *The Elements of Style*, which rarely takes longer than thirty minutes, is beneficial when approaching the art of writing strategically. This work is particularly valuable when considering vocabulary and grammar. Every word in this book tells, hopefully, as every word should tell when writing for the mass media.

Vocabulary

Words are the most basic tool for a mass media writer. They are the building blocks of imparting a message. There are several stylistic considerations for appropriate vocabulary when writing for mass media. Several of these were offered by Strunk and White.

Use simple words. When writing for mass media, the writer should encode the message into signs that are easiest for the audience to decode. Clarity is the most important consideration, rather than impressing the reader with our vocabulary. For instance in Earnest Hemmingway's writing, there is power in little words. He used simple words to evoke a meaning. Most great writers rely on simple words when they can evoke the desired meaning in a reader. On the other hand, comedian Dennis Miller, who was an unsuccessful announcer on Monday Night Football, when it was on ABC, often allowed his vocabulary to interfere with effective mass media communication. He used phrases like, "Insurmountable Sisyphean challenge," and Joe 12-Pack, sitting at home trying to watch football, had to refer a dictionary just to understand the commentary. Refer to the section on audience in Chapter 2. Whether or not Miller used terms like these to impress his viewers, his wide vocabulary interfered with his ability to clearly communicate the message to his audience. Thus, for example, a writer could refer to Miller's problem in two ways:

>Bad: *The spectators were daunted by his lexicon.*
>Good: *The audience was impressed by his vocabulary.*

Avoid fancy words. Just use simple words.

>Bad: *The antagonistic party extrapolated an insult from the remark.*
>Good: *The opposing party was offended by the remark.*

The mass media writer should use first-order and general words—English derivation rather than Latin. For example, which phrase sounds more natural: "He felt it deep down in his intestines" or "He felt it deep down in his gut"? What is the first word that comes to mind? That is probably the best word. This is consistent with Strunk and White's suggestion that **one should write in a way that comes naturally**. Borrowing from Stephen King, "Dressing up your pet in formal wear is embarrassing for the cat." It should be also embarrassing for the owner. It is best to just let the proverbial cat be a cat. Leave your words and ideas in simple form rather than trying to dress them up. Strunk and White suggest that we might want to trust our ear. How would it sound best? That is often our best bet.

> Bad: *The owner decided to let the pigs be unharnessed.*
> Good: *The owner decided to let the pigs loose.*

Use definitive, specific language. The writer is trying to paint a mental picture in the mind of the reader, so the writer should use words that are descriptive and specific. This way, the writer has more control over the image evoked in the mind of the receiver.

> Bad: *The woman was sad.*
> Good: *The woman was grieving due to the loss of her husband.*

Be clear to the audience. The most important consideration when writing for mass media is clarity. There is a difference between writing for mass media and writing for literature or art. An English professor may want you to impress them with your vocabulary, but Joe 12-Pack, who is just trying to figure out what time the monster truck show starts, does not. For example, describing the brave men and women that serve in the armed forces could be referred to as *soldiery*, but that term may not be as clear to the audience as the word *troops*. Another excellent example is the word *home* rather than *domicile*. When a receiver is distracted by vocabulary, it detracts from their ability to decode the message the writer is trying to send. Complex vocabulary can be distracting and can impede clarity.

Homonyms can also cause trouble. For example, the difference between what is "aurally" pleasing and "orally" pleasing, is the difference between a successful act of communication and an unsettling scandal. Mass media writers should try to avoid words that may lead to audience confusion. Stick with first-order words, not second-order words.

> Bad: *Seventeen academians made honor roll.*
> Good: *Seventeen students made honor roll.*

Mass media writers should avoid technical jargon or nomenclature. Ask yourself: for whom am I writing? In most cases in mass media, the answer to that question is "as many people as possible." If a tennis player wants to write a story about tennis for the general public, the tennis player should avoid specialized language or technical jargon that would come off as Greek to most readers. The article would be unclear to the general public, and possibly to many sports readers. The technical language of tennis might be appropriate for a tennis magazine, but a standard newspaper has a far wider audience than just tennis players. Do not use technical language solely to show that you possess some advanced knowledge, but rather use language that the general public can understand.

<u>Bad:</u>   *The musician improvised in the F# Phrygian mode.*
<u>Good:</u> *The musician improvised in an uncommon scale.*

When writing for printed mass media, a writer should use the word "said," when quoting a spoken source. Instead of using "The president suggested" or "The president contended," use "The president said." "Added" or "told" could work depending on the person and situation, but generally "said" is the verb a journalist looking to communicate with the largest audience should use. When writing for print, use the past tense "said." The event has already happened, so keep it in the past when writing for print. When writing for broadcasts such as radio or television, the writer will generally use the present tense "says." Never use the word "stated" or "according to" unless you are referring to information within a document: "The document stated…" People do not *state*.

<u>Bad:</u>   *Dustin stated, "I swear I did not do it."*
<u>Good:</u> *Dustin said, "I swear I did not do it."*

Word choice is important in mass media writing. Having a dictionary on-hand is always helpful. A dictionary can help a writer figure out whether or not they are using a word in the most appropriate way. If there is even the slightest doubt, a writer should check to see that they are using a word correctly. For instance, if a writer uses the word "precocious" to describe a clever, retired professor, they would be using the wrong word. "Precocious" does not mean just clever, but cleverer than their age—developed or matured earlier than usual. "Close enough" may be good for horseshoes and hand-grenades, but not for choosing words in our writing. In a description of an employee, *conscientious* is much different than *contentious*. If a writer is not sure of a word, they should either look the word up in a dictionary or avoid it altogether.

Bad: *Residents embargoed the fast food chain.*
Good: *Residents boycotted the fast food chain.*

Omit needless words—something Stephen King mentioned. Every word should be essential. Mass media writing should be concise. Remember, the writer's goal is to articulate a message in the simplest, clearest way possible.

Bad: *Every single day the child asked over and over again for a dog.*
Good: *Every day the child asked for a dog.*

Avoid colloquialisms. Colloquialisms are like local slang. If you do use one, do not put quotations around them. Try to avoid colloquialisms; they might be more appropriate for fiction writings, but not for journalism. Likewise, avoid euphemism, as discussed in the next chapter.

Bad: *The two friends had a reputation for being chill.*
Good: *The two friends had a reputation for being laid back.*

Use orthodox spelling. Avoid text talk. A writer should use *through* rather than *thru*. "OMG," is not going to work in journalism. That is the type of nomenclature that a writer should avoid when writing for the mass media. These types of phrases should be reserved for texting.

Bad: *The president said, "Ur a cool dood."*
Good: *The president said, "You're a cool dude."*

Spell proper names correctly. When it comes to proper names, be careful about what you get from the web. I once had a student write a paper about the rapper Vanilla Ice, whose real name is Rob Van Winkle. This student spelled the rapper's last name "Vanwinkle" and it didn't look right to me. I went on the web and checked the spelling. The Miami Herald had his name spelled "Van Winkle." I kept looking, and on the ninth webpage of the search results, I found it was spelled "Vanwinkle." I checked the source, and discovered the student had gotten the spelling from the web page of was an eighth-grade skater. If you are writing from the web, you must scrutinize those sources.

Use Spiel Czech. Word processors are very powerful tools—it is hard to imagine the life of a modern-day writer without them. **Spell-check features of word processing programs are useful tools.** A writer can write misspelled words, and spell-check fixes it. But a writer must be careful! Spell-check features in word processing programs do not catch all possible mistakes. Things such as compound words, sentence fragments, homonyms, and proper names can still sneak past. Spell-check is useful, but we can't trust the computer to do all our checking for us. Spell-check on computers does not necessarily differentiate correctly spelled proper names and incorrectly spelled proper names. If these types of mistakes slip through, they can damage the credibility of the writer. The writer is responsible for this basic level of copy editing.

GRAMMAR

If vocabulary is in the top drawer of a writer's toolbox, the second drawer of the toolbox would be grammar. Chances are, most people would consider their current understanding of grammar to be good, and it probably is. Our nation has a schooling system that focuses on learning grammar from our earliest days in kindergarten all the way to high school. Formal grammar is essentially just assigning names and categories to different words and parts of speech, and the only time we need to do this is when the parts are incorrect. Hopefully, at this point in your life you have a working understanding of grammar, but if not, there is always room to improve it.

Keep your sentences simple. When I think of simple sentences, I think of a subject and a predicate—nouns and verbs. If you take a noun and put a verb next to it, you have a sentence. A subject and a verb is generally all we ever need. A subject does something to an object (active voice as discussed later). Simple structure is like a safety net. Even if your writing is boring, simple sentences can help ensure overall clarity.

<u>Bad:</u>   *Run for mayor, he ultimately decided to.*
<u>Good:</u> *He ultimately decided to run for mayor.*

Pronouns should be in agreement with the verb tense. A writer should make sure to scrutinize over the proper use of pronouns, and remember that the number of the subject determines the number of the verb. You want an agreement between the singularity or plurality of the subject and the verb.

Bad: *They was driving at night.*
Good: *They were driving at night.*
Good: *He was driving at night.*

Generally when writing for mass media, use active voice. Active voice is when a subject acts on an object. Likewise, passive voice is when you have an object acted on by a subject. For example, instead of saying, "the man was arrested by police," which uses a passive voice, use "police arrested the man," which is active voice. Active construction is more forceful and to the point. There are, however, a couple examples where you might be able to use passive voice. One example of this would be if the object is more important than the subject: "Michael Jackson was arrested by the police." A while ago, I was working on probably the twelfth revision of the final chapter of a book I wrote, and there was something wrong with the last few sentences that I just couldn't grasp. The sentence was, "Web pages are used by activists to mobilize people." What should the sentence have been? "Activists use web pages to mobilize people." Active voice; subjects act on objects.

Bad: *The board had decided in an 8-1 vote to not divest their stocks.*
Good: *The board voted 8-1 not to divest their stocks.*

Complex sentences, or compound sentences, can increase variety in writing, although they should generally be avoided. Although we have been focusing on simple sentences, there are other sentence types you can use if it will not decrease clarity. In fact, you may want to vary sentence structure. Once writers begin to combine two independent clauses, they run the risk of creating a potential run-on sentence or comma splice. If we have an independent clause, one of the safest things to do is just put a period on the end of the damn thing and move to the next independent clause. Especially avoid combining two independent clauses that are not related, because they too run the risk of decreasing clarity.

Bad: *He made $200 and she made $100 and the company made $500.*
Good: *He made $200 while she made $100. The company made $500.*

Stephen King once suggested **fear is the root of all bad writing.** We tend to be timid instead of direct, and shy away from concrete language. We second-guess our message and whether we can articulate that message, and it makes this wishy-washy, unclear communication. What we need to do is be certain that we know what we are trying to communicate. **Quality writing is determined by its clarity, correctness, completeness, and conciseness.**

PUNCTUATION

Similar to grammar, punctuation is another one of those things that, by now, you either know it or you do not. **When it comes to the use of commas in a list, Strunk and White say that in a series of three of more terms with a single conjunction, use a comma after each term except for the last.** An example of this would be "The deranged man ran over a cat, a dog, an old lady, and a tricycle." You use a comma after each word on the list. However, even punctuation is open for debate. **The *Associated Press Stylebook* states that if the list is short, you do not use a comma after the last term before the conjunction**: "The deranged man ran over a cat, a dog, an old lady and a tricycle." In the end, whether or not you use a comma is either your, or more realistically, your boss's call. **Generally, in the mass media industry, the AP version is the accepted form** (See AP Exercises in the Appendix).

Bad: *The student bought a doughnut, a brownie, and an energy drink.*
Good: *The student bought a doughnut, a brownie and an energy drink.*

The following is a list of common punctuation conventions used in mass media writing.

Enclose parenthetical expressions between commas.

Bad: *The man who was very strong lifted the boulder.*
Good: *The man, who was very strong, lifted the boulder.*

Put a comma before the conjunction when joining two independent clauses in a sentence. Do not join two independent clauses with just a comma—that is a comma splice.

Bad: *The goat was chasing the cat, the ox was chasing the goat.*
Good: *The goat was chasing the cat, and the ox was chasing the goat.*

Use a dash to show a break or interruption, as opposed to a hyphen, which is conjoined. There is a difference between the dash and the hyphen, and this difference is often ignored by writers.

    <u>Bad:</u>   *The monster was hungry-it hadn't eaten anyone for days.*
    <u>Good:</u> *The monster was hungry—it hadn't eaten anyone for days.*

Do not put the title between the subject and the verb.

    <u>Bad:</u>   *Blagojevich, convicted felon, said...*
    <u>Good:</u> *Convicted felon Blagojevich said...*

Attribution at the end of the sentence is offset with commas.

    <u>Bad:</u>   *He's such a lightweight said the bumbling drunk.*
    <u>Good:</u> *He's such a lightweight, said the bumbling drunk.*

Attribution at the beginning of indirect quotation does not require a comma. What is the difference between a direct and an indirect quotation? An indirect quotation is an estimation of what the person said. For instance, if the president gave statistics that indicated the economy will perform better in the next quarter, a reporter could paraphrase the president and write, "The President said the economy will improve." When a writer is paraphrasing, it is an indirect quotation, commas and quotation marks are not required.

    <u>Bad:</u>   *Two of the councilmen said, they hate children.*
    <u>Good:</u> *Two of the councilmen said they hate children.*

A quotation within a direct quote is offset with single quotation marks. Comma and period also go inside the quotation marks on a direct quote.

    <u>Bad:</u>   *He said, "She said, "A woodchuck doesn't chuck metal.""*
    <u>Good:</u> *He said, "She said, 'A woodchuck doesn't chuck metal.'"*

If attribution comes after the first part of a quote, end the attribution with a period.

<u>Bad:</u> *"So what?" asked the stuntman "I'm not afraid of death."*
<u>Good:</u> *"So what?" asked the stuntman. "I'm not afraid of death."*

Question marks go outside if it is part of the sentence or inside if it is part of the quote.

<u>Inside:</u> *The President asked, "Will the secretary deal with this?"*
<u>Outside:</u> *Did the President say, "Will the secretary deal with this"?*

If attribution breaks up the sentence within a quote, it must be offset by a comma. If there are two sentences, you can also break up a quote. I would suggest not breaking up a single sentence with attribution, rather, put it at the end. If we are dealing with splitting up a single independent clause, chances are, they were two sentences.

<u>Bad:</u> *"We won't surrender," said the President "and we won't ease up."*
<u>Good:</u> *"We won't surrender," said the President, "and we won't ease up."*

We now move to discussion of paragraphs. Paragraphs (called **graphs**) in print journalist writing are short, in part to increase readability and facilitate easy layout. Print journalists and editors use graph breaks to break up the story. Each time a writer discusses a different speaker or a different source for quotes, they usually start a new graph. This is discussed in the chapters on writing utilizing inverted pyramid format (Chapter 6) and the chapter on writing print features (Chapter 7).

If a quote goes on for several paragraphs, you do not need to end the quotes with quotation marks until you are done with extended quotation. You still open the quotation with quotation marks; you just do not use them at the end of each graph until the quote is done.

Those are initial considerations to punctuation.

In this chapter we talked vocabulary, grammar, and punctuation in mass media writing. These are the tools in the top drawers of a writer's of toolbox. With these tools, a writer can begin the write good stories well.

CHAPTER 5:
STYLE: TELLING IT WELL

It is an old observation that the best writers sometimes disregard the rules of rhetoric. When they do so, however, the reader will usually find in the sentence some compensating merit, attained at the cost of the violation. Unless he is certain of doing as well, he will probably do best to follow the rules. After he has learned, by their guidance, to write plain English adequate for everyday uses, let him look, for the secrets of style, to the study of the masters of literature (Strunk & White, *Elements of style*, p. 2, http://www.cs.vu.nl/~jms/doc/elos.pdf).

In the game of chess, each move has to be made with precision, with anticipation of moves that will be made in the future. Mass media writing is about making choices, considering how those choices are going to influence future choices, and most importantly, how that is going to affect your audience. The writer should attempt to evoke the audiences decoding of the message in the intended way. The mass media writer's style will affect this decoding process. In this chapter we will be considering **style**, or how our writing sounds on the page. First, we will discuss **compositional style**, primarily informed by the work of Strunk and White. Second, we will address **form style**, with a heavy emphasis on Associated Press style. These provide a working base for considering what constitutes quality mass media writing—especially in journalistic contexts. The style of good mass media writing is always **clear**, **concise**, **correct**, and **complete**.

COMPOSITIONAL STYLE

Compositional style is the form we incorporate as we use the small building blocks from the writer's toolbox. Style is the sound the words make on paper. One must consider the work of Stunk and White when considering basic compositional style in the English language.

The stylistic guidelines of Strunk and White have had a great influence on writers of the English language for the last century. Stephen King, a great American storyteller, is an ardent follower of Strunk and White's stylistic suggestions. Remember, he says it's the one book on writing that doesn't fall into the bullshit rule. Strunk and White have helped educate several generations of writers. Ben Affleck praised Strunk and White's book when he said, "This book is an essential tool." This is Ben Affleck, who wrote and directed *The Town*. Ben is also an attractive example of masculinity. Ben continued, "It's been of great use to me and is probably responsible for my best writing. I owe my success to Strunk & White, only the mistakes are mine." This is coming from the guy who sat on the couch smoking weed while Matt Damon wrote *Good Will Hunting*. Ben won an academy award for that. My guess is that he could not have done that without his consideration of the stylistic suggestions from Strunk and White.

Many of Strunk and White's suggestions will help writers craft effective mass media messages. The organization framework and headings for this section incorporates the following central ideas from Strunk and White's *Elements of Style*:

Be clear. Choose a suitable design and hold to it. Make the paragraph a unit of composition. Use the active voice. Put sentences in positive forms. Use definitive, specific, concrete language. Omit needless words. Avoid a succession of loose sentences. Express coordinate ideas in similar forms. Keep to one tense. Minimize the personal. Write the way that comes naturally. Write with nouns and verbs. Do not over-write. Avoid use of dialect. Avoid the use of qualifiers. Do not write a breezy manner. Use orthodox spelling. Employ clear speaker attribution. Avoid fancy words. Do not take shortcuts. Avoid foreign languages. Prefer the standard to the off-beat. Incorporating these suggestions from Strunk and White can help an aspiring writer improve their craft.

BE CLEAR.

Mass media writing must *be clear. The most important consideration when writing for mass media is clarity.* This was expressed in the previous chapters. We need to be clear to our readers as well as to the other people we work with. Likewise, we need to be aware of misinterpretations. What we are trying to do is choose the signs that are going to invoke the meaning we want in our listeners, or the **intended message**. The **actual message** is the meaning that audience members' consciousness attributes to the signs, so we need to be very concise in our language—very simple. This is how our message remains clear and avoids misinterpretation. Likewise, when we are thinking about clarity, we must write in a readable way. Simple words, simple sentence structure, subject-verb sentence structure; keep it all readable. Complex sentences make it less readable. What we want to do, especially in straight news, is to keep our writing readable.

WORK FROM A SUITABLE DESIGN AND STICK TO IT.

A writer must be aware of the form of the genre of mass media in which they are writing. This awareness helps provide the conceptual and formulaic framework of composition. One of the unique characteristics of this book is that it teaches mass media writing in a variety of formats, from print journalism to feature film writing. The writer should research, brainstorm with lists, and compose with particular formulaic standards in mind. There are similarities between all types of mass media writing (clarity, concision, correctness, and completeness), but the organization of the ideas can be very different. Thus, the writer must be cognizant of organizational particularities and adhere to those concerns throughout the writing process.

One concept that a good mass media writer learns is that there are different ways to structure different types of stories. An inverted pyramid print or Internet story, which we will explore in the next chapter, is organized differently than a feature print story or a television news story or a film. The key is to decide on the appropriate organizational sequence and use it throughout the text as an arrangement anchor.

For example, suppose a writing assignment requires a mass media writer to craft a story with an inverted pyramid structure—the standard structure used for straight print journalism, public relations, or brief Internet stories. How is an inverted pyramid story structured? We will discuss this in depth in the next chapter, but a writer would start with the main points, and then move to the less important points. When writing an inverted pyramid story, writers should adhere to this structure in the paragraphs, the sentences, even *the words* that the writer decides to begin with. The first word of the story should be the most important. For instance, a story on the death of John Hughes, the director of the films, *Sixteen Candles, Ferris Bueller's Day Off,* and *The Breakfast Club*, should start with the idea that Hughes was a renowned film director and writer. If a writer crafted a press release about the death of Hughes, the first word in the **lead,** or the first sentence or paragraph of a story, of that story should have identified the most important part of the story. It should attempt to answer the questions **who**, **what**, **when**, **where**, and **why**:

- **Who:** John Hughes, director of popular American films such as *Sixteen Candles, Ferris Bueller's Day Off,* and *The Breakfast Club*
- **What:** died
- **Where:** in his home in Evanston, Illinois
- **When:** the 15th
- **Why:** heart failure

If a writer starts with the most important and moves to the less important, they are crafting an effective inverted pyramid lead. In sum, the writer should chose a suitable design and consistently incorporate that structural scaffolding throughout the story—even in the lead.

As said earlier, a lead is the first sentence or paragraph of the story. For an inverted pyramid, the writer will use a comprehensive lead, also known as a **summary lead**. That is when you say the climax of the story first—the writer just giving it right up front in an inverted pyramid story. Using inverted pyramid with a summary lead is a suitable design for a straight news release. A good writer will adhere to Strunk and White's suggestion that, "When the writer has to pick a design, they should consider the context and then write for that" design. Choose a design and stick to it.

MAKE THE PARAGRAPH A UNIT OF COMPOSITION.

Remember that in journalism, the paragraph is referred to as the **graph**, but it is still a unit of composition. For example, when writing inverted pyramid form, the first graph should be most important, the second graph should be the second-most important, and so on. A paragraph is a single idea articulated in one or more sentences.

USE THE ACTIVE VOICE.

Avoid passive construction. Active voice is when the subject acts on the direct object, not when the direct object is acted upon by the subject. Active voice construction is more clear and direct than passive voice. Generally, the subject is more important than the object and should come first. "The President responded to the crisis," not, "The crisis was responded to by the President." Again, this goes back to Stephen King; one reason people use passive voice is because they are timid. When you hear politicians say, "Mistakes were made," they phrase it that way because passive voice obfuscates responsibility. The active voice "I made mistakes" is too direct for most politicians. Fear and being timid are reasons people use passive voice. Active voice is clearer.

We might use passive voice to put the object up front if the object is more important than the subject. In addition, occasional passive voice may provide structural variety. However, these are infrequent occasions to make exceptions to the active rule. In general, use the active voice construction and avoid passive voice.

PUT SENTENCES IN POSITIVE FORM.

Do not write, "It is not raining today." Rather write in the positive form, "It is sunny today." Avoid writing, "He's not happy." Prefer writing, "He's sad/pissed off/whatever" that *isn't* happy. It is always clearer to use the positive. Is the subject crying? Is steam coming out of his ears? *Just say what is, not what is not.*

USE DEFINITIVE, SPECIFIC, CONCRETE LANGUAGE.

This is another reiteration about being clear. Avoid being vague. Ultimately, what we want to do is paint a picture in the mind of our readers. We might want to appeal to the senses; what did it smell and feel like? Don't say, "It was dangerous." Say, "There were bullets whizzing by, I could see blood on the ground." *Danger* is such an amorphous word; it is vague. Which of your senses made you think it was dangerous? Be specific rather than general. Don't say, "He felt threatened," but say *why* he felt threatened; "There was a man standing being him with a bloody knife, and red eyes, and he was ready to lunge." This way the writer does not have to tell us the subject felt threatened; the audience knows it. Likewise, strong descriptive language avoids excessive explanation of the feelings or emotions of the subject. Description allows the audience members to come to their own conclusions. Thus, the writer should use simple, colorful description when needed so that receivers have the information. They can then construct a picture in their minds that will leave an impression.

OMIT NEEDLESS WORDS.

Employ concision. Strunk and White wrote, "Every word should tell." Think about Super Bowl commercials. Those 30-second-long spots sell for millions of dollars.

How much is that *per word*? Omit needless words. Space is money! What is important about the newspaper? Is it the headlines? No; it is the advertisements. The newspaper business is a *business*, and that is why newspapers are 60-70% ads. What is most important? The ultimate bosses? The owners? Revenue. Cash. Profit. The bottom line is that space is money so every word should tell.

Concise writing requires work. Blaise Pascal once wrote, "I made this letter longer than usual because I lack the time to make it short." Editing for concision takes effort and time, but can make a writer stronger. Ernest Hemmingway sought concision. Hemmingway suggested that he could take a chapter and reduce it to a page. He could then take a page and seek to edit to a paragraph. He could take that paragraph and seek reduce it to a sentence. Hemmingway believed this process made his work more powerful. This is an important stage of a strong writer's editing process: finding excess words, and getting rid of them. Many aspiring writers include unnecessary language. For instance, the excessively wordy phrase, "This was a very significant finding." In this case, the finding was either significant or not. You don't need *very*. "It was a significant finding." In this case, the writer should go to the computer, make the changes, print up the copy, read it again, and search for more unneeded words. The writer dedicated to quality deletes them. Every word must tell.

AVOID A SUCCESSION OF LOOSE SENTENCES.

The writer should consider unity. Each sentence, and the order in which the sentences are presented, should compose a meaningful whole. In a loose succession of sentences, each individual sentence is unrelated to other sentences in the paragraph. The sentences should fit together somehow. The writing should not be choppy. The sentences should flow together. There should be a reason that each sentence is included in the order that it is.

EXPRESS COORDINATE IDEAS IN SIMILAR FORM.

This consideration is about **parallelism**. Parallelism in rhetoric or writing is expressing similar ideas with a consistency of form or order in the words of each sentence. For example, if a writer is crafting a newspaper article about a bad economy and uses the words, "financial difficulties," they should not later switch to the words "monetary struggles," or "fiscal dilemmas." In journalistic writing, it is not important to show people how many different words a writer can use to describe the same thing. There are writing contexts where that is okay, even encouraged, but in journalism and other kinds of mass media writing, it is not. A thesaurus is useful when a writer is trying to choose the most appropriate word, but not to express a similar idea with different words. Clarity is more important than impressing the readers. Thus, express an idea in a consistent form when writing for mass media.

KEEP TO ONE TENSE.

Do not change tense in summaries or the middle of a story. Pick a tense, and be consistent.

MINIMIZE THE PERSONAL.

The writer should place himself in the background. He must put his opinion aside for the sake of journalism and mass media writing. There might be a place for his opinion in an opinion piece, but not when writing for the mass media. The writer is trying to impart information and tell a good story. Audience members are not looking for the writer's opinion. It might creep into the text, but explicit didacticism should be avoided.

If there is a topic that a writer has a strong emotional opinion about, he should probably not write for the mass media about it. This is especially true in journalistic contexts. If he does write about it, he should make sure that he is being as objective as possible. For instance, I hate Nazis. I particularly hate *Illinois* Nazis. I do not think I could put my values aside when talking about Nazis. I'll leave the writing about Nazis to writers who can be more objective, or at least those who appear so. Personally, I cannot handle it. But if a writer was writing about Nazis, they should try to place themselves in the background. This will be covered in more depth on the chapter of mass media writing ethics.

WRITE THE WAY THAT COMES NATURALLY.

Remember, from the chapter on the writing process, that the first draft is supposed to be written how a writer would say it. A writer should relax and let the ideas flow after they have chosen a suitable design. A writer should just write it in a way that comes naturally. They can be conversational in the first time they write a piece. Formality can be added later in the editing process.

WRITE WITH NOUNS AND VERBS.

The mass media writer should rely upon a subject-verb word order. This compositional arrangement is simple and clear. There may be a place for more complicated or artistic writing, but not when a writer is crafting mass media messages. In the journalistic context, the writer should try to communicate news elements (who, what, where, why, and how) to the audience. The mass media writer should aspire to be clear, and in order to be clear, they should primarily rely on nouns and verbs as the building blocks in their message composition.

DO NOT OVER-WRITE.

This means not adding unnecessary details. The writer should avoid being redundant. The writer should avoid using too many adjectives or adverbs—if any at all. A mass media writer should be straight and to the point. I'm sure many students have found themselves in a situation where they think, "I just have to fill the page. I can get a thesaurus and just say the same thing three times." Writers should avoid this when writing for mass media. In journalistic contexts, the writer is ultimately writing for an editor who will encourage the writer to be terse. The writer must remember that space and broadcast time costs money—after all, that is the most important consideration to the owners of mass media corporations. The mass media writer should also avoid overstating or exaggeration. Once a writer starts exaggerating, people start questioning the sincerity of the writing. In journalistic contexts, the audience does not want the writer's judgment. The audience wants the writer to be descriptive and then let the audience members evaluate the information themselves.

AVOID USE OF DIALECT.

Incorporating dialect in clear mass media messages can be difficult. There can be some exceptions to this rule, especially in fictional dramatic writing. For instance, Stanley Kubrick used dialect effectively in *A Clockwork Orange*. He successfully incorporated slang words such as *ultraviolence* and *malvo milk*. However, some viewers may find the use of dialect confusing. Especially in journalistic contexts, the writer should avoid the use of dialect unless it is part of a direct quote.

AVOID THE USE OF QUALIFIERS.

Keep adjectives to a minimum, and try to avoid adverbs. Stephen King wrote that adverbs are not a writer's friend. Adverbs are the ones that usually end in "ly." They necessitate a judgment. The reader does not want the writer's judgment. They want to know about what the writer saw, what he smelled, what he heard, or, in a dramatic presentation, what is to be seen and heard. Avoid adjectives and adverbs. For example, instead of, "He said menacingly," use the crazy man's direct quote of, "I'm going to cut you in half!" A writer should not have to say, "'I'm going to cut you in half,' he said menacingly." The menacing-nature of the man is implied through his quote. It should be evident by the words: the writer should not need a qualifier.

DO NOT WRITE IN A BREEZY MANNER.

This is similar to when you meet someone who's overly friendly. Breezy writing meanders and is too informal for mass media. It is too chatty and overly friendly, like a wandering cell phone text chat between friends. This type of informal musing gives an impression of a stream of consciousness approach to writing, in which the writer does not take his writing assignment nor the time and attention of his audience, seriously. Breezy writing tends to also be wordy and too relaxed. It is inappropriate for mass media writing.

USE ORTHODOX SPELLING.

The professional and business context of mass media writing requires adherence to traditional spelling conventions. Traditional spelling will be clearer to both the audience and the other members of the production team. For instance, spell "through" rather than "thru." A writer's credibility is maintained when they use traditional spelling. Your readers will take the writing more seriously if you incorporate conventional spelling standards. Do not use the spelling you use when you text. For instance, do not use "ur" when you mean "you are." Use "tomorrow" instead of "2moro" and "love" instead of "luv." Likewise avoid emoticons and text abbreviations like LOL or OMG. The perspective reflected throughout this book is that there are different acceptable standards for different types of writing. Mass media writers should consistently employ traditional spelling norms.

Employ Clear Speaker Attribution.

Make sure your readers know who is speaking by using proper attribution. When there is extensive dialogue between characters, speaker attribution can become unclear. Thus, employ proper names instead of pronouns for speaker attribution when clarity about who is speaking is even slightly confusing.

Avoid Fancy Words.

We want first-order words. This was discussed in the previous chapter. There may be writing contexts in which it is appropriate to impress the audience with your use of complicated vocabulary or field-specific nomenclature, such as in academic writing. However, writers should avoid the desire to impress their audience with their vocabulary when they are writing for mass media.

Revise and Re-Write.

This consideration refers to the editing process. Strunk and White wrote that the writer crafts an initial draft, and then the writer edits. The writer revises and then re-writes, repeatedly. This was discussed in the chapter on the writing process. This is a positive attribute of this book: it prepares the writer for the editing process in the mass media business. When the writer completes their writing assignment, in most contexts it is going to go through at least five revisions. That is one of the most important things an aspiring writer can learn from the approach incorporated in this textbook. This textbook, along with courses utilizing this text, stresses the idea that all writing should go through numerous rewrites. If the importance of the revision process was underemphasized, I would not be doing my job. When students turn in their writing assignments in a class guided by this paradigm, they should have revised the mass media messages several times. Re-reading and revising can take as little as a few minutes; however, it is absolutely necessary if a writer is committed to quality writing.

Asking, *"What if I don't have time to re-write?"* is like asking, *"What if I don't care that my work is shit?"* All writers make time to re-edit it, even if it is extremely brief. If a writer has time to drink coffee or chew gum, the writer has time to edit it. A writer needs to be able to say to an editor, "I didn't have time to re-edit. May I have ten more minutes to run this by myself again? I don't feel comfortable yet turning this in." Stay committed to *quality*. Revise, re-write, revise, re-write, revise, and re-write!

USE FIGURES OF SPEECH SPARINGLY.

Avoid language cliché's, slang, or phrases that have a trendy popularity. Avoid "doublespeak"—which is also known as "euphemisms." These are the words we use to dance around something. It's like when we refer to something that's unpleasant, with a less unpleasant phrasing. We need to avoid them because they can obfuscate meaning. For instance, if the United States military in Afghanistan accidentally blows up one of its own soldiers, do we call the dead soldier an "innocent victim"? No, we use the euphemism "collateral damage." Doesn't that sound better? A hole in a street is not a "pothole," it is an, "asphalt deficiency." The bum that asked you for change is not "homeless," but "domicile challenged." We have to watch out for euphemisms so we can be straight in our writing. Clear them out of your writing.

DO NOT TAKE SHORTCUTS.

Always think about clarity. Do not do the easiest thing, but do the thing that makes the message most clear for our audience. This is always important. Writing shortcuts often decrease clarity.

AVOID FOREIGN LANGUAGES.

Sometimes foreign language is appropriate, like when you want to say *je nais se quoi*. You cannot really say that in English unless you want to say, "A certain something that cannot be said." The French phrase is better to use in that case.

PREFER THE STANDARD TO THE OFF-BEAT.

The writer should leave texting language out of their mass media writing. The mass media writer should not be cute with their language, unless they are writing in a comedic context. The mass media writer should aspire to be straight and clear with their language instead of clever. Likewise, mass media writers should watch out for language trends. For example, something like, "She was a hot mess," should be left out of your writing. "Obama was majorly dissed," is also too off-beat. Mass media writing should be straightforward and avoid trends.

These are some useful stylistic considerations from Strunk and White. All of these are a way to think about how your writing can be clear, concise, correct, and complete. While training mass media writers was not their primary goal (they wrote primarily with literature in mind), these stylistics considerations will help mass media writers be clear, concise, correct, and complete.

Bad writing comes from fear. Quality writers write without fear and become better writers. Aspiring writers must replace fear with a commitment to become a better writer. A growing writer uses fear to motivate themselves to become dedicated to their craft. The composition style suggestions from Strunk and White are useful tools in the journey to becoming a better writer.

Associated Press Style

Associated Press style is the accepted style for mass media writing, particularly in journalism and public relations. On the cover of a previous edition of the Associate Press Style Guide, it said, "The Bible for newspaper publications." There is a reason for that; it is the definitive source on proper style for journalism and public relations. A writer goes to the AP style guide for any questions concerning style. In the professional realm, knowing how to use the AP guide reflects credibility. If a writer's boss says they are using the wrong style, the AP guide would be the source for information about how to correct those errors. It is very important that the aspiring mass media writer learns how to use this book. Writers in the industry, whether in public relations, new print, broadcast radio or TV, should have the AP stylebook on their desk. If you have a question as to whether or not you should abbreviate Tennessee, for example, the answer can be found in that book. I offer here some basic and salient AP style considerations. In this section, we'll discuss the book as a **reference resource**, along with its considerations on **numbers**, **money**, **statistics**, **dates**, **times**, **addresses**, **names**, **titles**, **punctuation**, **titles of works**, **Roman numerals**, and **abbreviations**.

REFERENCE RESOURCE

First of all, whenever we talk about AP, a writer needs to know that they will have to look up the rules in the AP guide to check that they are using the style correctly. Thus, rather than memorizing all AP rules, the proficient mass media writer will know how to use the AP style guide. The book is a useful reference that should be kept handy. As a writer uses the guidebook, they will over time become more familiar with the style.

NUMBERS

Spell out the numbers zero through nine. There are exceptions when you are writing about the age of a person, percentages, dimensions, money, times, or scores. Double-digit numbers (greater than nine) should be written numerically rather than spelling out the words; an exception to this rule is if a number is used to begin a sentence. In this case, it may be preferable to re-write the sentence so the number is not first.

A writer should use a combination of numerals and words for higher units like millions or billions (for instance, 6 million). When the mass media writer refers to large numbers, they can use numerals for the relevant numbers and then the word for the denomination. For example, the writer can refer to 25,000,000 as "25 million." This is clearer for the reader. Large numbers can be rounded off when appropriate. For instance, rather than writing, "3,299,000" or "three million, two hundred and ninety nine thousand," a writer can write, "over three million." When a writer gets to thousands, and they are using figures, they should include the comma, unless they are talking about years or addresses.

MONEY

When writing about money, the mass media writer may use figures, but they can choose not to include the decimal portion of the figure, or the cents. They would not write $1.00, but rather $1. The exception would be if the mass media writer is writing for broadcast, in which case they would write it out as someone would read it aloud.

STATISTICS

Try to use statistics sparingly, and when you do use them, make sure they have power. Do not just throw them around as they tend to dull the reader's senses. Translate statistics into tangible terms. They do not say, "80% of dentists recommend Trident gum." Instead they say, "Four out of five dentists recommend Trident gum."

Even with basic math, mass media writers must be cautious. Do not overuse mathematics and numbers. Do not ever combine percentages. You cannot average percentages. Do not combine them.

As mentioned before, mass media writers may choose to round off numbers, especially big numbers. You do not say, "453," you say, "Over 400." Make it simple. This is the key with numbers.

Always think about the margin of error. If McCain is behind Obama 48% to 52%, but there is a 3% margin of error, which means six points potentially. So really, Obama could be as low as 45%. The margin of error can be significant. Recognize that.

DATES

For dates, use the day or the date, but not both. Whenever a writer is trying to figure out what phrases or figures to use, they should think in terms of the date of the publication. Use the day but not the date. If a date falls out of a 15-day window of publication, use the date rather than the day. Do not use both the day and the date. For example, "The protests will meet next Thursday."

The same general rule applies to the year. If the event happened one year prior, or is happening within the following year, do not use the year. Use the year when it is clarifies to do so. Days of the week are always spelled out; never abbreviate them. If the month is used with the specified date, then you can abbreviate it. Refer to the AP guide for rules about this. Some months are abbreviated; some are not. If the month is used by itself without the date, spell it out.

TIMES

Always use lower case *am* and *pm* for times. Do not use morning, evening, or afternoon—it is far clearer to use am and pm. For example, "The fair will open at 9:30 am Tuesday." To simplify things, use noon and midnight for 12 pm and 12 am. Be concise. Check AP if you are unsure. Have it on your desk as you write so you can double check.

ADDRESSES

Use figures for numbers and addresses, but do not use commas. For example, an address would be written, "1204 S University." The rule is that you can abbreviate a street if it can be abbreviated, but do not do so unless it is in a specific address. You can abbreviate when it is used as, "234 Main **St.**" Do not abbreviate it if you say, "The building was located on Main **Street**." If you abbreviate a state with a specific city and it is able to be abbreviated, look at AP to see what the abbreviation is. Do not use postal abbreviations; these are not proper in most cases for AP. Look it up instead. Also, when using multiple streets, do not capitalize the word "street."

NAMES

Another consideration in AP style is names. Spell the whole name out the first time you use it. For subsequent uses, just use the person's last name. The first time you use their name, you usually have some type of identification, their job description, etc., or what element about that person is relevant to the story. For subsequent uses of that name, just use their last name. Do not use Ms., Mr., or Mrs. because we don't need them. Titles such as Dr. you may use at the beginning, but not after that. Reverend is abbreviated the way Dr. or Sr. would be: **Rev.** When referring to a reverend, the writers should use "the Rev." If there are two people with the same last name, continue to use the first and last name throughout the story; this helps with clarity. On the other side of the coin, if you are talking about the Illinois Department of Transportation already, you may not need to include that someone works as an IDOT director, you can just say, "director." If a writer includes their particular name, the title would be capitalized, such as, "IDOT Director Smith."

TITLES

There are two types of personal titles: a true title and a false title. If it is a true title, it precedes the name. True titles are professionally recognized titles, like, "Vice President of International Affairs." False titles are those that describe their work. If it is a true title, it precedes the name and is not separated from the name by a comma. If it is false, then put it after the name and put a comma between them. If the title is separated from the name, it is going to be lower case. If it is a true title and it comes before the name, capitalize it. For example, you would write "President Al Bowman," or, "Al Bowman, president of ISU."

PUNCTUATION

The following is what the AP style guide has to say about punctuation in terms of **titles of works**, **roman numerals**, and **abbreviations**.

Titles of Works

According to AP, you use quotation marks to denote a direct quote, as well as titles of books, plays, poems, songs, speeches, lectures, etc. For instance, when you identify the name of a film, it is, "Gone with the Wind." When inserting a title of a work into a quote, place apostrophes around the title, such as, "I listened to 'The White Album.'" On larger volumes, like the Encyclopedia Britannica or the Bible, you do not need quotations. Again, *look it up in AP if you are unsure.*

Roman Numerals

Always omit the comma before Roman numerals.

Abbreviations

The first time you use the name of an organization, you spell it out. For instance, the first time a writer refers to an organization, they should spell it out, "Illinois Department of Transportation." Do not abbreviate it in parenthesis right after the word. However, the next time the writer refers to it, they can use the abbreviation IDOT. If it is a well-known organization, like the YMCA, PTA, or NRA, you do not need to spell out the formal organization name the first time. That is a judgment call. For example, if you are writing for *The New York Times*, you would not immediately abbreviate "Illinois State University" as most people in New York might recognize "ISU" as Iowa State University. However, if you are writing for *The Daily Vidette*, Illinois state's newspaper, you would immediately use "ISU" because on this campus, "ISU" is recognized.

Periods are used in abbreviations if the abbreviation spells out a word, but not if the abbreviation does not spell out a word. For example, refer to "NAACP" with no periods, but "S.T.A.R.T." with periods between each letter.

In this section we discussed AP as a reference resource, numbers, money, statistics, dates, times, addresses, names, titles, punctuation, titles of works, Roman numerals, and abbreviations (See AP Exercises in the Appendix). Overall in AP, be familiar with the book and keep it handy. You simply have to learn how to use it. The more you use it, the more you begin to learn it. AP is your stylistic consideration format when writing for public relations, TV, radio, and newsprint. Of course, if your boss says, "Do it this way," what do you say? "Yes, ma'am! I learned AP, but I am willing to do it your way." Your boss is your authority. Otherwise, use AP. Know it, learn it, live it.

Overall, in this chapter we have talked about style and your style toolbox, which consists of words, composition, and language. We have considered style, or how our writing sounds on the page. We discussed compositional style, primarily informed by the work of Strunk and White, and then addressed form style with a heavy emphasis on AP style. These provide a working base of considerations for a mass media writer that can help them determine what constitutes quality mass media writing—especially in journalistic contexts. Later in this book, these stylistic considerations will be re-examined and expanded to consider quality style in other forms of mass media writing. The style of good mass media writing is always **clear**, **concise**, **correct**, and **complete**.

CHAPTER 6:
INVERTED PYRAMID

In the next section, we will explore the organizational sequence for straight, hard print news writing—**the inverted pyramid**. As always, quality writing has several characteristics. **Good writing is clear, concise, correct, and complete**. A good writer should have an intimate working knowledge of these concepts, and maybe even get them tattooed on their arm.

The inverted pyramid was developed so that stories could be shared between newspapers no matter the editorial bias of the publisher. Inverted pyramid became popular when newspaper publishers first started using the wire services. The wire services, like Associated Press or United Press International, are organizations that gather news, and then news outlets subscribe to this wire for breaking information from around the world. When the wire services began and grew this breaking news was transmitted across a telegraph; "the wire." The wire is presumably non-biased—just facts. The news sources then take this information and use it to write their own stories or just copy and paste it into their publications. The organizational scheme also allowed for easy editing. These stories could be whatever length an editor needed to fill column inches in a newspaper.

The inverted pyramid is a story structure that moves from the most important information to the least important information in a story. (See Example of Straight Print News Story in the Appendix.) Thus, the first sentence of an inverted pyramid is the climax; it is a summary of everything that happened. This synopsis of the story is called a **summary lead.** In an inverted pyramid story, information is organized from most relevant to least relevant, and the first graph is a summary lead. (See Straight Print News Exercise in the Appendix.) A media writer should master this basic organizational sequence as a basic learning goal, and then learn to move beyond it. In addition, once the form is mastered, it will be a useful tool repeatedly throughout the career of the media writer. Once a writer knows how to use the inverted pyramid, they will remember it forever.

A writer should use the inverted pyramid for straight print news for several reasons. First, people have a much shorter attention span nowadays, so we need to give them their news fast. Also, inverted pyramid is easy to read. An audience member can read the first sentence, and if the reader wants more, they can continue to read. If a reader is not interested, they can move on to the next summary lead. It is easy for the editors. If something is irrelevant they can simply cut it out without losing anything. If an editor needs seven column inches and the writer turned in 12, then the editor can just cut it at seven inches because they know that what comes after that cut off is not as important as what happened before it.

Inverted pyramid works in other formats other than straight news. The ability to write in inverted pyramid style is useful to the print journalist, the public relations writer, the broadcast media writer, and the web writer. Variations of the inverted pyramid are often used in broadcasting. The inverted pyramid is a mainstay for public relations writing. It is clear, fast and easy. Inverted pyramid works well for public relations tasks—especially press releases. (See Example of Straight Print Media Release in the Appendix.) Knowing the inverted pyramid is like knowing the language of the reporters. When doing public relations work, reporters and journalists are often the target audience. These media personnel then get the message out to a larger audience. If a public relations writer can reach a reporter, they can reach potentially hundreds of thousands of people without paying a dime. Inverted pyramid also works well for copy writing in advertising.

Inverted pyramid is also very good for web writing. In writing for the web, the lead becomes a link. The link gets the readers' attention, they click on it, and they are taken to the full story on a linked web page. The audience reads the first few lines, and if they like it they keep reading. If they do not like it, they go to the next link. The fact of the matter is that inverted pyramid quickly gets the information to readers.

Inverted pyramid does have some restrictions. First, some writers place artificial limits on their creativity when they write an inverted pyramid story. A writer can make creative decisions when writing an inverted pyramid story. There are great writers who can craft amazingly entertaining and informative news with an inverted pyramid organization. The writer still has to decide which news values will be emphasized, what information will go in the lead, and how the story will unfold. Like jazz musicians, the media writer should master the basics first, like the inverted pyramid, and then move on to genre-defying work.

ORGANIZING THE STORY

There are several steps a writer should take as they begin to write an inverted pyramid news story. First, **research** is a critical stage in any type of writing, including inverted pyramid writing. This is emphasized in Chapter 3 on the writing process. Half of the battle for a reporter may be research, including conducting interviews. Aspiring writers will also develop these skills further in advanced courses on reporting. Next, **a writer can rank information as it is important to the audience.** If the writer bullets pieces of an interview, for example, the writer can rank the notes before adding the pieces to a story. In this process, a writer also ranks news values, putting information in descending order of importance. (See Straight Print News Story Facts in the Appendix.) Remember that the paragraph is a single unit of timely information, and in journalism, it is called a graph. The writer must also organize the **news elements** in the story. The news elements of a story are the answers to the questions who, what, when, where, why, and how. Then the writer must also consider the relevant news values when making decisions about what to include or emphasize. For instance, time may be important or not (timeliness). If a story is about an exhibition sporting event that has already occurred, the writer may not need to put the time of the event in the lead or even in the story. The writer needs to evaluate what news elements are most important while considering news values. What news values are important? Was it that the event happened near the audience (proximity)? Is it important because someone famous was involved (prominence)? The writer must scrutinize what news values are important to the reader. When a writer organizes the story, they need to think about the news elements and which news values need to be featured more or less prominently.

THE LEAD

The lead is the first sentence or paragraph of a story. In an inverted pyramid, the lead sentence should summarize the most important information. The summary lead, also called a comprehensive lead, should be the climax of a story. The summary leads should also include the most important news elements (who, what, where, when and how).

There are several general rules for organizing the lead. **First of all, leads should be short—generally less than 30 words.** It should be concise; every word should tell. If a writer composes a lead that is more than 30 words, a good editor will be able reduce it without omitting anything of value.

Second, mass media writing needs to be easy to understand. The writer should craft leads in the simplest way possible without extra words. Leads should also be composed using simple language. Again, the writer must think about their audience. What words will be easiest for the audience to understand? Try to use words that Homer Simpson would be able to grasp.

Next, leads should include active words and active voice; leads are active. This leads to the next element—leads should be simple sentences. The writer should avoid complex, compound, or convoluted sentences. Sentences that incorporate subject-verb order are clearer. These are general rules for leads. This applies to any type of lead, no matter what type of story a writer is crafting.

Everything else after the lead is called the body. The body of the story contains facts, background information, statistics, and direct and indirect quotations. The body of the inverted pyramid story obviously moves from most important ideas to least important ideas.

DIRECT AND INDIRECT QUOTES

When should the writer use quotes? Why does a writer use quotes? Quotes often lend a colorful piece of information from a perspective other than the writer's. Quotes may also reveal emotions of those most affected by a story. The bottom line is that the person speaking may be using the best possible words, and the writer can incorporate this utterance. The thing about being a reporter is the writer is rarely ever a witness; you are talking to the witnesses. These people can describe the scene and the emotion that they went through. This is a compelling reason to use quotes. Also, quotes can give the reader information they might not otherwise have. Quotes can also give a story a variety of perspectives.

The difference between direct and indirect quotations is that **direct quotes use a speaker's exact words, verbatim, versus an indirect quote where a writer paraphrases what someone said.** Direct quotes are in quotation marks while indirect quotes are not. Try to avoid brackets within a quote. Brackets indicate the writer had to interject something, and if you have to modify or clarify a quote, you probably should not use it anyway. I would recommend avoiding brackets within quotes at all times.

Using direct quotations may be the best way to characterize a situation, a state of mind, or a person's mood. In June 2004, former Vice President Cheney told Senator Leahy from New York, "Fuck yourself," on the floor of the senate. That is what Vice President Cheney said. This is the guy that shot somebody in the face and then had them apologize....If I want to talk about this event, and someone who saw it reports, "He was so mad, he used bad words," is it representative? The issue at hand here is whether or not to use a direct quote for, "Fuck yourself." I would recommend that you use it. I would want the public to think about what he actually said. What he said is a valuable direct quote; it shows his character and his actions.

This is also important when it comes to **colorful statements**— emotion filled words or phrases. I would recommend using them because they show what really happened. It will make it more clearly to the reader if they know exactly what the Vice President said. It conveys his personality, and his way of speaking. How could a writer paraphrase that? "Go make love to yourself?" That doesn't really say it, does it? Also, be careful when using quotes partially. Try not to quote just one or two words. As always, ask your boss or your editor what is acceptable. Your boss or bosses ultimately set the standards for what is acceptable or not. In addition, this example takes ideas about direct quotations to the extreme. A writer must consider what is appropriate for the audience. The word fuck might not be appropriate for the front page of a newspaper.

Sometimes, it might be clearer to summarize someone's quote to get their information across in a more direct manner. Also, in the above example, you may not be able to print the word *fuck* in a family magazine. In this case, you would have to paraphrase it with an indirect quote. To keep your quotes relevant and concise, you might just want to paraphrase them.

RULES FOR USING QUOTATIONS

When it comes to correcting your speaker's grammar and other slips, I would recommend it. If President Bush says, "Strategery," instead of "strategy," do we want to quote him on it? We could probably cut him some slack in that case; just correct it. We might want to paraphrase in this case. You can help your speaker be clearer and more representative, but try not to do this too much. Again, if you are unsure, ask your boss or your assignment editor.

There are also rules for using quotations. **First, you must be correct. Do not make quotes up.** Jason Blair, who worked for *The New York Times*, got caught making up quotes. He hurt the reputation of *The New York Times* and the journalism business as a whole. Do not make up quotes. Be accurate. Also, watch out for redundancies when you are setting up quotes. You do not want to give all of the information about your story in a quote and then just repeat what the quote said.

For example: *Jeffrey began to fear for his life. "I began to fear for my life," said Jeffrey.*

Before you give the quote, give the reader an introduction to the context of the quote. "According to," is only for printed or factual information. If a person orally gave the writer a quote, they, "say," or, "said." Also, give the person's title or name. The writer should put the attribution before the quote, unless they are continuing with additional quotations from the same speaker. For example, "Secretary of State Hilary Clinton said…" It can be good style to break up a two-sentence quotation by placing attribution in between two sentences of a quote. The writer should not assume people's feelings. Do not say, "He believed it would work," say, "He said he believed it would work." The writer should let the speaker say how they feel rather than suggest they might feel that way.

We will also use facts, background information, and description. **Description** is a tool where we tell our readers how it sounded, how it felt, what it looked like, etc. We want to use description as well as background information and direct and indirect quotes. We use description, sensory words, to put our reader there.

STRUCTURAL CONSIDERATIONS

Structural considerations are unity, variety, pace, and climax, as emphasized throughout this book. We address climax because it is the lead of our inverted pyramid story. Unity is very important for inverted pyramid as well as for other writing formats. When we are considering unity, there are several devices we can use. First, repetition of words can add unity. Repetition of words means using the same word. If you are talking about financial plans, do not change it to *fiscal* plans later in the article. Stick to whatever term you are using. In mass media writing, we are not trying to impress them with our words. We are trying to be clear. Second, transitions help unify a story. Transitions aid when switching ideas so that the reader does not feel like we are just jumping from one idea to the next. We need transitions to tell the reader where we are going. "Another," "in addition," and "also," are all usable transitions. Inverted pyramid is less dependent on transitions than other formats, but we should still have a consideration for it. Another way we can use unity is tone. Using tone to unify a story means retaining the same tone throughout the story. If it is a comedic piece; keep a unifying comedic tone. Quotations can also help unify the piece. You can use quotes from different people and then group them together.

Variety is another consideration, especially when using quotes. Is the writer using quotes by different people, or is it the same person the whole time? Are you mixing up quotations, statistics, and descriptions? Use different elements within the inverted pyramid to create variety. You can still use the inverted pyramid structure and provide different types of information in different forms.

The third structural consideration is pace. Most inverted stories will be quick in pace, because they are just the facts. In fact, the pace at the beginning of the inverted pyramid story should be faster and slow down toward the end.

Obviously, we want to be thinking about why this is a good story. In an inverted pyramid story, the climax is the lead. We want to think about why this story is important to our audience, and that information needs to go in our lead.

CHAPTER 7:
ETHICS AND MASS MEDIA WRITING

In this chapter, we will discuss the ethics of mass media writing. Admittedly, this is almost oxymoronic. To talk about ethics and mass media is like talking about "jumbo shrimp" or "military intelligence." At face value, the words do not seem to go together. However, the mass media writer should strive to answer to higher ethical standards rather than strive to make a profit. Unfortunately, the mass media business is a business and the profit motive often over-rides other ethical considerations. The key here, as Shakespeare suggested, is, "To thine own self be true."

Most importantly, we are going to talk about **world perspective.** This is what scholars call the ***lebenswelt***, or life-world, and how it influences what we write. Our life-world is our consciousness that is influenced by the collective experiences we have encountered. It is the sum of what our church told us, what our parents told us, what our peers told us, as well as the experiences we have been through. This thing in our minds called "consciousness" is what we use to interpret the signs around us. Remember how we talked about using the correct symbols to invoke the right meaning in the consciousness of our receiver when we write?

JOURNALISTIC ETHICS

Initially, whenever the writer faces ethical questions concerning their actions, they should be guided by what is often referred to as the golden rule: Treat others as you would have them treat you. Buddha posited this idea 2,500 years ago. A Jewish revolutionary who was executed by the Romans 2,000 years ago (an innocent victim of capital punishment) re-iterated this message. The Koran also communicates this idea. Thus, when faced with an ethical dilemma, the journalist should ask themselves, "How would I want to be treated?" Should a reporter stick a camera into the face of a grieving mother and ask, "Your son is dead. How does that make you feel?" How would you want your mother treated? Should a reporter take a picture of a person preparing to jump off a bridge or should they offer a comforting word to the anguished person? How would you want your brother treated? While this generalization is idealistic, it offers an initial guide for the aspiring news writer.

OBJECTIVITY

How we see the world and the signs we use are influenced by our experience. For example, having traveled extensively throughout Europe has influenced my view of the world. On the other hand, I have never been to a third-world country, and that also influences how I perceive the world. I have not seen the harder-edge reality that would help me more fully appreciate how lucky we are to have clean, running water. I take running water for granted. That influences how I see water in general. My view of the world partially through exposure to less fortunate parts of the world through mass media helps me appreciate the availability of fresh water in the United States.

Likewise, when I write, my previous experiences influence what I write about. I choose to write about something because I think it is important; I believe a particular subject merits writing about. The act of choosing a subject is, by its very nature, not objective. Even if we do not realize it, aspects of our life-world permeate our writing. This relates to the Heisenberg's uncertainty principle. Heisenberg originally looked at sub-atomic particles to see how fast they move. However, when Heisenberg and his team measured these particles, they had to isolate them in order to do so. In doing this, they affected the way the particles moved without interference. The point is that when mass media personnel are sitting in front of someone with a camera, does the subject react the same way if the mass media cameras were not there? Do they answer the same way they would if they were out at the bar with their friends later that night? The observer affects the observed.

Most writers of mass media have seen the television programs *Friends*, *Seinfeld*, *The Cosby Show*, or *American Family*. Life for most of the people in the world is not like that. Families are not like that. Often times, in television, life is presented in a way that is not true to real life. They stereotype people and groups. Some groups are not fairly represented. We have to identify that there is bias in media writing. Most mass media writers working in the United States right now have one thing in common: they have a college degree. Does having a college degree not influence your *lebenswelt*? If writers are from a like-minded community, it may affect what stories are written and the way they are told. We may think that we are not biased, but even choosing to make a documentary about a topic, or write a piece about a topic, making a decision to tell *that story* reveals our bias as it is influenced by our life-world.

Do these inherent biases influence the rest of society? If an audience gets an unethical portrayal of some event, does that influence the way they see the world? For example, did a little kid burn down his parent's trailer because he saw it on "Beavis and Butthead," or do "Beavis and Butthead" burn things because that is what kids do? The question is whether it's the media that affects society, or whether it's society that reflects media. This makes me think of Tupac's music; did he create the social ills by rapping about it, or did he just rap about what he saw? Tupac's music and life has influenced society. Tupac was influenced by his environment, and he was talking about what he saw, but may also have influenced people who listened to his music.

STRUCTURATION

The film *Basketball Diaries*, starring Leonardo DiCaprio provides another case in point. DiCaprio's character takes a gun to school and kills several classmates and his teacher. The question arose as to whether kids saw this and then did it (the Columbine shooters saw the film before they killed at their school), or whether this story was the product of a reflection of the times. According to Anthony Giddens, a British scholar, it is a two-part influence. Giddens conceptualized this as an interactive process (structuration) in which both factors influence each other. When a mass media writer is communicating to thousands, if not millions, of people, the writer needs to be conscious of the moral implications of their message.

Does mass media attempt to persuade audiences to consume more? Or is it reflected in the media because we over-consume in the status quo? Is it that we have to have the best car and the best clothes because of the media, or is the media just giving us what we want? I would suggest that it is a symbiotic relationship between these two ideas.

Diagram of the Structuration Process

SOCIETY ⇄ CULTURE

Thus, awareness of structuration, the concept from Giddens in which society and mass media are symbiotically supporting and reflecting each other, is a way we can appreciate the power of biases. The first step toward decreasing the effect of our biases is to recognize that those biases exist.

SANDMAN'S DILEMMA OF OBJECTIVITY

A writer can also decrease the impact of their biases by considering **Sandman's Dilemma of Objectivity**. Peter Sandman says that total objectivity is impossible, but it is a good goal to work toward. Thus, we should recognize our biases and work to negate the impact of those biases in journalistic writing.

Sometimes that may mean not writing journalistic pieces about subjects for which we feel very passionate. For instance, I hate Nazis. I do not know what I would do if I had to write a story about Nazis. I could present my argument, that they are hate-mongering racist bastards, but what would my opposition be? Would the idea of objectivity necessitate identification of the advantages of Nazism? I would like to be objective, and maybe that is possible for some people, but not for me. I like education; I think everyone, no matter who they are, should have the right to education. Therefore, I am biased about education. I like democracy. I like to vote and like free speech; therefore, I am biased about democracy. I can try to identify those biases and minimize them, but come on…. No one can be objective. Maybe it would be best if I did not accept a journalistic assignment in which I would have to be objective about the advocacy of education or democracy.

There are some places where lack of objectivity is good. Think about our American soldiers fighting in Afghanistan right now. Should we be objective about them? "Oh, look, another soldier died. That makes the score plus five for the Taliban." Does it not serve our interests to avoid objectivity in the case of men and women who are risking their lives for our freedom? No, I do not want to be objective about this. I want to respect our soldiers' lives and sacrifices and the way we talk about them regardless of my political opinion. I will not privilege a group of extremists who force children to kill as soldiers. These are my brothers, cousins, and family.

"We are fair and balanced." Bullshit. When is the last time you heard Fox News say, "The Taliban finally won a battle today. Good for them!"? Are they really fair and balanced? Al Franken wrote a book that had the subtitle, "Fair and Balanced," and he was sued by Fox news. He said he did not know why he was being sued, whether it was because he took their little tagline or because he took their joke. On some issues, I choose not to be objective. Do not, however, say you are objective when you are clearly not.

If you really have an ethical problem with what you are assigned to write, I suggest you go to your boss and tell them that, while you may be able to write the piece they requested, someone else may be able to do it better given your personal biases. I once worked with a man who said, "The facts do not speak for themselves." I agree. We choose which facts to feature and which ones to use. You cannot give them all the facts; you can only give them what you have column space for. By sticking to the facts, you can avoid biases, but even in doing this you influence what is included. Then, you are organizing them from most important to least important, giving value to the facts.

For example, if I write a piece about Nazis, I might do a lead like, "Illinois Nazis met today in Skokie, IL. They are members of a group that killed 15 million people in Nazi-occupied Europe, including 3 million children." That would be my lead; that is most important to me. See how even then I am conveying my biases. Inevitably, your *lebenswelt* affects your attempt at objectivity.

Remember, the *dilemma of objectivity* suggests that the writer recognize their bias. In doing this, maybe we should privilege the other side. For example, if I was doing a piece on Illinois Nazis, I would choose the most ridiculous quote I got from their side in order to make them look bad because I *hate* Nazis. Maybe what Sandman is saying is that I should privilege their side by giving them the same courtesy I would give my own allegiances. Maybe instead of starting with how many innocent children those scumbags sent to the gas chambers, I could start with how many people were at the meeting in Skokie, IL, and keep it at that.

DIALECTIC

In the social sciences, to bracket one's consciousness is called adopting a hermeneutic turn. In Buddhism it is called mindfulness. To bracket our consciousness means to step outside and look at our own consciousness from a privileged observer position. For instance, when considering an issue, we ask ourselves, "Why am I thinking what am I thinking now about this topic?" Then we try to consider the issue through the lens of someone else's conscious perspective. Maybe for the Nazi example, I could try to use someone else's lens.

To be as intellectually rigorous as possible, we need to think in terms of the **dialectic**. We need to be ready to change our minds, even if only slightly, when we consider a topic. The dialectic says that there are two sides to every conceptual coin. In history, there is a **thesis**, or some sort of idea. For example, assume I have to write an article about abortion—a topic which I already have my own perspective on. What I have to do is seek out a counter-factual for my thought about a topic, or an **antithesis**. From this I come to a **synthesis**. If I have a perspective, I should interact with people who do not share my viewpoint so that I can be more open to other stances or ideas. This may help me strengthen and/or understand my own position. I should be committed to trying to change my mind, even a little. This is commitment to an intellectual dialectic, and is a hallmark of rigorous thought.

Diagram of the Dialectic Process

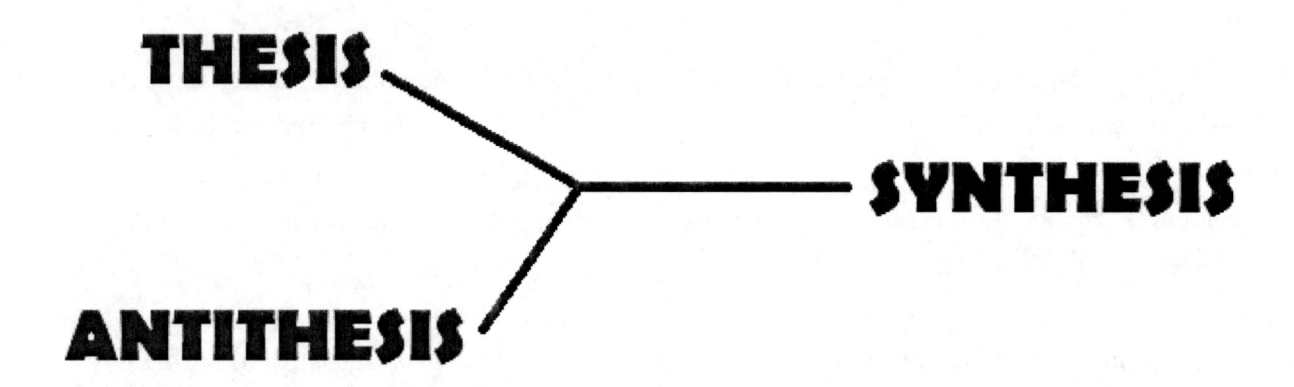

THESIS

SYNTHESIS

ANTITHESIS

We have all been in a conversation with someone who is just talking to themselves. They disagree with you, and they really do not care about what you have to say. If you are willing to change your mind a little, and be open-minded, then the person you are opposing will be open-minded and maybe change their mind a little, too. This is when real conversation occurs; this is conversational dialectic.

It is rigorously ethical to privilege the other side. Use more quotes from the other side. For example, when creating a documentary, do not just film your viewpoints. Seek out the best counter-arguments from the other side. Let the audience decide for themselves. That is when the best persuasion occurs. Recognize the other side. A commitment to covering the other perspective is essential in your writing and in everyday thinking. This will help minimize bias.

ETHICAL REFERENCE TO GROUP

The mass media writer should be considerate of how they write about members of various groups. Whenever we do a story about a group with differing characteristics—like men, women, older people, younger people, teenagers, people with disabilities, and ethnic groups—how do we refer to them? Our biases will be there. A writer should mention the group's identity only if it is relevant. If someone is a congressman, and they happen to be homosexual, the writer should not mention that unless it is relevant to the story. Also, try to avoid treating all people of the same group like there are no differences between people in the group. That is just not the case.

Avoid providing description that reinforces stereotypes. Bring up the differences only if it is relevant. For instance, if a governor of New York is sight-impaired, we do not need to constantly label him as that. Be careful with words, especially with minorities. Even using the word, "minority," is often misconstrued since white males are no longer the majority in this country. Do not use patronizing language. Do not be surprised when elderly folks are able to run a marathon. Avoid gender-specific words. *Flight attendant* is better than *stewardess*. A writer would be well advised to ask a member of a particular group for the preferred nomenclature. "It is better to be wrong in front of one person than embarrassed in front of millions" (Amber Dzierzynski).

To overcome biases in writing, we must know ourselves. As it says at the Oracle in Delphi in Greece, "Know thyself." This is the first step in working toward the goal of objectivity. This is a tough idea, but the mass media writer needs to be as objective as possible to minimize any bad consequences. Mass media writers influence how people see the world. This is why the writer needs to identify their worldview, their *lebenswelt*, so that mass media writers understand the impact of their unique perspective in their writing and on other people.

ETHICS IN ADVERTISING

Advertisers use knowledge about your psychological insecurities to sell you things you do not need. In a nutshell, that is advertising. Is that ethical?

Profit is the most important thing to commercial advertisers. When profit is an advertiser's number one concern, what role do ethics play? A woman that works for one of the largest advertising firms in this nation once told me that they have statistical research used to get kids to nag their parents for products. When she was asked about the ethics of her profession—creating the need for children to own material goods that they do not require, as well as discord in the relationship between child and parent—she said, "I don't know about ethics; I know that it works. It sells products." When thinking about advertising, understand that advertisers are out to make a profit and that ethics will fall by the wayside.

Artificial Need and the Culture of Consumerism

The concept of **artificial need** is important to consider when discussing mass media advertising and ethics. Herbert Marcuse, a member of The Frankfurt School of thought, first studied this idea. The Frankfurt School was a group of scholars in post-Nazi Germany that studied how the mass media was used to spread Hitler's message. You already know how I feel about Nazis… All I want to say is that Marcuse noticed how the Nazi ideology was spread through mass media. Then, he began to see how the mass media sold the **culture of consumerism** to the public. In a speech by Pope John Paul II in Poland in 1991, just after the fall of the Berlin Wall, he said to these former countries that the cult of communism should not be replaced by the cult of consumerism. We worship having new things. In America, one of the most important things to us is *having new stuff*. We do not care how many student loans we will have to repay in order to have the latest clothes from the Gap. We do not care if we sign a two-year cell phone contract just so we can have the newest and coolest phone that we can't afford.

I am part of this, too. I used to drive a 1989 Honda. I drove it until 2002. Then, all of a sudden, I thought, "I deserve better than this." I got sucked in by the idea that a new car was good. I felt I needed to have a car that met my professional status. Theodor Adorno was also from The Frankfurt School. He studied advertisements for automobiles. While doing this, he realized they are not just selling the new Mustang; they are also selling the idea that I need a Ford. Maybe even more important than that, according to Adorno, they are teaching me that I need *a new car*. He says that all ads teach me to want a new car—it does not even matter what model.

I have to admit, I am a sucker for this. My 1989 Honda Accord was not a chick magnet, and I wanted prestige. Luckily for me, one day, my Accord fell apart on the street and I had to buy a new car. What did I do? I went to the showroom and bought a brand new Prius. I did not go to the used car dealer to get a 2000 Accord. I went and bought a brand new Prius, and I was convinced that in buying this car, I was somehow *helping* the environment a little. I did not even consider the amount of energy wasted in making a brand new car.

This is the culture of consumerism—or dare I say the *cult* of consumerism—that we have fallen into. It is not a relationship with a higher power, or a king, or a church that makes us happy; it is a relationship to what kind of material stuff we have in our house. Advertising teaches us to define happiness this way.

Adorno also mentioned that "new" is the biggest element in advertising. Encourage us to want the newest cell phone, the newest apps, the newest styles in clothes, etc. Advertising tells us that the "new" is better than what we have now.

I have to admit; my mother has a problem. She has so much stuff that she bought online that I can hardly walk around in her house. She has recognized the problem and has gotten better (as in improved, not cured). Americans tend to be big-time consumers. We even want to put McDonalds and Camel Lights on every corner on every street in all countries around the globe. This seems most obvious when I travel around the world and then I come back to O'Hare Airport; we have a rampant obesity problem in this country because our mass media tells us that consumption will lead to happiness. Not to mention all the corn syrup and other crap they put in our food.

Suffice it to say, there are ethical issues in advertising. It is not the consumption that hurts us, because we also hurt the environment when we consume too much. We put the labor on the backs of third-world workers when we consume too much. We force kids in Vietnam to make shoes for us for a dollar per day. Many work 16 hours per day, 6 days a week and Nike says that is perfectly okay. There are major ethical issues with our culture of consumerism— our happiness set aside. It is like a drug in our society. Think of credit card debt. They do not *want* you to be able to pay for what you buy. They want you to pay the minimum balance, but they want you to owe them so that they can control you.

Our culture of consumerism is a kind of **indoctrination**. This is consistent with most current communication theories. The idea that advertising indoctrinates us can be defined by many theories. For example, advertising prepares us to believe that this behavior is not only normal, but our most desirable possible outcome should be material wealth. Diffusion of innovation theory also applies; we can see how products are absorbed through early adopters who then influence the masses to buy products. These early innovators are used to hook us all into waves of new products. The theory of a *spiral of silence* is also demonstrated in the mass media. Here, minority groups are silenced by the majority opinion and the system created by the majority power. In mass media, they want you to think that it is natural for everyone to define your happiness through material goods, and the mass media will silence the opinions of those who reject the idea or live an alternative lifestyle.

We need to consider other lifestyles of happiness that do not revolve around money. For example, I teach Media Writing, and make a healthy living doing so. However, money was *never* my motivation to teach. I am not motivated by the "stuff" I get from it either. Let me give you some advice: do what you love with all of your heart and dedicate yourself to it. The rest will fall into place. Do not read this book because you want money. Do not take your first job because you want money. Take your first job because it is something you love to do.

Society wants to teach you that you are here to make money, not to do what you love and express your thoughts, desires, feelings, and views of the world, and not to be happy in what you do ten years from now. In our culture, you do work, which is negative, to buy stuff that will make you happy. "Work," has been turned into a bad word. The reason we accept work as a bad word is because you will be able to gratify yourself later by purchasing material items. It is okay to serve the man as long as you can get off work, buy some SKYY Vodka, and drive away in your BMW. There is another way to look at the world: you do something because it helps people and because it fills you up with joy and motivation. Please do not mention this to this university, but I would do my job for free. The paycheck just happens to come with it. Seek your happiness and fulfillment first, and the rest will follow ethically. To thine own self be true.

REJECTING THE CULTURE OF CONSUMERISM

The culture of consumerism wants everyone to feel like a state of constantly wanting more is natural. There is another way to be. That is, do something that you love, that you care about—be it investigative journalism, television shows, or the art of video production. It could be it teaching. Come into the classroom in a way that will allow your students to feel empowered. Then, when you put your heart and soul into it, trust that money will take care of itself.

I have this buddy that owns a local college apartment rental company. He makes a ridiculous amount of money. He has a condo in Florida and yacht club membership dues. He is a member of five country clubs, he has several kids going to Ivy League schools, and he always says he just doesn't make enough coin. If he could only make more *money*, he would be happy. In delayed gratification, we are *never* satisfied. If the goal is always to get more, and we can always get more, then we are never happy.

I have a family, and I love them dearly. I hope that they, too, do not fall into the culture of consumerism. I hope they feel like they do not have to buy me things to show their love for me. But they do. For example, think about diamonds. I cannot express to a woman how much I love her unless I present her with a small rock dug out of Sub-Saharan Africa by the lowest paid laborers in the world while wars are fought over that diamond. People die for that diamond. You know who tells me I need a diamond to get engaged? De Beers. De Beers is a corporation that owns 90% of the diamond market. The need for engagement diamonds is an artificial need. I am not saying you should not accept a diamond or give a diamond to someone, but understand that if you do, you are a slave to artificial need just like DeBeers wants you to be. The idea that there is only one way to show your love for your fiancé—not with a ruby, an opal or gold, but a *diamond*—is a marketing scheme. [I bought my fiancé a diamond.] They have gotten into our subconsciousness.

I want to posit something; do you think Mother Theresa needed a diamond to tell those around her that she loved them? Did Saint Francis need a bigger car to feel satisfied? Did Gandhi need the newest designer jeans? If you have been exposed to the readings of Henry David Thoreau, he thought there were other things more important than *having*. He was a transcendental writer who thought that a spiritual relationship was most important. This goes back to the theory of the spiral of silence; the vocal minority is not vocal enough to drown out the status quo. The media tells the audience that the dissenters are wrong, or even worse, ignores the dissenting voices. There are other teachers in history who believe we did not need things to be fulfilled. Francis of Assisi taught that if you live simply, you will not be a slave to material possessions. He followed this one very famous teacher...a Jewish guy named Jesus. He also suggested we do not need to define happiness through material possessions. Gandhi also taught, "May we live simply so that others may simply live." There have been cultures of people throughout time that reject a consumer lifestyle.

What I am trying to point out is no one wants us to know there is another way to live. We almost had this when we went through the recession, when we realized we had too much stuff and too much debt. I hope we are starting to turn this corner. In Europe, most people have chosen to live more simply. They do not mind public transit, unlike us who just *have* to have our own car.

Does a fish know that it is wet? Not if it has never been dry. The point is; we never see anybody that is living a different way. We do not see people that ride their bikes to work instead of drive. If we did, we would realize that we do not need all the material stuff. Even worse, there is no class in university education that will teach you this. Critical media consumption is important. You will watch at least 10,000 hours of advertising before you die. It is important in the mass media that we highlight that the media is selling you a lifestyle, a *lebenswelt* (life-world): consumerism. They are trying to trick us. My daughter even knows about this. Maggie knows that the Disney channel is trying to sell her stuff she does not need. They are trying to sell her food that is not even food; it is just modified cornstarch and sugar. It takes teachers, parents, and enlightened media writers to teach our kids that they are "wet." Without these alternative voices, our children will be sucked into the naturalization of consumerism as a lifestyle.

The fact that you need to live the culture of consumerism is a lie. They make us feel like no one else in the world lives simply. "We cannot live simply *now*. We just cannot do that." Yes we can; we can make choices every day. There are alternate ways of living. There is a choice.

Remember when discussing advertising: the mass media creates artificial need. Artificial need occurs when the mass media tells us that what we "need," is what we *want*. I will do my best to help you convince people their needs are really their wants through the use of effective advertising. You will use those tools in a way that is comfortable for you. But scrutinize that question for yourself. "To thine own self be true" (Shakespeare).

CHAPTER 8:
FEATURE PRINT WRITING

There is a magic that can happen in writing. Writing can transport readers to another location and time. Writing also gives a writer power. A writer can put an idea into a reader's mind that they have not thought about before, or give an idea a new context. A writer can put the audience in another state of mind. Most significantly, a writer has the ability to challenge readers to think in terms of another paradigm. As an example, think about Hurricane Katrina hitting New Orleans in 2005. It might be noble to want to objectively question the facts about what should be done. But when we are actually there in the aftermath of the hurricane with dead bodies and our homes in pieces, we are in a different paradigm, or a different context, and we might have more subjective opinions. Writing is power, and quality writing has the power to create a melding between the mind of the writer and the mind of the receiver.

Writing has the power to create an image in the minds of our readers. In their minds, and in our minds, we are seeing the same picture, and that is magic. The subjects we discuss in this chapter will provide more tools through which the mass media writer, particularly writing in print, can create such magic. In this chapter, we will discuss print writing approaches beyond straight news writing using the inverted pyramid format, such as feature print stories. We will begin by discussing the importance of descriptive language. We then move to discussion of the narrative story approach and how it can be applied to feature print stories. We will then address other organizational styles. We will explore use of various leads beyond the summary lead. Finally, we will discuss other types of print stories.

USING DESCRIPTIVE LANGUAGE

Good descriptive writing starts with clear thinking. Remember, the writer has pictures in their minds about the story they want to tell. The writer needs to know what that picture is. Then, the writer needs to communicate clearly, concisely, and correctly. The process ends with clear writing because we are choosing signs, or words, in the clearest fashion to try to evoke the picture in the minds of our receiver. The writer can start with clear thinking and end with clear writing. To that extent, the writer should think about fresh images and articulate those fresh images with clear vocabulary. Descriptive writing should utilize simple words. It does not take big words to make a big picture. John Steinbeck was really good at this. He used simple language to articulate descriptions that created a picture in the reader's mind. Solid descriptive writing is useful in all types of writing, but the writer can be more descriptive in feature stories than in straight news.

Features are narratives that are designed to deliver news in a softer manner than straight news stories. They have a human interest angle and are entertaining but also have news value. When writing features, the writer should use descriptive language. Strunk and White mention using descriptive, concrete language to evoke meaning in the minds of receivers. When the writer is trying to build a mental picture for the readers, one thing the writer can do is establish a vivid location. Descriptive language helps the writer do that. For example, "The sun was bright and warm. The grass was lush and green. The smell of Old Style beer and popcorn wafted through the air. Baseball was here for the season." By using descriptive language, the writer can tell readers what the scene sounded, smelled, and looked like. The writer should try to describe the location in terms of the five senses. The writer evokes a mental picture in the minds of readers, and transports these readers to a scene. The magic in writing is created through the use of descriptive language. The writer wants readers to see a scene in their head as the writer thinks about it. To do this, we have to choose the right signs or words.

There is a balance between giving too much description and not enough detail. Sometimes ambiguity is good because sometimes we want our audience to fill in the blanks. I would suggest giving them the parameters of the scene and letting them personalize it. I can write, "There was a lamp on the wooden table," and that is probably enough description. What the lamp looks like is up to readers. It is up to them to interpret what kind of table or what style of lamp is on the table, and that is usually okay. We do not want to bury the reader in minute details, but we also do not want to deprive them of so much description that they cannot see the mental picture in their head. Let the reader supply some of the elements.

A key technique to using descriptive language well is to not rely too much on modifiers. For example, "He stuck out his large, prideful chin," is not as effective as, "He stuck out his chin." Do not over-rely on adjectives and adverbs. Sometimes, these are poorly used in place of good descriptive writing. Some figurative language can be okay. For example, using a metaphor can be helpful when comparing two unlike things. Readers get enough of the writer's framework in their minds to synthesize the writer's idea, but they also get to fill in the blanks. Again, do not over-rely on adjectives and modifiers. Metaphors can be okay when used properly, but they should not replace reliance upon descriptive language.

USING THE NARRATIVE APPROACH TO FEATURE WRITING

Features are a story. Often times in print writing, a "feature" is just a soft, soggy collection of facts. If a writer incorporates drama, it is going to make it a story versus a series of loosely collected facts. Therefore, drama can be used in any feature story. There should be a development of that story using dramatic principles. These were discussed in-depth in Chapter 1. Who is the protagonist? What is their will or want? Is there an inevitable outcome? Is there a major dramatic question? Are there complications that result in a climax and then end in a resolution? The writer should always think about the dramatic model when they are writing features; they should take the **narrative approach** (storytelling). (See Example of Feature Print News Story in the Appendix.) Using this approach allows the writer to share news with people and make it more interesting by sharing it dramatically. The writer can create a takeaway message that the audience will remember more vividly if the writer tells them a good story.

Narrative, or story, is generally the best organizational approach for writing print features. The writer should use the dramatic model and the story elements discussed previously. The writer should add the news values that make the story important to your reader. Just like movies, there can be good features and bad features, and the distinction rests in making use of the dramaturgical paradigm.

The ideal feature should grab the reader's attention and convince the reader to continue reading. The feature writer can grab the reader's attention with a soft lead. Then, in the second graph (paragraph), the writer can introduce the protagonist and identify their will or want. The writer is then tying the will or want of the protagonist to the major dramatic question that will carry readers through the feature story. In subsequent graphs the writer can write about the news value of the story.

Overall, the writer needs to craft a story, but also the writer needs to emphasize news value, discussed in depth in previous chapters. What does the story offer the audience? The writer should help readers identify what elements will apply to them as well as peak their interest in the story. The writer can highlight the impact, the prominence, proximity, etc. Then, the writer can get back into full narrative form by expressing the realization about the protagonist's will or want and what they will need to do to achieve it. This can be a point of realization for the protagonist.

A graph or two later in the story, the writer can include the complications that relate to the protagonist's will or want. The writer can dedicate several paragraphs to complications.

At the very end of the story, the writer can describe the climax, the answer to the major dramatic question. Finally, the writer can describe the resolution where the story and the protagonist reach stasis. Things are back to where they should be after the dramatic question is answered. Life is normal. The writer can tie the resolution back to the attention getter from the soft lead. When the writer uses this dramaturgical approach, they should include a climax and a resolution. The resolution can also tie back into whatever soft lead format the writer has chosen. The best features are those that tell a story, but they also identify the news values of the story.

Using a narrative approach keeps the readers interested in the whole story. In addition, features can create a scenario that puts our audience in another paradigm. Writing a dramatic story rather than just sharing the facts is more vivid, more real, and it all goes back to the fact that people like a good story. Readers remember information better when they receive it in narrative form.

OTHER ORGANIZATIONAL STYLES

As explained previously, a narrative approach and organizational sequence is an exceptional approach for writing feature print stories. Next, there are several other story organizational styles that can be used for feature print stories. These include narrative/news value hybrid format, news peg and nut graph approach, chronological format, hourglass format, and map format.

NARRATIVE/NEWS VALUE HYBRID FORMAT

The **narrative/news value hybrid format** combines a dramatic story and news values. (See Breaking Down the Elements of a Dramatic Feature Print Story in the Appendix.) The writer can start with a summary lead that emphasizes news values and then shift to a narrative structure. This organizational style can also be used in radio and television news. This particularly strong organizing sequence is a hybrid of narrative structure that emphasizes news values in the lead more than a simple narrative. This design combines the traditional structural features of the dramatic model (protagonist, will/want, realization, complications, climax, and resolution) with an emphasis on news values (timeliness, proximity, significance, prominence, etc.) to inform viewers/listeners as it entertains and persuades. This hybrid structure is an appropriate design for media writing and appeals to readers.

News Peg and Nut Graph Format

Many newspapers use the **news peg and nut graph format**. Here, the news peg is the aspect that the writer hangs the story upon. The peg explains why a story is important and why it is important *now*. The peg might also have some kind of news value or an appeal to the individual reader. Then, the nut graph is usually three or four graphs into the story. The third or paragraph has explains the news elements (who, what, when, where, why, and how). The nut graph contains an explicit statement of the news peg. A feature should contain a nut graph, and the news peg/nut graph arrangement can also be an organizing principle for a news story that is softer than straight news.

Chronological Format

Chronological format provides the story in the time order that it unfolded. Using chronology is much like using the narrative structure except that in the narrative format, we are stressing those dramatic elements instead of just telling the story as it happened. Sometimes we can use a summary lead and then go into chronological detail. This provides a detained explanation for readers of how exactly an event unfolded.

Hourglass Format

The next possible format is the **hourglass format**. This format essentially changes part of the way through. For example, the first five or six graphs may be in a straight news format with a summary lead, and then, using a transitional phrase to move into chronological format. That way, your editor can still use the first half as inverted pyramid straight news and cut it at the sixth graph, if needed, or they can run the full piece which will provide more detail to the readers. Hourglass is normally inverted pyramid for the first half and then another format for the remainder.

Map Format

A **map format** is much like a topical arrangement. For example, a writer may cover the military, economic, and social implications of a particular subject. Using this format, the writer lays out topics and then elaborates on them. Also, this format can be useful when doing piece on a geographic place, like the Chicago Art Institute. The writer can organize the piece by writing, "On the first floor there is Impressionistic art. On the second floor is Asian art..." etc.

LEADS

The best feature tells a story. It is going to be a dramatic narrative with the news values in the third or fourth paragraph. Then we talked about other types of feature formats. Now we move to feature leads. Again, a lead is the first sentence or first graph of our story. There are several types of leads.

The first type of lead is the **summary lead**. This is the lead writers use for straight news (inverted pyramid) format in which the climax and valuable news elements are presented at the beginning of a piece.

Another type of lead is the **multiple element lead**. Here, we have a couple different subjects we are bringing together under some auspices.

In a **delayed identification lead**, the writer would provide a startling quote as our lead but then maybe not reveal who said it until the third or fourth graph.

The **affective lead** uses emotion to grab the reader at the beginning of a story. It tugs at the heartstrings. When a writer utilizes an affective lead, they try to get readers emotionally involved in the story.

Anecdotal leads tell a story and have somewhat of a plot. The anecdotal lead gives an anecdote or story as the attention-getter. This is the point explained; the writer throws the complications up front to pique interest.

Descriptive leads set the scene. Descriptive words are a good tool here. The writer is trying to create a picture in the reader's mind right in the beginning.

Question leads use a question to engage the reader. I would suggest staying away from them; it is a stylistic thing.

Quotation leads use quotes to begin a piece. A weakness of this is that we may not be able to sum up the whole story with a single quote. The quotes are usually by a main character or the main character in the story.

Direct address leads grab the reader by trying to address them directly. It uses a "you," orientation. It is a way to directly speak to the reader.

Finally, **staccato leads** use repetitive words. Example, "Popcorn. Candy. Stars. How long has it been since you've been to the movies?" It uses non-complete sentences to create a feeling. There might be some instances where any of these options are most appropriate.

OTHER TYPES OF PRINT STORIES

In any type of writing it is more effective and interesting for the reader when a writer uses a dramatic approach. For example, if a writer is crafting a feature about a person, the writer can make them the protagonist in the story and incorporate story elements. If a writer is creating a how-to piece, then they can give readers a story that explains how the protagonist accomplished a given task. Or, if it is a hypothetical person, like the writer is doing a piece on something that needs to be done, the writer can present that information in the form of a story. The writer can create a protagonist and then tell readers what that person will face, what their complications are, and what will be their will or want. Always consider including a climax and a resolution. The following section will address different types of features.

PERSONALITY STORIES

One way of understanding a person is to know the battles they have gone through in their life. **Personality stories** are stories about a person. These are complications from the dramaturgical approach. The writer can tell readers a story about that personality with a good narrative. The writer can explain for readers what the complications have been for the subject and how they overcame obstacles to achieve a goal. Quality features about a personality also explain the news value of the story.

HISTORICAL STORIES

Historical stories are those that discuss history. History is remembered because it is composed of good stories. Historical figures engage in battle, defend or abandon principles, face complications, and either achieve their goals or do not. But the exploits of historical figures are entertaining narratives.

A writer should make an incident is an entertaining story. If you are going to tell a story about history, you might as well tell it in narrative form. Research can reveal entertaining episodes. Who likes history when it is just the facts? Most people do not. Facts are mostly boring and difficult to remember. These stories are often good around holidays and anniversaries.

LOCATION STORIES

Place or travel stories are those about traveling. Rick Steves has a show on PBS that I think of when I think of travel or place features. If I was going to talk to you about going to Paris, I could talk to you about place after place, but would it not be more effective if I told a story about my own experiences? In narrative format, I could write about how at first I was lost, but then I learned to get a museum card and directions at a particular train station, and I learned to travel on the public transit system to see certain places. I could describe how I was able to find my way to Notre Dame, had breakfast in the Left Bank in the morning, took some buses to get to the Louvre and the Arch de Triumph, and ended up at the Eiffel Tower in the afternoon. The story could provide the information necessary for other American tourists to find their way to these locations while providing an entertaining read.

BRIGHTS

Another type of print news story is a **bright**. Brights are short, entertaining stories that are highlighted by factual information. They are almost not a story at all. The writer gives the reader the news values, and tells the reader why the issue is important today. For example, you can give a story about previous presidents and their attempt to create socialist policy and then compare that to President Obama's proposal of public health care. Brights generally present just the facts in a nutshell with few transitions.

FOLLOW-UP

Another non-straight news format is the **follow-up story**. The follow-up story is the second-day story that runs when something changes or is added to a previous story. It generally provides some controversy and puts that controversy in the lead. A reporter may use this format to continue writing about a particular event without appearing to present old news.

OBITUARY

There are also other formats to writing other than those that we have discussed. The first is **obituary** writing. Obituaries are reports about deceased that run when a person passes away. Often times, if you are just sitting around with nothing to do, your editor at your newspaper will ask you to start writing the obituary of someone who has not died yet. For example, if you hear that a celebrity or known person has a fatal disease, it is not a bad idea to start working on a life bio so that if something happens to them, you already have half the story written. In an obituary, you are talking about their biography, their life, their complications and successes, and also when any memorial services will be held. If you start out as a journalist at a newspaper, you will probably start out writing obituaries, divorce announcements, court proceedings, etc. An obituary should include general biographical data about a deceased, identify surviving family members, and information about memorial services. Obituaries can also provide information about family requests for donations to a cause in remembrance the departed.

STORIES ON SPEECHES

In terms of speech pieces, the writer is presenting information about what happened during that speech. What is the most salient information that a writer can present about the speech that was given? A writer should consider the actual and residual message (addressed in Chapter 2). The salient information will give the reader a residual message that lasts with them. The writer should find the most important theme or themes in a speech and use such themes as the central focus of the story.

OPINION PIECES

There is a time and a place for writing opinions: an opinion piece. These can take the form of editorials, guest opinion pieces, or even letters to the editor. The ability to write a compelling opinion piece is a useful tool in a democracy in which even average citizens have opportunities to express themselves in print. Usually an opinion piece is structured in a more traditional way, where we have an introduction to the idea graph, an attention-getter with a thesis statement, a preview of the main points, providing evidence, and supporting information with logic. Then, in the conclusion, we summarize our ideas and tie that to the attention getter. (See Opinion Writing Exercise in the Appendix.) There is a place for opinions in writing, but not in straight news. The writer is trying to inform in regular print news stories. We want to give our readers a description that will put them in that place. Avoid interjecting your opinions in straight news stories, but build a compelling argument in an opinion piece. Good writing is good writing in opinion print pieces, as with other writing forms. The writing process is the same, and the central principles of clarity, concision, correctness, and completeness are important.

In this chapter, we discussed print writing approaches to straight news writing using the inverted pyramid format. We began by discussing the importance of descriptive language. We moved to discussion of the narrative story approach to write feature print stories. We addressed other organizational styles, and then explored the use of various leads beyond the summary lead. Finally, we discussed other types of print stories. Writing has the power to create an image in the minds of our readers. In their minds, and in our minds, we are seeing the same picture, and that is magic. The subjects we discussed in this chapter provide more tools through which the mass media writer, particularly writing in print, can create such magic. We are working on being better writers so we can better create that magic.

CHAPTER 9:
LEGAL ISSUES IN MASS MEDIA WRITING

It is important to touch on the common legal issues involved in media writing. If you are planning to pursue a career in media writing, I suggest you take a specific course on media law. However, a few key introductory points are worth mentioning for anyone expecting to write for the mass media. I will only skim the surface of these concepts, as the depth of content on the topic is capable of filling an entire course. Should you pursue a career in media writing, you will end up taking part in more in-depth discussions of these basic ideas.

RESTRICTIONS TO FREE SPEECH

The first important point when discussing media law is the **first amendment law**, or freedom of speech. It says the government shall make no law interfering with rights to political speech. Plenty of first amendment debates are generated in the study of media law, such as whether or not corporations should be treated as individuals, and the topic can offer interesting and enlightening discussion. Suffice to say, the first amendment simply says the government cannot restrict your free speech. This includes the development of editorials, documentaries, or any kind of political speech or mass media.

There are legal restrictions to non-political speech, however. The first restriction of speech is **obscenity and indecency**. As a writer of the mass media, it is important to remember that the airwaves are public. Therefore, the courts and the Federal Communication Commission have deemed it appropriate to say that indecency should not be broadcast over the airwaves. This law applies to public television and radio. Many of us watch cable and know that it does not have to follow these restrictions. Different laws apply to cable that allow television shows such as "The Shield" and "Nip Tuck" to be delivered to homes. Cable companies voluntarily feature adult appropriate content later at night and deliver shows like "South Park" after 10 pm with a disclaimer.

Libel is another commonly used term in media law. Libel is something that hurts the perception of someone's character or their reputation. The important part of libel that distinguishes it from other slanderous remarks is that it is something *untrue* that hurts someone's reputation. An example of libel would be if a newspaper published a fallacious story about someone stealing money from their employer. If a story is published and it is proven to be untrue, the writer of the story will be sued, along with the newspaper, magazine, or television station who allowed the piece to be aired. However, the individual whose reputation has been damaged must provide several pieces of information to sue. First, the individual must prove that the information presented is untrue by showing that there was **actual malice**. In other words, it must be proved that the reporter published the piece intentionally to hurt an individual's reputation. Only one response is available against charges of libel: the truth. The best response against a charge of libel is, "It is true." If what a writer communicates is true, it is not libel. This makes it incumbent on a mass media reporter to ensure you do not get sued. A writer can respond with a claim of ignorance, expressing that they did not know the information presented was wrong, but the best defense is to respond that the information is true. There are additional facets that apply to libel, but these are the core elements behind the law that must be considered when writing for the media.

When it comes to laws and commercial speech, **false advertising** is also illegal. The Federal Trade Commission is supposed to monitor all advertising and take action if anything is presented falsely, but unfortunately there are still plenty of questionable claims in many advertisements on television. Advertisers are known to push the boundaries, but there are laws in place that prevent false advertising. Additionally, in some states, it is illegal if public relations pieces (i.e., press releases) are false as well. It is important to constantly be aware of these laws and that any commercial speech should be completely free of lies. A mass media writer should not present false information.

COPYRIGHT VIOLATIONS

Another important legal consideration is copyright. **Copyright** stops you from stealing another person's work or property. If a writer is going to use someone else's work, they or the organization they work for need to get permission and/or pay the original creator of the piece. There are two exceptions to this law: federal documents and information utilized for educational purposes. If I am using a film, for example, to demonstrate class concepts, I do not have to pay the company or ask permission because it is used for academic purposes. Another example is if I make a documentary that teaches younger kids about the consequences of bullying. I may use copyright material to supplement my work because I am not making the documentary to create profit, but for educational purposes.

Another copyright issue that has become more and more prevalent with the increasing popularity of YouTube and other Internet sources is music copyright. Several years ago the

Supreme Court decided a source could use up to eight seconds of a song or film without violating copyright. Later, the courts changed the standard and decided there can be no use of any portion without permission. We live in a democracy, so we do have influence, but ultimately the courts decide what is copyright and what is not. Therefore, I would suggest that when you are in the workplace, refer to a lawyer regarding your questions of whether something is a copyright violation or not. Even more directly, ask your boss. Your boss should know whom to call to verify the legal law, which changes frequently.

There are a few factors to consider when you are deciding whether or not something is a copyright violation. Think about whether the intention is to make a profit or is for educational use, and think about the nature of the copyrighted work. If you use a piece from Ken Burns' *Civil War,* he may not care. If it is music from your friend's garage band, they may not be upset either. When considering whether something is a copyright infringement or not, it is also important to consider the parts of the piece used. Is it used independently or within the context of the whole? In the major motion picture *Pearl Harbor*, the director used footage from a documentary about Pearl Harbor. This was the case that brought the copyright issue to the Supreme Court and ultimately where they decided that a source can use up to eight seconds of someone's work without it being copyright infringement. Another test for copyright violation is the affect it has or could potentially have on the market. For example, if use of the Pearl Harbor documentary footage in *Pearl Harbor* the movie caused sales of the original documentary to plummet because so much was available within the movie, then the copyright violation might be taken more seriously. Again, always ask your boss if you are unsure. The first best response is, "It was true," and then second best response is, "My boss said it was okay." That is called plausible deniability.

PLAGIARISM

Plagiarism is another legal consideration. **Plagiarism**, also known as **misappropriation**, is taking information without citing sources. Misappropriation is when a writer relies too much on one source of information. When a writer researches, they have to research until their information becomes common knowledge.

I wrote a book on Pope John Paul and image restoration discourse. One of the important issues of the book is that Pope John Paul said the Jewish people have been discriminated against by members of the Catholic Church at various points in history. During my research I discovered that the pope played soccer on a Jewish league when he was a boy in school. This point was important when reflecting on John Paul's relationship with people of Jewish faith. So when I used that information the first time, I cited the source of that information. As I continued doing additional research, I found another source that noted John Paul's participation on the soccer team. After discovering this second source I went back and added it to the citation. Eventually I found a third source with the information regarding John Paul playing for a Jewish soccer team. I thought, "Of course he did. I know that." After discovering this third source, I went back to my citation and I removed the citation because I did not need it anymore. I had three independent sources that informed me he played soccer on a Jewish league as a kid. The information was common knowledge to me at that point. My rule is this: three times a citation and the information becomes common knowledge. You will have to make this distinction for yourself, but I say three is adequate. For example, a writer does not need a citation for the fact that the Declaration of Independence was signed in 1776. It is common knowledge.

A writer can be fired or lose credibility if they get caught committing misappropriation, plagiarism, copyright violation, libel, or indecency. Check the Internet for whether or not something is plagiarized. You can take five words and search them on google.com. Google will tell you if those five words exist in any order somewhere else. This involves propriety of ideas. This is why a writer must be rigorous when it comes to appropriation and citation. Writers need to protect the sanctity and validity of knowledge and the origination of individual ideas. If a writer gets as many sources as they can, they will avoid plagiarism and misappropriation. Again, there are many more legal considerations and issues that are not covered here. I have only offered a brief overview to get a writer started.

CHAPTER 10:
BROADCAST MEDIA WRITING

We are moving into the realm of broadcast media, which is quite different than the print realm we have already discussed. In this chapter we discuss several considerations when writing for broadcast media, the similarities and differences between broadcast and print writing, elements of oral style, broadcast formats, broadcast leads, broadcast format writing guidelines, style in copy, attribution in broadcast media, and trends in electronic media. If you commit; you can be the best writer that you can be. This is true for broadcast writing as for all other types of writing.

BROADCAST WRITING CONSIDERATIONS

First, in print, the words are seen, not heard. In broadcast, they are heard and not seen. This means that our audience cannot go back and look at something if they miss it or if it is confusing. In print, the reader controls the rate of consumption; in broadcast, the receivers do not have that luxury. Here, the producers control the rate of communication as well as opportunities to review the message. In broadcast, we can use words on the screen to create emphasis. This will be particularly important when we communicate with pictures. Whenever you write for broadcast, you need to read that copy out loud as you prepare it. As you read it, include inflection, proper tempo, emphasis, or any other feature that could add time to the presentation on air.

The second important consideration is that there is a one-time consumption chance in broadcast. This means that presentation is not in the control of the receiver. The broadcasters control the sequence and rate in which the message is delivered. We have to be more concise about what we present and how we present it. Again, the message may be re-broadcast, but the receiver has no control. Some of that is mitigated in television broadcast because we have DVRs and on-demand, or things like TiVo. The point is we only get one shot to broadcast the message to our receiver, to share the message with the audience, so we need to be even more precise.

The next consideration is that there is limited feedback in broadcast. In verbal communication, if your receiver does not get the point, there is an opportunity to clarify because the speaker can receive feedback (i.e., facial expressions). We do not have this in broadcast. There may be emails, blogs, or letters to the broadcast company, but this is all indirect feedback. In terms of feedback, corporations use sales as an important measure of message effectiveness. Ratings are also a measure of message effectiveness. Sometimes corporations or media outlets might use surveys or focus groups, but typically sales and ratings are the standard.

The last element is that in broadcast, we have a large audience of individuals. This means that we need to shift our orientation to a "you," orientation. Our message can be casual and conversational as opposed to the formality of print. We can use contractions in broadcasting because they sound more natural. As we think about people listening to our message, we want to be conversational and much less formal than we are in print.

SIMILARITIES AND DIFFERENCES IN BROADCAST AND PRINT WRITING

These characteristics all separate broadcast communication from print communication, but there are several similarities. First off: *good writing when good writing no matter what the context*. We should always have those four considerations when writing for mass media: clear, concise, correct, and complete. No matter what broadcast format, the most important is clarity: clarity to our audience and clarity to the people we work with. Concision is even more important in broadcast media. Every word should tell because time is money. As we think about how much it costs to run a commercial during the Super Bowl, every second must count as it may cost tens of thousands of dollars. Being correct is basic; we need to make sure that they get the right information. Finally, being complete is always important because we must include every element that the audience needs. We need to include all the information that we think is important for them to make a judgment or opinion or to be informed about a given topic. You should always be clear, concise, correct, and complete.

Also similar between print and broadcast are the four structural considerations: pace, variety, unity, and climax. Pace is important in broadcast as we mentioned earlier because the audience does not control the rate of consumption. Variety means mixing it up a little bit. To some extent, that is why we like actualities. Changing elements keeps the attention of the audience. Unity will be important because the sum of the whole needs to be greater than the sum of the individual parts. It should all fit together. Climax is still important in broadcast media; we need to make sure that the major dramatic question is answered, the punchline is presented, or that the solution to our problem is presented.

Another similarity between print and broadcast is drama. We want to tell a good story. Whenever we structure broadcast messages, we should always consider the dramatic approach. Who is our protagonist and what do they want? Here is the deal; you can write a straight informational radio story, but that will never be as good as if you can structure it with some drama. You want to identify a protagonist and articulate their will or want. Often the protagonist can have a realization that they may achieve this will or want if they were able to do something. Thus, we are going to turn to the complications that stood in their way.

It does not matter what it is (for instance, if the local PTA is making policy on dress codes) we can just give the facts, but it is so much more interesting if we talk about the complications in terms of a story. Emphasis on story enables a writer to connect with the audience. Maybe the parents are worried that they will not be able to afford the new clothes, or that some students are concerned that they are being suppressed individually. The writer needs some kind of climax: did the school instate the dress code? Then, we need some denouement; in this example, what will happen from now on with the dress code. The dramatic approach is the foundation of this class. Telling a good story well necessitates us to always consider—be it radio or TV or a commercial or a film—that we think about a good *story.*

The writing process in broadcast media is also very similar to that of writing for print media. We think about our topic, we research, and then we re-write and revise. This is the process we go through before we even get the first acceptable draft. Then, share it with others and re-write again. We must consider again that we have many listeners or viewers in broadcast and only one chance to reach them.

News values are also still important when writing for broadcast media. We want to think about why our audience would want to listen to our story. Thus, we have to consider proximity, magnitude, impact, oddity, and prominence just like we do when we think about writing for print.

Despite the similarities between broadcast and print, there are some contrasts. In broadcast, the content and pace is fixed by the writer. In print, the receiver controls these things. Likewise, time spent with the message is controlled by the reader. They also can decide whether or not they will consume the entire message or whether they will just flip the page. This is unique to print. Also, there are some vocabulary challenges when writing for broadcast. If the reader encounters words they do not understand in print, they can access another source to clarify it. In broadcast, they cannot.

In broadcast messages, all aspects of delivery are chosen by the writers and producers. The writers and producers decide how fast, how much, and when the message is delivered. They control variety and sequence and pacing as well as emphasis. The writer strategically determines what elements should be in the message and then the producers who determine what gets on the air. Again, there is not as much feedback.

Deadlines when writing for broadcast media can also be different. Deadlines are more frequent in broadcast than in print. We may have a 5 pm deadline for a story, but then we need to update that story for the 10 pm newscast. Think about 9/11; the New York Times is only printed once a day. They printed that story, but then were locked for 24 hours from updating it until the next day's issue came out. Think of how many updates there were to that story during the course of the day on broadcast: every *minute* provides a new deadline. Every time a new piece of information came up, they broadcast it on television.

In broadcast, you really can tell a story more than we can in use of the inverted pyramid. We want a story in broadcast, and we have more opportunity to do so. Format is also different in electronic media. Also, cost is hugely different between broadcast and print. Most electronic media costs more than print. The thing about newspapers is that usually people do not read them all. In broadcast, we consume it all. It is a matter of supply and demand. There is less time and less space in broadcast and it has the potential to reach a larger audience. Also, the receiver can be a little more passive in consuming broadcast media. You can talk on your cell, drive a car and make pancakes—all at the same time—while you listen to the radio. Print is not like this.

ORAL STYLE

Oral style is important in broadcast because our audience is hearing it, not reading it, particularly in radio. When thinking about oral style, the first important consideration is clarity. Clarity is even more important here because there is no feedback from the receiver. Some techniques can be used to increase clarity stylistically. It is important to know your audience and their background. For example, if you are writing for NPR, you are going to write differently than in writing for MTV. Likewise, different talent personalities will have different character than others. Understanding this can increase clarity.

Oral style is more informal and more casual than in print. That is the difference between oral and print. If that is true, than we really need to scrutinize our language. Our words need to be accurate and precise; we need to use words the audience knows. They do not have the opportunity to look the word up. If we distract them with an unknown word, we could lose them. Simple words are important. Vocabulary should be straightforward. Avoid general or abstract language. In time limits, we want to be conversational but we want to be concise.

The writer should use connotative and descriptive words. In connotative words, there is some other element that goes with the words; words that, by association, are more descriptive. When we talk about descriptive, we want to put our audience there. We want to paint a picture in their minds. Onomatopoeia are words that sound like the quality they are describing. The words bubbling, crunch, and clash are examples of onomatopoeia. Onomatopoeia is another good descriptive strategy.

Using active voice is also very important in broadcasting. It is more forceful than passive and also more clear. Make sure your subject acts on the object; the subject performs the action, not receives it. Inversely, in sentence structure, the object is not acted upon by the subject. Rather, the subject acts on the object. That is active voice. Passive language slows and weakens our message. We can add variety by rarely adding passive structure, or, of course, when the object is more important than the doer. But, in general, use active construction.

Personal pronouns are allowed in oral style; you can use first and second person pronouns to address your audience. "You," orientation is often used in oral style. "We," is also used in broadcast media. Be careful with pronouns, but personal pronouns in oral style are fine. It is even more important in broadcast media that we use simple sentences. Complex sentences cause our audience to get lost. If we are reading, we can go back, but in broadcast, we cannot. Therefore, we must speak even more simply than in print. Do not have open independent clauses. A writer should eliminate lengthy interjections at the middle of the sentence. Avoid having a long list of nouns as modifiers. Always use simple sentences. Use subject-verb-object order in your sentence structure. Stick to this structure in broadcast, it will be more clear.

Also, we need to use transitions and **vocal cues**. Our receivers in broadcast cannot see a comma. Therefore, talent needs ellipses, which provide a pause. In broadcasting, vocal cues perform the same function as punctuation in writing. We need to rely on transition so that our receivers can see that we are moving on to a new paragraph. In broadcast, you may underline a word or phrase so that it is read with emphasis. Also in broadcast, you want to use a moderate pace. Do not go too quickly. Do not use negative construction; it is an obstacle to clarity and it is confusing. Always use positive construction. Avoid homophones—words that sound like other words (i.e., oral and aural). Homophones are confusing and can be misinterpreted; be careful with them. If you must, think of another word that is clearer. Avoid redundancies—things that are repetitive. They waste time and add clutter.

Avoid **doublespeak** or euphemisms. This is even harder when talking about political correctness. For example, it used to be called "friendly fire," when we accidentally shot someone on our own side in a war. Then it got changed to "innocent victims," and now, it's "collateral damage." We want to avoid doublespeak. This is often difficult when we try to be politically correct. Avoid clichés. They are overused and lazy. I mean, how many "Cinderella stories," can we have in sports? Clichés are lazy and should be used very rarely. They can be used, but use them rarely and carefully. Be inventive.

Oral style is sometimes criticized as being too simple, but it is about getting a message across clearly. Oral style is often too focused on being too entertaining. I would suggest that the two purposes are not mutually exclusive. I think that we should give our listeners rational reason why they should listen but also an emotional element for why they should listen. Using drama can increase this blend of news and story.

BROADCAST FORMATS

There are some general considerations for different broadcast formats and scripting. First of all, when we talk about writing any type of broadcast format, we are going to use a standard 8.5 x 11 sheet of paper. Second, only use one side of the page when you script. We want to make it easy for the talent to read; not have them confused and lost while turning over pages. The word **talent** refers to people who are on camera or on mic. Often times, they are just reading copy, they are not reporters. Plus, turning over pages will be picked up by the microphone or boom. The third consideration is do not crowd your script. Space things out if you need to. Clarity is the most important consideration when writing for mass media, and we need to be clear to the people we work with. I am all about saving trees, all about protecting the environment, and re-using paper. I re-use paper, front and back, but do not try to save paper when you are writing scripts. The most important thing is whether or not it is clear. Therefore, spread things out if you need to and only use one side of the paper.

There are a couple more considerations to scripting in broadcast. First, do not use a dateline before the beginning of your piece. We are going to assume that it is the most up to date version. In print, we use a dateline to say when and where the story was filed, but not in broadcast. Second, always use *present* tense. Try to give the story in present tense, especially when dealing with attribution. Third, avoid complicated proper names. Try to simplify them for your readers if you can. Again, you would not say, "former president William Jefferson Clinton," you would say, "former president Clinton." Leave out excessive explanation. Give your audience only what they need and let them fill in the rest. Always use active voice.

BROADCAST LEADS

When we talk about structure for broadcast leads, there are a few considerations of format and style. The lead is the first sentence or paragraph of the broadcast news story. Again, we are going to make it present or future tense, rather than past. In broadcast leads, the writer should use simple sentences. The writer should avoid complex or confusing sentences for the lead. In broadcast, it is very important that the writer attracts the attention of your audience and maintain that attention. They could easily flip the channel or the dial to another station or program. The writer can lead with the most compelling aspect of an event or information. Examples of writing leads for particular broadcast formats are presented in later chapters on particular broadcast formats.

I would suggest that you use a three-part format: content, explanation, and effects. I would suggest that the best organizational sequence for a broadcast piece is a *story*. Identify your protagonist, with a will or want, their realization, overcoming complications, and then a climax in which the tension related to the dramatic question is answered, finished with a dénouement—where everything returns to normal and we look to the future. The cornerstone of media writing is that we should tell a good story and tell a good story *well*. This is important particularly in broadcast; we need to really grab our audience and a story is the best way to do that.

BROADCAST FORMAT WRITING GUIDELINES

Whenever we write for broadcast, we want to consider several stylistic elements. They include writing in the present tense, delaying identification, reading the copy out loud, using action verbs, paraphrases and sound bites, putting attribution first, breaking up lengthy series of modifiers, and repeating of key elements.

The writer should use present tense when writing broadcast news. It is more current and more engaging than past tense. Remember, "news" has the word, "new," in it. If a story is old, then it is history. This makes broadcast news stories about *the now*. When the writer uses the present tense, it satisfies the news value of timeliness.

Delay unimportant names until after an explanation. For instance, if a woman was hit by a bus, but no one knows her name, we do not identify her until later in the story. The woman is not necessarily newsworthy in that case, the more important fact is that a bus hit a woman. Now, if Bill Clinton was hit by a bus this morning, we would put that in the lead because that expresses the news value of prominence.

Also, you always want to read your copy out loud before the broadcast. This is going to enable us to identify where words are cumbersome for who is going to read it. This also gives you an opportunity to identify the time on the story, and the time is very important. We want to be timely. For instance, national feeds come at the hour. Reading copy out loud allows for considerations of oral style. When it is copy, it is just text.

The fourth consideration is that we are going to use action verbs. Instead of forms of the verb "be," we are going to think about action verbs. This is going to make our writing more direct, more forceful, and clearer.

Utilize paraphrasing and sound bites. This gives us variety and perspective. Paraphrasing allows us to give quotes in a more succinct way. Remember, listeners cannot hear quotation marks on the radio. When you do directly quote, use an actuality. We need to give verbal cues that act as punctuation. This leads into avoiding punctuation. Do not rely on punctuation; our audience cannot see it and we need to use verbal cues instead.

When writing for broadcast, always put the attribution first. Rather than saying the name and then the title; put the title before their name. Also avoid introductory clauses. These are phrases that are offset by a comma. For example, "before the ceremony began, Rod Blagojevich, governor, slipped on a banana peel." If a writer is considering including an introductory phrase, they should generally just save it for the end of the sentence. Do not separate your subject and your verb; keep them together. For instance, "Blagojevich, on the other hand, slipped on a banana." Try to put, "Blagojevich slipped on a banana peel, however...." Do not add parenthetical phrases that will keep them apart. Likewise, put titles before the name of the noun; it is more clear.

Always break up a lengthy series of modifiers. Again, modifiers are not our friend. Rather than use modifiers, use descriptive language that paints a picture in the mind of our viewers that allow them to ascribe a modifier themselves. If the scene is haunting, talk about the darkness, the dust, the creaks, and moans; let the reader determine if it is haunting. Also avoid negatives. Try to say things in the positive. You would not say, "It is not sunny outside," you would say, "It is cloudy."

The final element here in considerations for broadcast structure is repetition of key words. Once you use a word or phrase to describe something, stick to that, do not try to get complicated and flowery. You have all had English classes where writing means coming up with many ways to say the same thing, but broadcast writing is different. One of the overall structural considerations is unity, and we should always stick to phrases that are unified throughout our piece.

STYLE IN COPY

When you are writing for radio or television news, or maybe a commercial or a feature film, there are several things you want to do when writing your copy. The first is use phonetic spelling. The AP Style Guide has suggestions when it comes to phonetics, particularly for broadcast. Phonetic spelling means you spell out words that could be pronounced in a simpler, verbal form. For example, "Pharmacy," might be phoneticized as, "Farm-uh-see." Remember, the syllabic breakdown of words in the dictionary is not necessarily phonetic as much as a pronunciation guide, so consult AP for phonetics if you have questions. Often the phonetic spelling of a word is in parentheses after the word or name.

This is particularly important when it comes to proper and foreign names. Also, we need to think about our talent. Ultimately, the consideration here is clarity. Would it be clearer to them if it was phonetically spelled out? Err on the side of clarity. It is a judgment call, but consider your talent.

Use short titles and keep them before the name. Shorten the title as much as you can. Terse is the key. "DOC Commissioner," is much better than, "DOC co-commissioner for appeal and consumption for impaired vehicles." In terms of common name usage, as mentioned earlier, the writer does not need to write out, "William Jefferson Clinton," as most are familiar with, "Bill Clinton."

ATTRIBUTION IN BROADCAST MEDIA

When it comes to attribution in broadcast, we must make a clear distinction between attribution in print and in broadcast. In print, we use, "said," for attribution, in the *past tense*. In broadcast media, "says," is the attribution we are going to use: *use present tense in broadcast attribution*. This is very important. In print, we would say, "The President said the economy would get better." In broadcast, we would say, "The President *says* the economy will get better." Again, in writing for radio and television news, attribution is in present tense.

Also, when doing attribution in broadcast, do not put the title between the subject and the verb; put attribution *first*. You would not say, "Blagojevich, former governor of Illinois says…" you would say, "Ex-governor Blagojevich says." *Put the attribution before the subject in broadcast.*

Do not use abbreviations if possible. This is another big difference between print and broadcast. Unless it is a very common abbreviation, avoid it. If you want to use abbreviations like, "am" then write, "A-M," so that they know to read the letters. For example, in "YMCA," you would print, "Y-M-C-A," for radio announcers so that they say the acronym. Do not abbreviate places. Spell out cities, states, streets, etc. Do not abbreviate days of the week. Do not abbreviate titles like "Jr." or "Sr." and do not abbreviate companies such as, "Pepsi Co." Spell out "Pepsi Corporation," in radio or television. Err on the side of spelling everything out.

As far as number usage, clarity is the critical consideration for broadcast. Some of these might be different from our AP guidelines, but these are not the guidelines we use for print. In broadcast, write out 1 to 20 with words. Above 20, use a numeral. Then, write out number names such as "billion," or "million." Always be clear about it. If the number is 4,376,344, write out, "4 MILLION, 376 THOUSAND, 344 DOLLARS." If the number is not that important, just say, "OVER FOUR MILLION." Always write out fractions. Write "THREE-FOURTHS," instead of "3/4." Also write out numbers that are Roman numerals. The goal, again, is to make the copy as clear as possible for the talent.

Write out addresses like they are said. For phone numbers, put dashes between the numbers so they know to say each number. For example, "8-7-6-4-5-4-3-6-5," so they don't say, "876 MILLION, 454 THOUSAND, 365." The year is written as normal.

GATEKEEPING

When you are writing for broadcast in media, you need to think about making choices. The gatekeeping function theory says that the people in radio are making decisions about what is important and what is not important to tell our audience. They cannot possibly tell us everything, so they must choose. There is a choice to be made as a news writer and that is: what are the most important elements of the story. Some of the media's job is to distill things down to the most important form to share with our audience.

TRENDS IN ELECTRONIC MEDIA

When we think about electronic media, we want to be aware that there has been **convergence**. Convergence means that there is now an inter-relation between formats. I can consume many different media formats at the same time. That means for you, as broadcast writers, we have to be able to write for as many mediums as possible. That is part of our approach. We always want to consider the three cornerstones of good mass media writing. First; clarity. Is it clear? Then, we want to look at our structural considerations: unity, variety, pace, and climax. Finally, we want to write a good *story*. If we are doing those things, then no matter what media format we are writing for, we will produce quality writing. Convergence means you need to be able to write for different formats.

Diffusion of audience is also another important trend in current electronic mass media. **Diffusion of audience** means that we have to work harder to get and keep our audience's attention because the number of people consuming electronic media continues to go up, but the number of people watching each particular channel is going down. For example, I can access a show produced by FX on many different sources. This means that if for any reason I cannot tune in to FX, I can still watch FX programming. Therefore, the number of people watching FX may be going up, but even FX has to compete with their own product on different available formats.

There is also more **shared information** between newspapers and the Internet. This is due in part to convergence as fewer companies own more of the media airwaves and corporations. Disney owns ESPN, ABC, The Family Channel, The History Channel, Marvel Comics, and other properties. Likewise, if you are a reporter for ABC, you are also working for The Mouse. The Mouse may call on you to write something. You will be called on to write more and more things, and there will be shared staffs. You may work selling ad time and creating the ads that air as well as managing your customer's account. This is why we always want to think about clarity, correctness, concision, and completeness. We need to think about our structure, and we need to tell a good *story*.

We have to be ready to write across platforms because you will be called on to do that later on in your career. I realize that it is a challenge to shift from the stylistic format between one form and another. It is one of the challenges that we face in our particular approach. Remember, clarity is key; always learn from what you have done and continue to strive to improve. Always do the best writing that you can.

The aspiring writer's most important goal as they work with this text must be to become a better writer. Do not worry about your grade. Rather, worry about doing the best work you can do. Devote yourself to doing all that you can do to become the best writer you can be. The rest will follow. I had a student that came to me one semester and she was so concerned about the grades that she had gotten on the first two assignments. I will go on the record saying this—I had some bad grades as an undergraduate—and I have gotten to teach at Stanford, Yale, Princeton, and Northwestern and have earned five degrees and professional certification in film production from New York University. Grades are over-rated. I said to that student, "Do you promise to do the best work that you can do for the rest of the class?" And she said "Yes." So, I took a post-it and I wrote, "Laura: B." After that, she simply did the best that she could because she was confident that I would give her that B if she tried. Then, at the end of the semester, I was adding up her grade, and she actually earned an "A." she was doing the best work that she could. She knew that if she tried as hard as she could to become the best writer she could be, she would get the B, and she completely out-did herself when she forgot about grades and committed to being a better writer. That is excellence. *Eretre* (greek): to reach, that is virtue.

In this chapter we discussed several considerations when writing for broadcast media, the similarities and differences between broadcast and print writing, elements of oral style, broadcast formats, broadcast leads, broadcast format writing guidelines, style in copy, attribution in broadcast media, and trends in electronic media. If you commit, you can be the best writer that you can be. This is true for broadcast writing as for all other types of writing.

CHAPTER 11:
RADIO NEWS

In mass media, regardless of what you are writing, good writing is good writing. We are now moving on to exclusively writing for radio news format. In good writing, we are always clear. Is the format that I am using clear to my audience and clear to my message? Also, is it clear to the people I work with? Good writing is concise; it uses the least amount of words possible for the message. It should be accurate, and it should be complete. These principles apply to radio as well. In this chapter we will discuss radio news leads, organizing a radio news story, structural considerations in radio news, news values in radio, radio news style, radio news research, script mechanics, and handling sound.

RADIO NEWS LEADS

We are now moving on from discussing broadcast writing as a whole to discussing writing for radio, and, specifically, leads for radio news. In radio leads, you always want to use present tense to make them seem timelier. When we talk in the present tense, it satisfies the news value of timeliness. We also want to use simple sentences. This gets mentioned *ad nauseum* when talking about mass media writing, but it is an incredibly important point. We also must be clear and concise. We do not have time to give the listener filler—if they do not like it, they will change the channel or station and then we cannot reach them. The writer needs to attract the audience's attention and keep that attention. There are other types of leads other than summary leads, and many of these are very effective when writing for radio.

RADIO NEWS STORY ORGANIZATION

In terms of structure, a three-part format tends to work nicely. First, we give them the context, then explanation, and then effects. As you all know, I have a particular preference to structure when it comes to broadcast writing—story format. Radio or television format, story structure will be effective.

When you think about writing, do not forget about telling a good story. We want to use climax in terms of dramatic development and always consider what that climax will be. The cornerstone of what we use to write should be that of the dramaturgical approach—telling a good story. In a radio story, even if you only have a minute, you can still tell a good story. Is there a will or want by the characters in the story, the protagonists? What is the inevitable? Is it a win or a loss by a team? Is it a new policy a school is enacting? Is it that they are rescuing people that were hurt in the tsunami? Whatever it is, phrase it as a dramatic question. For example, "When they first began the quest, they were hoping that they could save a lot of people. The question was, how many people could they get to in time?" That is the correct use of drama and the inevitable to tell a story in a radio headline. There is always a realization in and of the dramatic question where the protagonist realizes what it will take to achieve their will or want. As they try to do that, they face complications. Those complications should increase in severity until finally, the tension related to the dramatic question is most acute and then answered in the climax. After climax, you need a resolution. We need to close the story and head to the next thing. Do not forget about dramatic development. The writer should attempt to draw out the dramatic elements in a story. The writer should always try to draw out and emphasize the most interesting aspects of a story.

STRUCTURAL CONSIDERATIONS AND RADIO NEWS

Other than the elements of the dramatic model, there are other structural considerations that always apply: unity, variety, pace and climax. Variety includes changing it up, using different voices and actualities. In radio in particular, we need to use actualities to give the audience a variety in the story. Keep your actualities between 8 to 15 seconds. Pace is also very important in radio. When writing for radio, we need to use a moderate pace and think about the talent reading our text in an appropriate pace. We need to be clear between our talent and production; it needs to have a comfortable pace for them as well. With a lead in broadcasting, we do not want to include as many facts as we do in a lead in print. This is because the facts are harder to remember and our audience cannot go and look at it. Maybe we should focus on one or two elements instead of throwing facts at them that they might miss. In radio, too much info in one sentence is hard for the audience to digest. Only use one or two elements in your lead and spread the rest out. Radio leads are softer. Unity is demonstrated through using relationships between the national and local. Also, vocal cues and transitions can provide unity. Again, we do not have paragraph breaks so we need to use transition words and phrases to unify the piece. These are called segues. We already talked about using specific vocabulary. This is not the time to go out and grab your thesaurus. We want to stick to the same terms and words for the same concepts in order to increase unity and make it clear and comprehensible for our audience.

NEWS VALUES IN RADIO

The first and most important thing about using the new elements in radio is not to inundate your audience with too many elements right up front. Your lead should have less news value, per se, than it would in print. I also want to talk about the **gatekeeping function** of radio news. Gatekeeping function says that the people in radio news are making decisions about what is important and what is not important to tell our audience. Some of the function of radio news is to distill things down to the most important form to share with our audience.

As far as news elements in radio, decisions have to be made. In terms of criteria, we need to consider what is important. We will consider news values just as we do in print, although we are going to be more selective for radio. The most important news value for radio is **timeliness**. Timeliness means it just happened. The radio can tell us about right now. Print, most of the time, tells us what has already happened. For radio, we must consider if it is happening *now*. **Significance** means that the story is relevant to the greatest number of people. Significance is a combination of **impact** and **magnitude**. Impact is how deeply it affects someone and magnitude is how many people it affects. If I lose my car keys, it does not have much magnitude, but if a thousand people lose their car keys, it does. Again, if my house burns down, that is a large amount of impact, but not a lot of magnitude. If ten thousand people in California lose their homes to fire, than that is a large impact and a large magnitude. There are different phrases to use for news values, but the concepts are most important.

Timeliness and significance are probably the two most important considerations you will use when writing for radio. You will have to decide which story and which elements are most timely and most significance. Also, if you are writing for a local station, the local angle is most important. If the local stories are going to be most important to their audience, then we need to include them. For example, if you are writing for a station out of Peoria, then the closing of Pontiac Prison is very important, whereas that story does not have a whole lot of national significance. Always think about what is important to your listening area. It is important to attempt to position personal feelings second to the needs and interests of the audience. What is significant to the writer may not be significant to the audience. Always consider the audience.

Conflict can be very important. In an oral culture, stories were how we transmitted information. It makes it easier for us to remember if it is in story form. *The Odyssey* was passed through thousands of years in oral form because people could remember it. That story also reflects values and practices of Mediterranean cultures, and when receivers heard information in the story, it was easier for them to remember. Writing is about making choices, and that is what news values are about.

Radio Style

We have discussed stylistic considerations for broadcast; all of those apply to radio. However, I believe it is worthy of merit to mention some of these things again. The first one is that we be concise. Short sentences are best. Short is better because every word takes time and we only have a certain amount of time to tell a story. If you only have six minutes per hour for news, you might only get three or four sentences. You need to be terse and tell a strong story. As Strunk and White said, every word should tell. Get rid of excess wordage. The second stylistic consideration I think is important to remember to be less formal. Write like you would talk to a friend. To that extent, you can include contractions and use more of a "you" orientation where you directly address the audience. Third, always employ the present tense. Even if an event did happen in the past, the radio news writer needs to communicate what is happening now as a result of what happened then. Novice broadcast news writers often struggle with this idea. What is happening right now gives the story timeliness.

Always use present tense for attribution; "says." Use present tense verbs. Also, use titles before the proper name. You should always employ active voice: subject-verb-object order. The object is not acted upon by the subject. Rather, the subject acts on the object. There are exceptions, but generally this is true. Stories can change over time, like, for example, when there is an update. We might need to make yesterday's news current. You would make the story "now," by adding new pieces of information or new developments. Remember, radio has the ability to update a story whereas most print sources go out once per day maximum.

Radio Research

When doing research for radio, you as a reporter are responsible for the facts. In accordance with the gatekeeping function, you are deciding what is important to include and what is not. (See Radio Public Service Announcement Exercise in the Appendix.) Then, you are going to get opinions and accounts from witnesses who were there at the time, or those who have an educated opinion. What you want to do with your research in actualities is to get usable quotes. You will need to be nosey in order to do this. You will need to go to the locations of disasters or unfortunate things (or good things) and experience them.

First of all, writers can look at the news wire and newspapers to gather information. The writer can also listen to a police scanner or call the police station to get facts. Radio news writers must be curious and do the footwork like a detective to get the information to share with the radio audience. The writer should get an actuality from a person in an authority position in relation to the story. For instance, if a story is about a fire, the writer could find the fire chief or official spokesperson and talk to them. The writer should find out what is going on from somebody who would know and who would be happy to tell us. Find someone who feels that it is their job to interact with the media. The people who will be most willing to talk to you are those who put the event together, or who run the location, or who sponsor the event. Find usable quotes: ones that add something, not just reiterate what we are already saying. Actualities should be no more than 15 seconds when doing a one-minute story. When you are interviewing, you want something that makes the story sound more interesting. Our actuality could add controversy or make it more interesting. Ask them what they think, feel, or believe, but do not assume for them. They key question is: What will people find interesting in an actuality? an actuality is what people would find interesting.

SCRIPT MECHANICS FOR RADIO NEWS

In radio news, you want to make sure that you type all the way across the page. Do not use shortened columns for text. (See Straight Radio Story News Example in the Appendix.) Other kinds of radio writing (non-news) may use a two-column layout. This is particularly useful for television commercials. You have a source column, and a copy column. In radio news, there is only one column. The standards that we use were made in the golden days of radio, but we still use them. First of all, you will have one-inch margins with one column. All radio layout is double-spaced, which makes it easier to read. Number your pages. In split column, you will want to use sound cues, music cues, and source-cues.

In a radio news story, you want to employ a **slug**. A slug is like a title that describes what the story is about. This makes it easy for the talent and the people you work with. Also, talk about actualities. Stations vary on identifying actualities, but your boss is ultimately the deciding factor. Everyone is different. To be most clear to the people you work with, you want to use the standards of your place of employment. You will probably use "Start," to indicate where the actuality starts as well as "End," with the last several words of the actuality so that the talent knows they must start reading again. It also tells the technical people when to switch the audio control back to the talent on-mike instead of rolling the actuality. The writer should also identify the length of the actuality within the story.

Some places will require you to use all caps for the script. Unfamiliar words should be spelled out phonetically. In terms of punctuation, we want to help our talent so that they say it correctly. Write out numbers in a way most clear to the talent. Avoid abbreviations and use phonetics to be clear to the talent.

HANDLING SOUND

This is a big topic, but we need to deal with several considerations when handling sound. These ideas are particularly relevant for radio, but also apply to video.

The first one is characteristics of sound and using sound to tell a story. There are two types of sound we can use in radio: artificial and natural sound. **Artificial sound** is that which is produced for the piece. Natural sound, or **nat-sound**, is sounds that occur naturally in the environment. I think a piece that WGLT did a few years ago that won an award about a protest at a shopping center. The writer had natural sound of the chanters marching and talking and it made the story seem more real. For sound, we are talking about radio, television, and film.

There are several characteristics of sound. The first one is **pitch**. Pitch is the frequency or the wavelength of the sound. Lower pitches are relaxing and calm and higher pitches are more fast-paced and annoying sounding. Use of long vowels and short constants have different pitches. **Timbre** is the physical complexity of the wavelength. Is it brassy or soft? The writer can make use of dissonant sounds like a bubbling brook. A third consideration of sound is **volume**. Low is soothing and high is disturbing. In the background, you can start a sound and then increase or decrease where you say, "bring up to full," or "bring down behind." The louder something is, the closer it is to our audience. In particular I want to think about sound in radio commercials. A fourth consideration is **distance**. *On-mike* means the subject is in the foreground. *Off-mike* means it sounds like there is distance because it sounds like they are far away from it. Fade is a useful tool, especially in music. "Music full," means full volume and then "fade to under," means fade to under the dialogue. A fifth consideration is **acoustical setting**. This is changes to sound made by surroundings. Reverb is echo. We can use technology to manipulate the sound. A sixth consideration is **rhythm**. In musical sound effects, we will use a certain rhythm. Finally, the last consideration is **juxtaposition**. Juxtaposition means combing sounds to create a picture. For example, if you hear a drum, you might not know where you are. If you hear a drum, cheerleaders, and people cheering, you know you are at a sports event. By putting music and sound effects together, you can create a certain impression. Juxtaposition is an aural montage.

Sound effects can be used in writing for radio or television. Sound effects have many uses. They can bring the listener into the story. They can also establish a locale. They create a mood; if you have sounds of crickets and a bubbling brook, that creates a mood. You can also use sound effects to establish climax or time. If you hear a clock tick, you know time is of the essence. Sound effects can also cue entrance and exits. Transitions are also another thing that can be indicated by sound effects. Do not overuse sound effects; too much is confusing. Sound effects should augment the message, not detract from it.

In terms of **music as sound**, it can be very important. There are musical signatures that tell us exactly what we are watching. Think of the film *Jaws* and those famous low-notes, or *Seinfeld* and the crazy whacky bass line, or *Friends* and "I'll be there for you." These types of music instantly indicate to the audience what they are watching. I always think of *The Office*, which has such a cool little song. When I hear it, I'm with my friends at Dunder-Mifflin. Music can create a good bed for commercials as well. Do use it in moderation; the music is secondary to the message. Music can also be used as a transition. Music also can be a sound effect to evoke a certain mood. When you specify a song to be used, be clear and specific. To say, "Reggae," is one thing, but to say, "Bob Marley's 'No Woman, No Cry,'" is much more specific. Music, like sound effects, should augment the message, not detract from it.

In terms of cues for sound, we use "fade in," "fade out," "bring to full," "cross fade," and "segue." Voices can also act as sound. You can have one narrator or two. You can use different voices for different things.

In this chapter we discussed radio news leads, organizing a radio news story, structural considerations in radio news, news values in radio, radio news style, radio news research, script mechanics, and handling sound.

CHAPTER 12:
TELLING A VISUAL STORY

As the mass media writer thinks about writing across different media such as commercials, documentary, television, film, and news, they want to think about telling a *visual* story well. Telling a story with pictures goes back to the principles of telling a good story well. Quality writing is clear. The visual elements should add to the clarity. The message must evoke the signs the mass media writer desires the audience receive. The writer must also be concise; to be concise means that every frame must communicate a message. The juxtaposition between one shot and another is the cleanest, shortest way to get a point across. Identifying which visual stimuli will convey a writer's message is also very important. Strategic ambiguity can be used in television writing, but only when the writer is specifically and clearly trying to be ambiguous. Otherwise, the writer should plan on showing images that will evoke meaning in the consciousness of the receivers. Finally, the writing should be complete by giving the audience information that allows them to effectively comprehend the message. Quality writing necessitates being clear, correct, concise, and complete.

The mass media writer should always try to tell a story using the dramaturgical approach, especially in a narrative using visuals. Visual narratives can be very effective. The Brinks Home Security commercial is a good example of telling a visual narrative. Even without the words, the message can still be clearly understood. It is terse and complete, telling a story about how to keep a family safe. The family experiences complications and clearly has a will or want. The climax occurs when the Brinks man saves the day. Again, a visual narrative is telling a story with pictures rather than words. Words are used, but are secondary to the visual elements in the story. The story must include a protagonist, who has a will or want that leads to the dramatic question. Complications, a climax, and a denouement must also tie into the visual story to make it clear, correct, concise, and complete. The writer should always think about using the dramaturgical approach with visuals.

STRUCTURAL CONSIDERATIONS

In terms of structure, it is important to follow the principles of writing: **unity**, **variety**, **pace,** and **climax**. **Unity** is an important structural consideration when telling a visual story. Consider whether or not the pictures used work together or if there are extraneous shots. In the film *Where the Wild Things Are,* for example, there is a shot of a gun in a scene that is never referred to or used in the story again. The shot of the gun is extraneous, meaning it does not fit with the rest of the scenes or the story. Unity is making sure that all the pictures work together to tell a story.

Variety is also important to consider. Are the shots changed up? Are they showing different angles and viewpoints? Without variety, the story becomes stagnant and potentially boring.

Pace is another important structural consideration. Are the pictures shown in a pace that makes sense in a particular scene or part of the visual narrative, and does the pace still convey the meaning of the story? Some films are based off of books and not necessarily written for the big screen. The original book *Where the Wild Things Are* is only a dozen or so pages long, so the pacing must be stretched out to avoid thinness in the visual narrative. Otherwise, a fast pace could water down the richness of the original work.

Most importantly, **climax** goes back to the dramaturgical approach. Do the visuals effectively contribute to the story's climax? Does the shot selection create tension that builds to the moment of the highest tension? A good writer must always think about telling a visual story using these principles.

CAMERA POSITION

The director always decides how he or she is going to use the camera, including what shots are shown, what angles are used, and what visuals ultimately result. This is often a negotiation between the director, editor, and producer. With that in mind, however, the writer can offer suggestions. Often, those suggestions are taken into account and used in the film. Camera angles must be clear and descriptive in the writing so that hopefully the story will be shot as originally intended. When thinking about camera angles and visuals, there are several tools at our disposal as writers.

CAMERA DISTANCE

The first element is **camera distance**. This is essentially how far the camera is from the subject. The close-shot and the long-shot are most often used as descriptors here. The **medium-shot** is generally a shot of the head and shoulders, but can also be framed somewhere between the knees and the head on a human. A medium shot is distance-neutral and can provide a bulk of information. It is psychologically neutral as well. These specific angles can (and should) be suggested when writing a story so that the visuals enhance the words. This is especially true in commercials, documentaries, and film. There is a range within these shots, such as a close-up or an extreme close-up. A **close-shot** is when the camera is focusing tightly on one element. A close-up actually allows us to focus the audience's attention and, more importantly, increase the tension of a scene. By using a close-up, we are stressing that the object of the shot is particularly important.

In a **long-shot** the camera is very far from the subject and thus seems as if the position of the audience is far from the subject. The long-shot is also called an establishing shot or a wide-shot. It gives us a lot of information and is used to provide context and establish the scene. Often, an establishing shot is used before the shot is moved in closer. This way, the audience can get physically oriented to the scene. The long-shot also psychologically distances us from the subject, allowing us to zoom in to emphasize points and zoom back out in a wide-shot to establish location before moving on to the next scene. In this way, the audience is psychologically ready to move to the next shot.

CAMERA ANGLE

Camera angle is the vertical orientation between the camera and the subject. Most of the time, visual storytellers use **eye-level shots**. Eye-level shots are psychologically neutral, but a particular angle can denote a power distance. If the audience is at the level of the subject, it is in a neutral power position. In a **high-angle shot**, the camera is above the subject. A high angle of Rod Blagojevich psychologically denotes that he has less power than the audience. In **low-angle shots**, the audience is below the subject and psychologically denotes power. For example, in the film *Pulp Fiction*, there is a scene in which Jules, a threatening killer, talks to Brad, who will be shot by Jules. When Jules talks to Brad, he is shot from a low-angle that emphasizes that he has power over Brad because he has a gun. On the other hand, the storytellers use a high-angle on Brad, denoting his lack of power. Not only is it metaphorical in nature, it is also psychologically effective. Camera angles can be suggested in writing in order to more effectively tell a visual story that has the psychological impact originally desired by the writer.

Chapter 12: Telling a Visual Story

CAMERA MOVEMENT

The perspective of shots can be altered by zooming the camera and moving the lens. Camera movement, however, should not be overused. Consider the film, *Casino,* in which an excessive use of camera movement made some scenes difficult to watch. *The Blair Witch Project* is another classic example of camera movement that may be too overwhelming, and could potentially even make the audience sick. Most changes of view should be in the editing rather than the camera movement. In live or low-budget visual narratives, however, camera movement may be used more.

Zoom is a special lens that changes the field of view continuously without losing focus. Zoom-in places the audience in the scene, increases intensity and, like a close-up, provides more detail for visual scrutiny. In addition, the filmmaker forces the audience to look at a certain thing with a zoom-in. If the storytellers move from a wide-shot before zooming in to pan, he or she is putting the scene in the audience's face and then telling them where to look. Inversely, movement can go from a subject of scrutiny and zoom-out. Zoom-out has the reverse effect because the movement pulls the audience out of the action psychologically by disengaging the audience from the subject (where the attention was originally focused). It also effectively sets the stage for the conclusion of the scene, allowing the audience to let go psychologically before the story moves on.

Pans involve moving the camera in an arc from a fixed position from left to right. If the camera pans across a space, it shows the size or depth of the room. It also can denote movement. When two characters move from one side of the room to another and the camera pans with them, the director is demonstrating that the movement is important.

Vertical movement on an axis is called a **tilt**, and is when the camera is moved above or below an axis. On a tilt the camera is moved up or down and most often establishes size. Tilt and zoom can increase the emotional impact of the subject. A swift-pan is a really fast pan that provides a connector to scenes or shots.

A **dolly** is when the entire camera is moved in or moved out. A dolly is unlike a zoom because it brings the audience to the scene, whereas a zoom moves the scene closer to the audience. When a dolly is used without a track or wheels it can add movement that offers a realistic feel. Hand-cams are commonly used in documentaries and provide a more realistic experience.

A **truck** is when the entire camera is moved parallel to the action. Trucks are often used in old cowboy movies, where the cowboy is riding a horse and the camera is on a truck driving alongside them. A truck moves the camera horizontally parallel to the moving subject.

Another kind of camera movement is the **boom**, also called the crane or cherry-picker. This is where the camera moves vertically on an object. Like a tilt, the emotional payload engages the audience. Often times, at the end of a movie, a boom will be used to disengage the audience psychologically and move them up and out of the scene.

TRANSITIONS

When telling a visual story, you will need to describe what happens between each shot. You have several options you can use to visually transition. The first one is a cut. A **CUT** is where you have one shot, and then immediately, with nothing between them, you have another shot. With a cut, a shot just changes from one to another.

Another transition you can use is dissolve. **DISSOLVE** is when one image slowly disappears at the same time that another is appearing. Dissolves are useful because they indicate that time has passed. They are kind of like a fade, but there is no "to black," you just gradually move into the next picture until it is fully visible.

We also have fade-in and fade-out. **FADE-IN** is where we see black and then slowly, an image comes in. **FADE-OUT** is where we see a picture and then it gradually fades to black. Another type of visual transition is defocusing. **DEFOCUSING** is where an image is shown and then the subject within that image goes out of focus as the focus of the shot moves to another object or person within that shot. A good example is in *Casablanca* where Rick is drinking and contemplating and then the shot moves out of focus from Humphrey Bogart to a photo of Paris. This usually denotes a memory or a flash-back. Dream-sequences also use defocusing frequently. They are similar to dissolve, except the focus moves to something else in the middle of the transition.

A **SWISH-PAN** is when the action within a shot quickly pans to another area of action within a shot. A **WIPE** is where one picture pushes out another picture. They can be diagonal or horizontal or vertical, but it is when a line moves across the screen and reveals another picture as it goes. Martin Scorsese uses wipes a lot. He will show a shot of Henry Hill and then a circle will move out to replace the picture with something else. Homer Simpson, when making a fictional feature film in a certain episode of *The Simpsons*, says that the "star-wipe," is the greatest transition of all time...where the shape of a star pushes out to the next frame. More serious writers and mass media producers will want to avoid the star-wipe. D'oh!

There are other types of transitions that use digital creation. I particularly like the **AUSTIN POWERS TRANSITION**. This is where they will be fighting crime and then it will cut to a shot of everyone dancing on a sound stage with music and then it will go to another location in time. Next time you see any of those films, note the transitions; they are great. These are some of the transition options you as a writer have when writing scripts and storyboards.

EDITING

In visual storytelling, the shots are the building blocks of the scene. The **poetic function** is where the symptomatic axis (what is happening) reflects on the paradigmatic axis (what the shot means). Each shot has an individual meaning, and together, the sum of their parts should be greater than the whole. Consider a close-up of a man's face that is hungry and drooling. Suddenly the picture of a pie is shown, and then the shot moves back to the man's face glaring at the pie. Here, the shot in between (the pie) discloses the meaning of the man's face: he is hungry and wants the pie. Now, take the same shot of a hungry man drooling and growling, but this time the image in the center is a scantily clad woman doing an exotic dance, and then man's face is shown again. This sequence of scenes now has a very different meaning as compared to the first shot. Likewise, if the shot in the middle was a little boy on a playground, the meaning would be entirely different.

Each shot plays a part in expressing the meaning of another. This is where the symptomatic axis meets the paradigmatic axis: what the shot means is defined by the way the shots are sequenced. Originally, when people started filming, cuts between shots were not used. A train would be shot roaring by and that would be the end of the shot. At some point, someone realized if a shot of a train was filmed and then edited to show a shot of a woman tied to the tracks screaming as if she was afraid she would be run over, then back to the moving train, anticipation would be increased dramatically. Eisenstein and Griffith were two innovators in the field of juxtaposition. Editing in filmmaking drives the tension in the story. Consider the film *The Great Train Robber*, which is one of the first films to intercut using sequences of shots to tell a story during the editing process. Each shot has a meaning in and of itself, but when the shots were placed into a sequence with other shots, the scene's meaning was effectively communicated to the audience.

Visual storytelling involves associations that are formed quickly. Sometimes when pictures are shown, the audience does not immediately know how to interpret them. The writer is responsible for creating meaning through shots and evoking the desired message in the receiver. Juxtaposition of shots describes how shots change from one to another. This is where the poetic function comes into play between the symptomatic and paradigmatic axis. Comparison is an important element derived from the combination, defining the meaning of one shot based on the shots around it.

Controlling Tension with Editing

Keeping in mind the power of juxtaposition, the sequence of shots gives meaning to the whole. This process is done in editing. A protest occurred in China a few decades ago in which a group of students were peacefully demonstrating. The army showed up and started shooting and gas bombing the protestors. People ran and screamed throughout the streets. This same story was shown differently in China. The Chinese news showed a group of students running and screaming, then the army showing up, then students peacefully protesting. This exemplifies how the editing sequence of shots can completely change a story's meaning. The Western version means that people were protesting and the army showed up and fired shots, which eventually lead to total chaos. In the Eastern version, chaos filled the streets until the army showed up, which eventually led to peace. Writers must be cognizant of this so messages are communicated accurately.

Ultimately it is important to understand that close and extreme shots create tension: eye-level and long-shots release tension or take the audience away from the action. The mass media writer must know and use these tools in order to invoke a meaning in your receiver. Think about what the audience will be seeing with your words and why. When building a sequence of shots, the writer must know that changing the scene provides transition points, which will be discussed later. As a writer, you need to think about telling your story visually.

CHAPTER 13:
SCRIPTING THE VISUAL

Clarity is always the most important consideration in writing for the mass media, but is particularly important in script writing. We need to be clear to our production team and clear to our audience members. We will use clarity when scripting for radio or television commercial announcements, television shows, and feature films. A script is like a roadmap for the production team. Any time you get in your car, you usually have a destination in mind. In terms of a story, we generally know where it is heading, but this is a way to give our team exact directions in order to get to a desired end.

GENERAL CONSIDERATIONS

Whether we are writing television, films, commercials, or documentaries, there are some general writing considerations we should follow. Earlier in the history of visual scriptwriting, writers had to format these by hand. Now, there are computer programs that make formatting much easier. Unfortunately, many of the best of these programs cost money. There are many free programs on-line, or, if not entirely free, they are free for a trial period. When a writer works for a company, the employer will more than likely provide some type of scripting software. When it comes to scripting, whether it is a story-board layout, two-column layout or a one-column layout, it is important to remember that *there are no fixed rules*. Ultimately, your boss and the people you work with will use their own standards. A supervisor's preferences are very important. Ask the people around you what your company's specific guidelines for script formatting are. However, there are some general considerations that we will always use.

The first one is that a mass media writer should type all work. The writer should always distribute computer-printed copies. Uniform neatness equals clarity. Secondly, you will use standard paper size—8.5 by 11. This reduces confusion and makes a letter-sized piece of paper standard. Third, always use only one side of the page. Recycling is good, but scripting is not the place to be ecologically conservative. We do not want our talent flipping the paper over on air; it is loud and can decrease clarity. The next thing is to always have multiple copies. It is preferable to distribute at least one copy of the script for everyone who is involved in the production process. This makes it easier and clearer since everyone has their own copy. Here the writer should consider the light crew, the shooting crew, the talent and everyone else involved with the production.

Finally, when it comes to script headings, there is no industry standard. Sometimes, on the title page, there will be a series title and the name of the television spot. If it is a commercial, it might include the product title. If it is a series, it may have the name of the television series as well as the episode name. Usually, the title page also has the name of the writer, director, and producer. You may also identify the length on the cover. The time and date of the program may be included as a form of heading. You might include a music list that has the included music soundtrack. You might want to put the name of the production as a header on every page. This is in case the pages get separated in an organization that runs multiple spots. If you use headers, people who are working on it know what assignment they are working on. The front page also usually includes the date that version of the script was last edited. Although a slug may be included, it is only for the production crew to read.

There are additional considerations that we must consider when writing a script. In terms of punctuation, be clear to your audience. Most punctuation rules apply, but you want to keep your talent in mind (i.e., the announcer or actors). The writer must make it clear how the writer wants them to read the dialogue. In audio presentation, the audience cannot see the punctuation; they can only hear it. Things like transitions, pauses, and emphasis need to be noted in some way by the writer. You can emphasize words or phrases and indicate pauses by using punctuation in your script. When using numerals, you want to employ the same script mechanics used in writing for radio. Your talent is reading off the script, and it needs to be clear to them how to read it. Do not use abbreviations. Overall, filmmaking is a collaborative effort, and if everyone collaborates effectively, the whole will end up greater than the sum of the parts. The key thing is that making audio-visual programming is a *team* effort, and so you must be clear to your team. Presentational ease is the goal, and the way you are going to get this is by having every member of your crew in-the-know. How you do this as a writer is by being clear when constructing your script.

STORYBOARDS

When we write commercials, PSAs, advertisements, films, or television programs, we usually use storyboards. Aside from the general considerations we mentioned in writing scripts, we need to think about the storyboards that accompany it. **Storyboards** are a script for our story that use pictures frame-by-frame to explain all the elements of production. Each cell may include a sketch, an attached photograph, or a digital photograph inserted into the storyboard's digital format. The good thing about storyboards is that they are effective for nonproduction people. For example, if a local car-wash owner wants to shoot a business commercial, you can create a storyboard series for him and show him that commercial to entice him to invest. He does not even have to know the mechanics of script writing to see what kind of commercial you have planned. There are some computer programs that will actually take those frames and animate them. Storyboards are uniquely important because they clearly communicate the story to people not familiar with industry script format. However, the main reason storyboards are used is because a film crew costs thousands of dollars a day, if not tens of thousands. Storyboards help decrease the uncertainty of the final product, and to increase the clarity for the director, for the writers and for the rest of the productions crew.

When it comes to storyboards, the number of cells will vary for each story, but however many you have, make sure you number the cells. You need to number them so that you and your crew can talk about each one clearly. Each shot may be different in complexity, and usually, you will indicate changes between shots as well as changes within them. It does not matter how good your art is, all that matters is that a visual point is clearly portrayed. If you want a scene to be a wide-shot of a person, draw a wide-shot of a stick figure. You can draw that art and then put them into cells in the page. The sound and action within the storyboards should parallel the pictures. Make sure that the sounds that accompany that picture go under that cell in the storyboards. Also, on each shot you will have descriptive information underneath the cell. You will use descriptions like "tight-shot," "crane-shot" or "two-shot" to say what the camera is doing when each visual cell is presented.

When writing your storyboards, you will use a transition at the end of every cell description. You have several options you can use to visually transition between shots, as described in the chapter on visual storytelling.

When writing your storyboards, always make sure you describe both the visual shots with transitions as well as the audio under each cell visually. You want to give full descriptions to the fullest possible detail. For example, when using music, do not just say, "pensive guitar," say "Lorena McKennet." When using voices, do not just give text, say what type of voice—male, female, old, child. Always number your cells and do not forget camera directions. There are no universal rules when it comes to storyboarding; you will need to talk to your specific organization or company. In addition, you may use a storyboard alternative like a **photo board**, where hard photos are used as the visual cells. The writer could make a slide-presentation on Microsoft PowerPoint that acts as a storyboard. A writer could also use a split-column format under each visual cell for audio and visual. Traditionally, we will use only one column under each visual cell to increase clarity.

SPLIT-PAGE LAYOUT

Sometimes commercials and PSAs are written in a **split-page layout**. Split-page divides the page in half: on the right is the technical side for the production crew and on the left is what the talent is going to say. Split-page format originally evolved from radio, but it is particularly helpful in multi-camera productions. Programs like Oprah and The Daily Show use split-page format; this is so the technical crew can see the visual cues in their own "technical" version of the script. Sometimes what is on the right becomes the script for the teleprompter. With split-page format, you will divide the audio and the video. The right side has all of the information that the talent needs to know; most often, they do not have to pay attention to the "technical" side on the left.

For your layout, you will double-space everything except video instructions. *Always adjust spacing so that the audio and visual are parallel.* What you have on the left needs to match what is on the right. For all scripting, if you have to spread things out for clarity, do it. This is not the time to save paper space—we want to be *clear*. In audio, there are different ways to do this. Unlike in radio, we may not need a source description on our talent side. Anything that is not spoken should be CAPITALIZED so that the talent knows not to read it. You can put parenthesis around directions or put them in all caps, but feel free to include them as a writer. Directions may be how to read the script or how to move. Just like in television news, you will note all the on or off-camera voices.

On the video side, use all caps for directions except when you do titles. When you include titles, you want them to be in upper and lower case because the location will actually appear as a CG on-screen. Denote these caption or titles with "CG:" at this point. It may end up being "FONT," or "SUPER:," for super-imposed, but unless noted by your boss or editor, use CG and then a colon and then what will be seen. You can use abbreviations for video terminology.

SINGLE CAMERA LAYOUT FOR TELEVISION AND FILM

When thinking about the writing format for television spots, it is appropriate to use single-camera format. Most popular dramatic and comedic series use single-camera layout. In the television single-camera layout, the standards are pretty much the same as film scripting. They have evolved and been informed by writing for theater. In this sense, they have much more technical direction. The same production companies that make films are often the ones who often make our television programs—Columbia, Viacom, Paramount, etc. They all make television shows that are sold to networks. Because it is often the same company, there are often the same scripting standards.

Like feature films, most television shows come from a series of separate camera shots. When you write a film or TV show, you have to keep it simple. Do not overwrite the camera angles. You write what to shoot, not how to shoot it. That is the director's job. The director decides where the camera moves and how it is shot. The script writer and writer make suggestions. Film making is a collaborative effort, but the director gets the final say in these decisions.

I hate to break this to you, but writers have very little power in the industry. Sometimes even the best writers are frustrated because what they wrote does not look at all like what ends up on the screen. We have to remember that the script is a *map*—a set of guidelines. Remember when I said the script is a roadmap? When you go somewhere you have not been, you need some guidance. Just because your map or your GPS says, "Go this way," does not mean you will be able to. Maybe the person you are with needs a pit-stop. Maybe the road is closed. In *True Romance*, Quentin Tarantino wrote the story in a non-linear fashion. But when they shot it, they started at the beginning. It was not the same as it was written. The filmmakers decided that they wanted to change the structure and the ending. What you write will not always make it to the screen—that is just the process. The director has the power to make changes, but the writer can only make suggestions.

When scripting visuals, the script can be written through the master-scene approach or the shot-by-shot approach. In **shot-by-shot**, the script will show what the camera does every time it moves to something new. This is not what is used for most television spots and commercials. **Master scene**, by contrast, is what is used in most film. This means that the script has suggestions as to what the audience should see. If you are writing a film and turn in a script that is a shot-by-shot, chances are you will be laughed at. You'll probably come off as a novice in the film industry trying to do the director's job. Instead, they want to see a master-scene script that reads in terms of what the audience will see within the scene.

If you look at the script for Quentin Tarantino's *Pulp Fiction*, which is available online, you will see the master-scene approach being used. It does not say what the camera *does*, it just says what we *see*. The script begins:

Chapter 13: Scripting the Visual

```
1. INT. COFFEE SHOP - MORNING 1.

A normal Denny's, Spires-like coffee shop in Los Angeles.
It's about 9:00 in the morning. While the place isn't jammed,
there's a healthy number of people drinking coffee, munching
on bacon and eating eggs.
```

Most film and television is shot in an order that is best for logistics. What this means is that, you will shoot a random series of non-related shots that will later be put together in editing. Assume that you are shooting a movie and there are four scenes that take place in a classroom: one scene is at the beginning of the film, one in the middle, one near the end, and one at the very end. Chances are the production crew would want to shoot all four of these classroom scenes in the same day, even though they do not appear chronologically together. Otherwise, the crew and cast would have to return to the classroom, put back up the lights, reset the cameras and so on. Simply put, it is more convenient to shoot it this way.

PRELIMINARY PAGE

In our script, we will have a page that precedes the writing and dialogue. This page acts like a title page and is called the **preliminary page**. In all caps, you will see the name of the program, television show, film, documentary, commercial, or whatever it you are writing. You may also have the series name and an episode number if it is for television. The name of the writer is definitely included, though you may also have the names of the producers and directors depending on how the preliminary page is written. Then, you will see a date on the script. This is very important. The date you see on the preliminary page is the *last* or *most recent* time the script was edited. This tells us which copy of the script we are using. Remember, scripts go through dozens, if not hundreds, of edits. We need to make sure everyone is shooting off the most recent edition.

SECONDARY PAGES

In addition to the preliminary page, you might have other "introductory" pages. **Secondary pages** offer more introductory information. In the script for *Pulp Fiction,* Tarantino uses a secondary page that has the definition of "pulp":

```
PULP [pulp] n.

1. A soft, moist, shapeless mass or matter.

2. A magazine or book containing lurid subject matter and
being characteristically printed on rough, unfinished paper.

American Heritage Dictionary: New College Edition
```

This definition acts as an introduction to the work, setting the unique mood of the story. On the next page, Tarantino uses a table of contents that shows where different moments in the story appear in the script, complete with page numbers. Secondary pages may also appear that describe the characters and their attributes, wardrobe, or setting. We do not actually put these kinds of details within the script—that would clutter it. If we spread it all out, it becomes much clearer.

You can also **date-revise pages**. These are dates that will appear on certain pages when new changes are made so that your cast and crew are aware of what has changed. Again, in the master-scene approach, the dialogue and what the audience sees is identified, but how the camera moves is left out. The shots that make it into the film are selected by the director on location. This differs from the shot-by-shot approach, because that script will tell what the camera does in every shot as well as the provide dialogue and whatnot. When you write a master-scene script and it goes to production, the director might decide to re-write it as a shot-by-shot to come up with a better game plan. That is the director's job, however, not the writer. There are exceptions to this. For example, much of the *Pulp Fiction* script, as well as most of Tarantino's other films, tend to err on the side of shot-by-shot rather than master scene. This is because Tarantino *is* the director, so when he is writing, he will give himself more detail because he will eventually be the one shooting it.

SCRIPTING TERMS

Again, let me reiterate that it is the writer's job to determine **what** the audience focuses on, but it is director's job to determine **how** to draw the audience's attention to it. You as a writer can make suggestions, but make sure that you are not telling the director exactly what to do.

When making camera shot suggestions, a writer can use the term ***angle on*** *[object]* to suggest what the focus of the shot is. ***Favoring*** something suggests that, though there may be other things in the shot, a certain person or object should be at the center or forefront of a shot.

Another consideration for the writer is whether the camera is going to change from one angle to another. **Wide-shots** are often used to psychologically disengage the viewer, decreasing the emotional intensity for the audience. The writer could keep that in mind while scripting the story or ending a particularly emotional scene. **Point of view**, or **POV**, is another angle that can be used to compliment the story, because it shows us a character's literal view of things.

Reverse angle is when the camera cuts between two people speaking. This allows the audience to see how one character reacts to what the other says. Another angle is the **over the shoulder shot**, which is pretty self-explanatory. A **close-up**, or **close shot**, may refer to a shot of a person's head and shoulders. A close-up draws the audience's attention to a particular element and increases emotional intensity. These particular effects of various angles, shots, or transitions were further explored in Chapter 12 on telling a visual story. A **two shot** is when two separate shots are consecutively shown in order to show a relationship between the things in each shot. For example, if the first shot is a character looking up, and the next shot is a close-up of a shotgun hung up on the wall, the audience can assume that the character is looking at the shotgun.

SCRIPTING RULES

There are general rules for scripting that you will almost always follow. Again, all of this is subjective and depends on your production house as well as what your boss requires. If you have concerns, err on the side of clarity and check with your supervisor or editor.

Before we get into an in-depth dissection of scripting rules, I just want to say that you need to make sure to *always number each page of your script*. Think about it: if you are shooting and are trying to get your crew to shoot the same scene, they need to know what page of the script you are talking about. Having them hand-count each page every time they wanted to get on the same shot would be ridiculous. You want to be clear to the people you are working with, and this means giving them page numbers to work off of.

One of the best ways to understand how a screenplay is composed is to look at the scripts of other famous movies. Here I have included an excerpt from Quentin Tarantino's screenplay for *Pulp Fiction*. Pay particular attention to the layout and format of the script, the scene descriptions, the stage directions, and the suggested camera directions:

Chapter 13: Scripting the Visual

3. INT. CHEVY (TRUNK) - MORNING   3.

The trunk of the Chevy OPENS UP, Jules and Vincent reach inside, taking out two .45 Automatics, loading and cocking them.

                              JULES
                    We should have shotguns for this
                             kind of deal.

                             VINCENT
                        How many up there?

                              JULES
                         Three or four.

                             VINCENT
                        Counting our guy?

                              JULES
                         I'm not sure.

                             VINCENT
                    So there could be five guys up
                              there?

                              JULES
                         It's possible.

                             VINCENT
                    We should have fuckin' shotguns.

They CLOSE the trunk.

                                                            CUT TO:

4. EXT. APARTMENT BUILDING COURTYARD - MORNING   4.

Vincent and Jules, their long matching overcoats practically dragging on the ground, walk through the courtyard of what looks like a hacienda-style Hollywood apartment building.

We TRACK alongside.

                             VINCENT
                        What's her name?

                              JULES
                              Mia.

    The first thing we see in this excerpt is the scene number "3.", followed by the setting and time of the scene in all upper case. This is very important. Again, if you are talking about a specific scene when shooting, it is easy to go down the page and just find the number of the scene rather than trying to describe it. The scene numbers should appear at the *right <u>and</u> left margin*. We want to put the scene number on the margin to denote the scene number in a place on the script layout that will be different from the other numbers around it. Oftentimes, scripts may have several sets of numbers on the script within the scene. If the scene number itself is offset, then it is easier to find.

Sometimes, certain scenes will be omitted during the revising process. If this is the case, you might still leave them in the script with the script number and mark "omitted" underneath the scene number. Do not take the scene out and then re-number every single scene afterward. It is much easier to simply let the omitted scene keep its number so that all the subsequent scene numbers remain the same. Again, this is about clarity to our team.

The next thing we always want to keep in mind in scripting is the scene heading, scene description, stage directions, and camera directions. Again, these may be formatted different ways, but there are some general guidelines for clarity. Before the scene description comes the **scene heading**, or **slug**, which appears in ALL CAPS. In our *Pulp Fiction* example, Tarantino has written "INT.", specifying that the scene is taking place in the "interior" of the Chevy's trunk, and that it is the "MORNING". Then, a reiteration of the scene number "3." is aligned to right side of the page. Now, the reader clearly knows the scene number, the setting of the scene, and the time of day it takes place.

Following the slug, there is a **scene description** that elaborates on the details of the scene, such as the setting, time, mood, characters, action, sound, or sound effects. This description is written in upper and lower case letters and with single spacing. In Tarantino's description paragraph, we are told that the trunk of the Chevy opens up, and Jules and Vincent reach inside taking out two forty five automatics, loading and cocking them. Notice how the words "OPENS UP" are in all upper case. This is because it not only denotes some kind of action within the scene, but also affects the camera's initial view of the scene considering the camera filming from inside the trunk. Also, if the reader is meeting the characters for the first time, the names of the characters may be written in ALL-CAPS within the description, though this does not apply to our excerpt.

Within your scene description, you will also have **stage direction** and/or **camera directions**. An example of stage direction can be found in the scene description of scene 3 when Tarantino writes "Jules and Vincent reach inside, taking out two .45 Automatics, loading and cocking them." Here he is giving stage directions to John Travolta and Samuel L. Jackson, telling them what to do during the scene. An example of camera direction is in the scene description of scene 4 when Tarantino writes "We TRACK alongside." Here, he is offering a suggestion of how to use the camera to shoot the scene.

Stage and camera directions are grouped by a single-space format and a double space separates these directions from the scene heading. There is a difference between the heading and the descriptions, and this spacing format visually "blocks" them together. This makes it very clear what Tarantino wants. It tells the costume people what they need to have ready; it tells which actors need to be on set, what kind of lighting will be used, etc.

The **dialogue** is placed after the scene description. This is typed in a narrower column at the center of the page. We do not just tab inward and finish a line; we have a truncated margin on the left and a truncated margin on the right. Because it is so far off from the rest of the script format-wise, the reader can immediately look at any script and know that truncated formatting means dialogue, and thus will not confuse it with the scene description. In the dialogue, the name of the character speaking is centered in all capital letters. In the excerpt, we see that "JULES" has a line that is spoken, which is written in upper and lower case letters with a single space format. "We should have shotguns for this kind of deal." After Jules's line, "VINCENT" with his character identifier in all caps and centered, responds, "How many up there?" Although things like truncated margins and capitalized names may seem like a trivial detail, these are the kinds of things that make scripts more clear. The reason we have conventions of format is so a writer can write his screenplay in a way that the people who are going to be working with it can easily read it.

One last formatting rule is to know where to write **parenthetic directions**. In the dialogue column right underneath the character's name, there may be parenthetic directions for the talent, which are directions given to the actor describing *how* to say the dialogue. For example, note the parenthetic direction "checking his watch" from scene 6 of the *Pulp Fiction* script:

```
                JULES
           What time is it?

               VINCENT
          (checking his watch)
      Seven-twenty-two in the morning.

                JULES
       It ain't quite time, let's hang
                 back.
```

Another example of a parenthetic direction is in scene 2:

```
               VINCENT
          Royale with Cheese.

                JULES
             (repeating)
```

>   Royale with Cheese. What'd they call
>   a Big Mac?

Here, Jules is given the parenthetical direction to repeat what Vincent had just said. This way, Samuel L. Jackson, who plays Jules, knows to deliver the line, "Royale with Cheese," like he is trying the name on, repeating what Vincent has said. Again, these directions go between the name of the character and what is said by that character.

At the end of scene 3 in our first *Pulp Fiction* example, you'll notice the **method of transition** is placed on the right edge of the acceptable columns. Tarantino chose a "CUT TO:" transition, though he could have picked other transitions like "DISSOLVE TO:" or "FADE TO:". When writing transitions in your television or film script, the transition will appear in ALL-CAPS all the way to the *right*. We will double-space after a scene before the transition cut and double space after it before the next scene heading. Another example of a transition appears at the end of scene 2:

>   JULES
>   Uuccch!

>   CUT TO:

3. INT. CHEVY (TRUNK) - MORNING   3.

Here, Jules ends Scene 2 by saying, "Uucch!" Then, a double space is used to separate "CUT TO:" which denotes that the transition between Scenes 2 and 3 is a cut. Then, another double space is used before the scene heading for scene 3, "INT. CHEVY (TRUNK)- MORNING."

OTHER SCRIPT FORMATTING ISSUES

When writing in a single column format, a writer must pay attention to which parts are single-spaced and which parts are double-spaced. Generally a writer double-spaces between all major items in order spread the script out so it is clear for the reader.

Transitions from one scene to another are always double-spaced, as seen in the gap between "CUT TO:" and the "4. EXT. APARTMENT…" slug in the first example. When dialogue is exchanged between two or more characters, two spaces separate the dialogue of one character from another whenever a different character begins speaking. Camera directions may be separated from the scene description, as seen in the gap between scene 4's description and the suggestion "We TRACK alongside." There is then another double-space between that direction and the dialogue. In conclusion, the most common places a writer must double-space is between the slug, the scene description, the directions or suggestions to the film crew, the first character identifier, every time a different character speaks, and the method of transition at the end.

All in all, the key is to not clutter. Allowing for a generous amount of space will make all of the different script elements more clear. There is a massive amount of literature available on single-camera layout that you can use, but there is also a wide variety of scripting software available. For example, Celtx is a free downloadable program on the Internet that formats your work to a single column script as you write, though I personally use a program called Final Draft. When I first started writing, I used to just open a copy of a Spike Lee script because I liked the way he wrote, and tried to copy his format. Now, computer programs make this process so much faster. Final Draft and Celtx know that when I give a transition, I will be moving to a scene header, so they automatically format in ALL-CAPS and moves to the left margin. When I hit enter again, it assumes I am doing scene description and formats it accordingly. Likewise, if you enter again, it will format your dialogue.

The important thing to remember is that script formatting varies. Final Draft is the software they use for shows like *CSI*, but they format the script a certain way. So in Final Draft, they offer a specific template that is used in *CSI*. This format is just slightly different from what they use in *Law and Order*, which is slightly different from how Tarantino wrote *Pulp Fiction*. Final Draft and Celtx are great programs to use for scripting, but ultimately whatever format you use comes down to whatever format your production company uses.

FROM PAGE TO SCREEN

The important takeaways in scriptwriting are that we still use a slug to identify locale, we still use description of people and scene from line to line, and we might identify the camera focus. We might suggest favoring, which suggests the camera focus rest on a specific character for emphasis. Remember, these are all just suggestions we make as the writer. Like anything, practice makes perfect when working with this form. We have talked about many different kinds of writing, and the more you write them, the better you will get. The challenge for you is to take an idea and translate it effectively to the page. The suggestions the writer gives bring life to the screen and vice versa. Keep in mind how the written page would translate to the big-

Chapter 13: Scripting the Visual

screen in a megaplex if it were produced. (See Film Script Pulp Fiction Example Exercise in Appendix.)

In script writing, describing the action will be your biggest challenge. You will need to look at what is happening in each shot. Again, what you write may not make it to the screen, but you do always want to consider what the overall product should look like. Be open to the collaborative process, as it may lead to changes that will affect the overall look of the story in a positive way. For example, if John Travolta, who plays Vincent Vega in *Pulp Fiction*, wants to change a line from, "We need shotguns for this deal," to, "We need shotguns for this shit," then that may happen. To get Travolta and Samuel L. Jackson in the same scene is just awesome casting. They are part of the collaboration. You have to trust your talent as well. Your script is the personification of an idea. Many artists contribute to the process. Actors need to be able to ad-lib and add their own talent to the film as well.

Consider what the focus of the shots are going to be. You as a writer think about where the audience's attention needs to be and the director will figure out how to move the camera to portray that focus. McKee suggests that when writing a shot, the writer should ask, "What do I see in the screen? What are people looking at in the picture? How can I describe that to them?" We as writers need to use vivid description and we need to name things. We need to use action verbs, and to only make suggestions when it comes to actual camera directions.

In your slug line, sell your script but do not interrupt the reader; allow them to be able to read continuously. When you write a screenplay, you are trying to put an image in the mind of reader. Ultimately, your screenplay is what the production company will consider in determining whether to make your film or not. You want the readers, whether they are producers, directors, or agents, to be able to see the image in their mind.

Describe the action of *watching the scene*. When you write for screen, you are always talking about *now*: the action. Always suggest to your audience that we will continue to *move*. Avoid general nouns with adjectives. It is better to describe rather than to use ambiguity. Use good descriptions instead of boring nouns to tell our audience what is happening. We are telling stories with pictures. When thinking about screenplay, we are asking the reader to see certain things and using these pictures to tell a great story. From now on, whenever you watch TV or a movie, think about how it would look on the page. As a writer, you need to start thinking visually and clearly so that you can provide a road map to the people you are working with.

In this chapter, Quentin Tarantino came up a lot, but it is important to remember that he was working at a video store when he wrote his first film *Reservoir Dogs*. Some of the best screenwriters of our time were "nobody" when they wrote the script that became a huge international best seller. If these people can do it, so can you. When Oliver Stone wrote *Platoon*, which won the Academy Award for Best Picture in 1986, he was *driving a cab*. If you dream of writing film or television and you have the will to do it—you can. The limit will be on your own *will*. Natural-born talent is rare, but through countless hours of hard work and an unbreakable willingness to succeed, you can sharpen your craft and achieve the dream of seeing your movie on the big screen.

CHAPTER 14:
TELEVISION NEWS

This book will now enter the realm of telling a news story with pictures. In this chapter we will discuss television news and audience gratification, scheduling news, writing television news stories well (television news and drama and structural considerations), writing the television news story (leads, organization, types of television news stories, organizing stories, kinds of stories, and style and copy for talent), the building blocks of television news, news writing computer programs, and ethics and television news writing.

TELEVISION NEWS AND AUDIENCE GRATIFICATIONS

We will talk about many aspects of television news, but we will start with television management decisions. People watch news for various **gratification functions**; there are reasons they watch the news. Some of it is **information seeking**; we want to know what is happening. We watch the weather to see if it is going to snow. There is also a gratification of **surveillance**; many people want to know what other people are doing. TMZ serves this function; we want to see how celebrities are living. **Curiosity** is a gratification function. When editors make decisions about what to feature, they are **going** to make decisions about what the audience is going to see based on gratifications. Therefore, when writing or filming for television, the writer needs to think about these things so they can give their news director what their station needs.

SCHEDULING NEWS

Scheduling news has changed greatly in recent years due to the **proliferation of the 24-hour news cycle**. It almost seems now that if there is not news, they have to make some up. Networks will manufacture news if nothing is going on. There is continuous news programming and local news airs at 5 pm, 6 pm, 8 am, 10 am, and sometimes they even cut in at certain times throughout the day. This means that you have to constantly update your story. You cannot tell the same story you told at 5 pm as you do at 6 pm; you have to update it and add more information or a new perspective.

Let us break down the news program. A news program is usually allotted 30 minutes. Six of those minutes are commercials. There are 24 minutes left. How many of those are dedicated to sports? About 5 to 6 minutes. That leaves 18. Weather is another 5-6 minutes, so we are down to 13. Then, there is the little oddity piece about, for example, the California couple who invented sunglasses for cats or the squirrel that can water ski that takes about three minutes, which leaves 10 minutes left. The health beat for the older crowd, which is a newly added segment that we see frequently because of the generational aging, takes another three minutes; now we are at seven minutes. Seven minutes for national, state, and local news. That is not a lot of time, so every word must tell.

Generally, television news stories are only 45-90 seconds in length. It is important that the length of a story is exact because each story fits into a larger program. National feeds and advertising also increase the importance of getting the time of a story accurate.

WRITING TELEVISION NEWS WELL

The elements that comprise quality television news writing are the same elements that comprise quality writing throughout various media forms. The television news writer must be *clear*. One caution about story length in television news is that the writer should not give too much information too quickly, lest the audience be unable to digest the information or retain it. That is why often in television, the writer usually does not use a comprehensive lead; the writer needs to give audience members time to digest all the elements. Some repetition can be good in broadcast, especially the more important elements. If a writer, for example, is writing a broadcast story that details the showing of an upcoming documentary about the closing of a local prison, the writer could mention the will or want of the director, and what complications the director went through while making the film. Then, the writer should mention the time, date, and location of the showings so the audience can decide if and when they want to attend. The audience needs to have time to digest the information the writer and crew are sending them.

The television news writer must also be *concise*; every word should tell. Generally, television news stories are only 45-90 seconds in length. It is important that the length of a story is exact because there is other news before and after a particular story.

The television news story should be *complete*. The television news writer should give the audience all essential information. Finally, the television writer must be *accurate*. The writer must give them correct information.

TELEVISION NEWS AND DRAMA

Even if the television news writer works in an entertainment-driven news world, they can strive to give the audience the best story possible by using the structure and values outlines in this book. If a writer works on a story, they can provide solid news while entertaining the audience. The writer can also serve higher goals instead of just slaving for The Man for a paycheck. The dilemma is how the news writer can ethically make these compromises. The writer should dedicate themselves to good writing. The writer should always consider the features of a good news story: who is the protagonist? What is their will or want? What is the dramatic question? What is the realization that they have? What are their complications? Then, finally, what is the climax; the answer to dramatic question. It will entertain the audience if the writer tells a good story. In terms of structure for television news, it is recommended that the writer use the narrative structure with all the elements outlined in the dramaturgical model, when possible. Writing skill should come second to story-telling craft in television news.

STRUCTURAL CONSIDERATIONS

Likewise, the television news writer should always think of the four structural considerations; unity, variety, pace, and climax. The writer should spread out the news elements so as to not overwhelm and confuse the audience (pace). The writer can incorporate these elements throughout the television news story especially when the writer also has the tools of visuals elements (variety). On the other hand, the writer must consider unity, or how the pieces hang together so that the sum will be greater than the individual parts. The writer should think about who their audience is and consider the news values; timeliness, impact, proximity, personalization, prominence, conflict (drama), and oddity. The writer will want to use these values to consider which elements of the story they would like to present in making choices about the structure. These criteria tell the writer which parts of the story to tell and which to emphasize, as well as where to put them.

WRITING THE NEWS STORY

In terms of news length, hopefully the writer's assignment editor tells them how long their story needs to be. The writer should use variety in their story, but not use a pace that is too quick for their audience. The writer will have to negotiate that with the other news staff and the director.

TELEVISION NEWS LEADS

The **lead** is still the first sentence or graph of the story. Leads for television are usually softer than straight print leads. The television news writer usually will not want to write a comprehensive lead. The writer should not want to give all the information right up front or they could lose the audience's attention. Also, audience members cannot digest all the news facts at once. The writer should spread the news elements out so the audience members can digest them slowly and make sense of the story. Comprehensive leads are usually inappropriate for television news because they give too much information too quickly. Attention getting is almost more important than telling the audience all of the facts right away.

When writing television news, generally try to identify **where** and **when** the events are happening. Usually, when, and where may even be identified in the lead. When and where are very important in television news. Those two are often in the lead. Television news excels at answering questions about *now*. **Where** and **when** is important to this idea. *Who* is also important in the story, but it is often delayed in television news. First, the writer might use descriptive information about that person, but not necessarily their title. For example, "An Illinois State student was found dead Tuesday night." The writer should describe *who* but not place it up front. The writer will reveal *who* later. However, the writer might want to identify the subject (who) first if the subject is a prominent person. **Impact leads**, those that feature the most significant aspect of the story first, can be very useful. In terms of attribution, we want to identify them first before the quote. The writer should generally start with the source.

Another quality lead in television news is the **umbrella lead**. An umbrella lead unites several angles about a particular topic. It also contains lead-ins for the various stories. For example, pretend a blizzard is coming to ISU next week. The lead could introduce a combination a number of stories about the weather, like the meteorological aspects, how the weather will affect students, and how the local road crews have to be activated. Each one would be an independent story from different reporters, but the umbrella could introduce viewers to all of the stories as an anchor turns to coverage of the weather. (See Television News Exercise in Appendix.)

The types of leads discussed previously in the chapter on print features are also useful for television news. **Affective leads** are a little more emotional. **Rhetorical question leads** can be effective. A **straight lead** pits one or two of the news elements that are most important. The

throw-away lead has some type of setup that peaks the audience's curiosity, but there are no news values or information in it. There is also the **feature lead**, which is the soft news lead. These leads were discussed in the chapter on print feature stories and include direct address leads, anecdotal leads, and descriptive leads.

In addition to a lead, there can be a lead-in before the lead. In television, a lead-in is a transition in which the talent introduces the story and sends the attention of the audience to another anchor or the reporter. An example would be if the anchor sent the audience's attention to the weather person by saying something like, "And now to Karen with the weather. Karen, how is it out there?" Writing a lead-in may be the responsibility of a television news writer.

KINDS OF TELEVISION NEWS STORIES

There are various kinds of television news stories. One of them is the **disaster story**. Here, the writer might want to present different angles of the same disaster. An **investigative story** is one that attempts to find information about a given topic. A **soft news** or **feature story** is one that is not breaking news. There is the opinion piece, although most television news outlets with the exception of Fox News use this form less often. News tries to stay away from opinions, although they used to use them more often.

ORGANIZING THE TELEVISION NEWS STORY

In terms of organizing, there are different organizational sequences the writer can use for their television story. These include narrative, narrative/news value hybrid, chronological, and effect and cause sequences.

Narrative

A narrative organizational structure uses the features of drama, outlined in Chapter 1 and re-iterated throughout this book. The strongest organizational paradigm reflects the dramatic model: tell a good story. What is unique about this approach is that story (narrative structure) is that it helps the writer tell a good story. There are other organization formats for television news stories.

Narrative/News Value Hybrid

A particularly strong organizational sequence is a hybrid of narrative structure with an emphasis on the lead on news values. This design combines the traditional structural features of the dramatic model (protagonist, will/want, realization, complications, climax, and dénouement) with an emphasis on news values (timeliness, proximity, significance, prominence, etc.) to inform viewers/listeners as it entertains and persuades. This hybrid structure is an appropriate design for media writing that appeals to listeners/viewers. This narrative/news value hybrid emphasizes important aspects of a news story in the effort to inform audience members of newsworthy aspects of a particular news item.

Chronological

Another organizational sequence is chronological. Here, the writer gives the events in the order that they happened. This is different from the dramatic approach because there is no explicit dramatic question. The writer is not choosing the elements that add dramatic impact. In the dramatic approach, the writer highlights certain elements in order.

Effect and Cause

The television news writer can also use an effect and cause sequence (in that order). This sequence first tells the impact of the event and then tells what elements caused it. Another arrangement sequence is action-reaction. In action-reaction, the writer reports an event that has happened and then the reactions that are happening as a result. For example, if Congress passes a bill on 401Ks, then the writer could tell that story and cut to retirees, bankers, and investors reacting to this action.

Thus, there are different organizational sequences the writer can use for their television story. These include narrative, narrative/news value hybrid, chronological, and effect and cause sequences. There are other organizational sequences for television news, but these are several of the most useful for the television news writer.

TYPES OF NEWS STORIES

The first type of news story is **live news**. In live news, the anchor is live on camera. The writer could use an anchor on camera with a box (a feature inserted or *chromo keyed* into a video shot with special effects technology) over the anchor's shoulder, which is a type of live news. A story could feature live narration, where the voice is off-screen but feeding live. This can be mixed with sound-on-tape, or pre-recorded audio that matches external video, as with actuality pieces, or sound bites.

One of the most common formats of live news is a **VO/SOT** story. A VO/SOT (voice over with sound on tape) is a story that starts with an anchor on camera and moves to an actuality or sound bite, which is also called a SOT (sound on tape). This is a relatively simple type of television news story that is an appropriate for the beginning news writer. (See Straight Television News Example in the Appendix.) The viewers would first see an anchor on camera, possibly with identifying font generated on the bottom of the screen. Then the viewers often see external video, shot from actually locations where events took place. The audience would hear voice over narration, delivered by the anchor over this external video footage. Often, an actuality or sound bite is presented, in which an interviewee is featured. The interviewees voice is hear as sound on tape (SOT). The interviewee is identified with computer generated font that includes their name and possibly their credentials or involvement in a story. The story may also return to a shot of the anchor, possibly with a graphic box placed (keyed) over their shoulder. This box is a computer-generated graphic that may feature words related to the story and a visual element from the story such as a photograph of some element from the story. In addition, a VO/SOT may feature partial screen graphics to full screen graphics. The key elements of a VO/SOT is that the anchor provides the bulk of the spoken copy, either on camera or as voice over narration, and there is SOT, or a sound bite.

There are other types of news that are not particularly VO/SOT. Television news could also feature a reporter live from a different location, like a video feed from a remote. This remote coverage could be mixed with live anchor interaction.

Another type of news is **recorded news**. Recorded news is put together off of shot-sheets. It is put together a as a **package** (PKG). Here, the whole piece is pre-done and with audio and visual recorded beforehand. Location video is still shots of a location or event. Usually, you want about 20 seconds per shot. When gathering video, you want to think about getting a variety of shots so that you can use what best fits your story. Often times, you will hear a reporter's narration or VO over that. Then, we have sound bites in recorded news. Natural sound would be sounds that occur as we are filming. We also have graphics and font. Graphics and font identify the location, identification, or scene. Package stories have all of these elements.

STYLE AND COPY FOR TALENT

The writer should always try to write copy, the text that will be read by the on-camera talent, which will be read aloud in the clearest possible way. A stylistic suggestion is that the writer should always write out numbers in the copy that is to be read aloud. When the writer wants the talent to say individual letters, the writer should put dashes between them. For example, you would write "Y-M-C-A" for YMCA, just like you would for a radio broadcast. For a short pause, use a comma, and for a long pause use ellipses. The key when it comes to style and copy that will be read is clarity. How can the writer present copy in a way that will be easiest for the talent to clearly share with the audience?

The writer should keep in mind that a television news script is in split-page format. Technical commands and information is on the left side of the screen, and the copy block, the copy to be read by the on camera talent, will be on the right. Most computer programs allow for easy differentiation. Likewise, the copy-block on the right hand of the page will generally be the copy that is put on the teleprompter for the talent during the news broadcast.

BUILDING BLOCKS OF TELEVISION NEWS

There are various approaches to television news. In news, the writer uses the visual and the aural. The television news writer needs to think about the visual aspect. What is the audience going to see? The visual might identify who is talking. The key thing in television news is to use the audio and the visual together to make something greater than the sum of their parts. The writer should always think about whether what is being heard by the audience matches what they are seeing. The writer should want to use the two together. The audio and the visual play a symbiotic relationship in television news. When an anchor is speaking, you can use visuals to augment the story. If we are talking about a documentary about a prison, then the VO might be saying where the prison is located while the visual shows a map with the prison locale on it. Try to think strategically about using these together.

There are several visual building blocks the writer can use. First, the anchor can be on-screen. The writer can include a reporter stand-up. In a reporter stand-up, a reporter is on the scene of a news story or in the station and talks directly to the camera (to the audience). External video can be mixed into the story and the reporter can provide voice over narration. Graphics are also available for the writer, whether they are identification graphics with font, partial screen, or full screen graphics. Often there will be a small graphic somewhere on the screen that identifies the television station or outlet. News crawlers are also often featured on the bottom of the screen, providing additional information about the story or information about other major breaking stories. Increasingly, movement in graphics is used to add visual variety and augment a sense of pace. The writer can use combinations of all of these to create engaging, informative television news stories.

There are also several audio choices for the writer. These are similar to the audio choices listed in the chapter on audio. First, the talent can be on-mike (on the microphone), meaning they can be speaking and the audience can hear it. Second, the audience may hear sound-on-tape, or the audio recorded with external video. The audience could also hear narration over external video. There may also be some natural sound, possibly mixed with narration from the talent.

For the sake of providing examples of how these tools can be used in a VO/SOT television news story, we will provide a breakdown in the context of a television news writing program.

News Writing Computer Programs

There are a number of computer programs that are used to write television news. The particular features of these programs differ, but they make writing for television news easier and they allow consistency within a particular network, television station, or group of stations. One such program is E-Z News, which is used at TV-10, the daily television news program broadcast from Illinois State University School of Communication.

E-Z NEWS

Here is where we are going to explore the various elements in shots and the various types of shots. E-Z NEWS is a software program that will help the writer craft a news story. (See E-Z News Tutorial in the Appendix.) There are several commands a writer needs to know to use the program. The first one is anchor. Anchor is written **ANC**, identifies when an anchor is on-cam. **OTS** is an over-the-shoulder box. This means that we see the anchor, but over their shoulder is some type of graphic. When using an OTS, you will need to specify what is seen in the box. **SS** means "still-store," or static graphic. This is when we see one graphic on the entire screen. **1-shot** means that there is one person on camera. This is denoted by default when an anchor is on-cam. The next one is back-on-camera, written **BOC**, and it is used when returning from a VO to a 1-shot. **VO** means voice-over. Voice-over is when someone's voice is talking over other pictures. **SOT** stands for sound on tape, like the audio clip of someone's quote.

A package, written **PKG,** is a pre-recorded news story. **LOC** is a CG locator that tells the crew where the clip is. CG stands for computer graphic; it is when we see words on the screen on top of shots. **NAM** is a CG name that is super-imposed. When someone is speaking, we have super-imposed letters of their name or a title over the footage as they speak that tells who they are. **2TAL** means there are two names super-imposed on the screen. When using a **2-shot**, we will see two anchors on camera, but only one anchor will be speaking. This is denoted in the description of the shot.

At the top of your story will appear a slug, similar to the kind we use in radio. This slug is not necessarily the title of the piece. A slug just helps the talent and crew to identify the story.

TELEVISION NEWS AND ETHICS

The most important element of all for the people that own the company is the viewer's attention. They want to sell the viewer's attention to advertisers in hopes to gain a profit. Several years ago, Viacom bought CBS. Viacom is a group of shareholders who had money and realized that CBS could generate more profit. So they cut CBS's national, state, and local programming time, increased commercial time, and put it in-program promos. Informing the audience about the day's news events was not at the top of their priority list in making this plan. Their main objective was money: profit. I do not want to be jaded, but I do want to remind everyone that media sells a lifestyle, a *lebenswelt*, to the American public.

Glenn Beck, for example, has compared President Obama to Nazis. Glenn Beck is an entertainer. Rush Limbaugh is an entertainer. Some viewers who watch Beck love him because they say he is right. I have friends who watch Beck so they can know their enemy. They can all watch it, and argue about it, and have fun. [Beck is on Fox News, not the Fox entertainment network.] What is important to Beck and his network (Fox News) is that people watch his show, not that they are informed. When he makes controversy, he hopes that people will watch it and talk about it. When Beck's sponsors (i.e., Walmart) began to pull advertising funds when he was on CNN because of his controversial tirades, they stopped allowing him to talk and gave the money to another network. The mass media is about profit. When stockholders feel their shares are valuable, they do not care if the audience is getting quality news. Stockholders care about profit. If they lose money, they do not ask, "Well, did we at least inform the public?"

In general, all major news outlets reflect the perspective of their owners and journalists. The deeper question is: what is the perspective that is presented? If the audience agrees, they feel the news is objective. This was discussed in depth in the chapter on ethics. If audience members disagree, they view the coverage is slanted. Most major news media in the United States reflect a pro-corporate bias.

For example, *Men's Health* magazine featured a headline on the cover that said, "Eat your way to better abs." I thought, "That sounds like a plan! I want abs like Brad Pitt or Jesus. If I can eat and get them, sign me up." Well, I thought it was going to be this huge article, so I flip through, and I finally get to the page, and it ended up just being a little box that said, "Eat as much lettuce and peppers as you want." They did not care about the article. They were just trying to sell me the magazine so they could push the advertisements. Television news does the same thing. They want to gain the audience's attention to sell those audience members to advertisers.

How can the news writer be ethical in caring about the mass media but not write for profit? There are several ways. For example, CNN was owned by Warner Brothers, which made money on their entertainment division, and then augmented the price of their news division for use as a quasi-public servant. The easiest way to share news is by using the dramaturgical approach and telling your audience a good story. Consider your audience and the fact that people like stories. Telling story attracts and maintains an audience so the news outlet can sell the exposure to the audience to advertisers. The writer should entertain the audience as they inform. The risk, however, is that entertainment becomes more important than informing. This problem is exasperated because newspapers are dying. They face the same dilemma. This can lead to increased tabloid journalism. All audiences want to be amused. Unfortunately, that also can lead to a preference to entertainment in news broadcast at the expense of informing.

In this chapter we have discussed television news and audience gratification, scheduling news, writing television news stories well (television news and drama and structural considerations), writing the television news story (leads, organization, types of television news stories, organizing stories, kinds of stories, and style and copy for talent), the building blocks of television news, news writing computer programs, and ethics and television news writing.

In writing news, the writer will always want to go back to those basic elements. Is the news story clear, concise, complete, and accurate? Always take into consideration the elements of the dramatic model as well as the structural considerations of unity, variety, pace, and climax.

CHAPTER 15: ADVERTISING

In this chapter, we will discuss quality commercial advertisement writing. While the focus is primarily on television commercials, many of the concepts can be applied to other mass media commercial advertisements. For instance, many of the concepts discussed in this chapter are relevant for radio spots. When crafting commercials, including television commercials, a writer should always employ the four structural considerations of mass media writing; unity, variety, pace, and climax. When we talk about unity in commercials, we want to make sure that everything works together to create a whole that is greater than the sum of its parts. Unity is particularly important in commercials because we want to be as concise as possible. Every second and every inch costs money in mass media.

Variety needs to be considered as well. The writer should change characters, shots, and music to keep the audience's attention. Audience members have so many channels that the audience could change the station at any time. Writers need to keep audience members interested. In commercials, the pace is a consideration as well. This is the rate at which the message unfolds. The writer needs craft the announcement so that it is slow enough for the audience to understand it, but not too fast that the commercial overwhelms the audience. An example of this was in the exemplar discussed in Chapter 2, the FedEx commercials where the pace is strategically fast to express the idea that FedEx will get a package to a location fast. On the other hand, Corona ads are slow-paced to convey that it is a relaxing product.

In terms of climax in commercials, we always want to consider what the climax is. Just because a writer is only writing a thirty-second spot does not mean the writer cannot give the audience a climax. In a commercial, the climax may be the punchline of a joke, the solution to a problem or the moment at which the product is introduced.

FUNCTIONS OF ADVERTISING

Now, we move on to the nuts and bolts of advertising. Advertising has two functions. The first function is to get the audience's attention. The second is to motivate action. The takeaway is that commercial writers should get the attention of the audience and then sell them a good or service that they do not need. That being addressed, we will discuss how to construct and be critical about mass media commercials. The idea is that commercials and advertising affect our decisions. I am not asking you to move to the woods and eat acorns; I am trying to show you the media sells us things we do not need. We can live more simply and not get scammed by what commercials are selling. I do not have to go to McDonalds. I can make food at home. There are choices, and we need to highlight that there are choices. I will admit that I go to the movies several times a week that are sold to me by the blockbuster advertising machine. However, you do not have to sell out completely to the man.

TYPES OF SPOTS

The first type of television spot is a commercial. A **commercial** is any paid or barter placement. Particularly, these sell people goods or services. Most of what we call "commercials" is exactly this. They are often simply referred to as "spots." (See Television Announcement Example in the Appendix.)

The second type of television spot are **PSAs**. Public Service Announcements are air-time given to nonprofit organizations by television stations. For example, this may be for the Red Cross or anti-drug ads. There might be public service announcements that show the taboo life of a drug user to encourage teens to stay away from substances. I would recommend you start by taking an organization you love or have interest in and try to make a PSA for them. I understand we all need to pay our rent or mortgage, but we should try to make money doing what we love in order to help people. This is a great way to advance your cause.

The third type of television spot is the promo. A **promo** is an announcement for a television network or product. This would be like a preview promo that says, "Tune in next week for *The Office*." Often times we see them in news programming or in sitcoms. They may be giveaways or announcements about the station in general. For example, "WHOI joins the ISU Lady Redbirds to bring you 'Hoops for Hope.'"

BRANDING

In the last two decades, branding has become increasingly important. **Branding** is the recognition of a deep sense of brand identity that accompanies a product. This means customers associate the product not only with a specific brand name, but with a character or personality that accompanies the brand. To keep customers, advertisers seek to make brands part of our lifestyle.

Campbell's soup ads are a good example of branding. When you are sick or your child is cold, there is nothing that makes them feel better. The marketers of Cheerios pushed the idea of kids and wholesome goodness for several years. Now the people at Cheerios have also moved in the direction of associating heart healthiness with their product, likely reflecting recognition of an aging demographic in their target audience. They are selling little O-shaped cereal, but they are also selling the idea that Cheerios and kids go together. I was watching *Sesame Street* with my daughter and they had a character in a high chair eating little o-shaped cereal. It could have been any type of whole-wheat os, but because of successful branding, I associated it with Cheerios.

Think of Johnson & Johnson baby products; it could be any baby soap or lotion, but there is something trustworthy and wholesome about that brand. In another example, I personally associate the idea of "cheese" with Kraft. It is also how we refer to cotton swabs as Q-Tips, even though it is a brand, not a product. Kleenex is another example; we do not call it a "facial tissue." *That* is successful branding. The thing itself becomes associated with the product name; that is when advertising is great. Advertisers seek to associate a feeling with a product. Am I too old to mention the Budweiser frogs? I am not sure what that was even supposed to mean, but it made me laugh, and therefore, laughing is associated with drinking Budweiser; it's a feeling.

Branding has also branched off into different ideas as well. For example, there was a prominent Apple iPod commercial that used the song "1234" by the Canadian artist Feist. That was successful at conveying the simple nature of the iPod as well as to sell Feist's first record. I did not buy the iPod, but I did buy the album because the music was associated with a feeling in my psyche.

Sometimes, an ad will be used to combine the idea of entertainment with a product. My son Woody convinced me to buy cheese crackers because they had a special edition Star-Trek box that had Captain Kirk on it. Literally, he associated Star Trek with those crackers. Likewise, the inverse of this process is **product placement**. This is when they place products within the entertainment. In the film *Talladega Nights*, Will Ferrell's character Ricky Bobby thanks Baby Jesus (not grown up Jesus) for a delicious meal of, "Domino's, KFC and always-delicious Taco Bell." Product placement in entertainment programs is an effective way to get a product in the minds of audience members and is also a way entertainment producers can increase revenues. Another example is a deal between the producers of the original Jurassic Park film and Mercedes-Benz automobiles. The producers received a large sum to feature Mercedes-Benz vehicles in the film.

Branding is effective. If done correctly, it can be very efficient in creating life-long customers. Of all the money made in America each year, 2% of all of it goes to advertising. The reason is because advertising works. Think of McDonald's and that catchy little tune, "I'm lovin' it." My kids do not even like the food that much, but they know that when they go to McDonald's, it will be a good time. McDonald's has an annual advertising budget of about $2 billion. Forty percent of that advertising is directed at children. McDonald's effectively brands.

This is a true story of branding: someone who works for Red Bull found out I like to drink it before lectures. A representative was outside my classroom waiting for me with a free six-pack. When they gave me free products, they were attempting to reach all of my students. When I carry Red Bull while lecturing, my students can see the label. My students then associate Red Bull with academic excellence. *That* is branding. This is not traditional mass media, but it is branding.

FORMAT

In commercial script, there is usually a split-page format. In addition to split-page format, like in television news, the writer can also use storyboards in attempts to convey their vision. Sometimes in commercials, single-column format may be used, but traditionally it is the storyboard and split-page. When the mass media writer is thinking about their television commercial, they should think about telling a story with pictures and words.

AURAL ELEMENTS

The mass media writer will want to use the aural elements of the commercial to complement their story. Aural elements include narration, dialogue, music, and interviews.

As with television, these aural elements may be even more important in radio advertisement. Radio advertisement differs from television advertising because it is exclusively dependent upon aural characteristics. Imagery in radio advertisements has to be constructed from aural elements. The words, music, and sound effects are used to tell a story without the benefit of visual elements. The discussion of handling sound in Chapter 11 on radio news is particularly relevant here.

Often in local television or radio commercials, the budget simply is not there to bring in actors for dialogue, so a spokesperson or real-life interview is used. Here, the mass media writer could use non-actors as the voiceover for your audio narration. When interviewing your talent/client, you would not use a script. Instead, you would have a rough interview format of questions that get them to say what you want to air. You would ask questions like, "Why are you uniquely qualified to offer this good/service?" Or, "Why is your customer service number one?" You would use these interview answers as voice over. You would do the "writing" per se in the editing process. It is often good to ask the client questions before the interview in order for them to be prepared. One way to structure the commercial is to see what the interviewee thinks is important and let them give you their ideas. The writer can use the most effective and articulate ideas of the client as possible structural lattice.

Also when thinking about aural elements, we have nonverbal choices such as music, natural sound, and sound effects. Music sets the tone for the piece. Most of the same considerations we discussed for radio and aural elements are the same for television commercials.

OTHER CONSIDERATIONS FOR COMMERCIALS

In addition to what we have discussed, we also want to consider **purpose**. There are always three possible purposes of a mass media message: **to persuade**, **inform**, or **entertain**. All communication may have a sermonic function. Aside from this, a writer needs to know whether the primary purpose is to inform, entertain, or persuade, your ultimate goal is to get them to act in some way. Even entertainment can be used to grab attention and then motivate action.

The writer always needs to consider their **target audience**. The target audience is the demographic group the writer is trying to reach. For example, you would not market the Xbox games containing graphic violence during reruns of *The Golden Girls* or *Murder, She Wrote* because the target audience for those programs is probably not young males, the likely target audience for violent Xbox games. You want to think about placing the advertisement to reap the audience that you seek. The key thing for the writer to remember is even if you get a small percentage of the audience to see the commercial, and an even smaller percent to go to the store and buy your product, it increases revenue. Placement is important. Likewise, the mood of a spot should reflect the target audience. The target audience should be able to establish an emotional tie with a product and/or program.

Chapter 15: Advertising

The way a writer crafts the ad and what they have in the ad depends on the target audience. The writer might create different commercials for the same product that target multiple demographic groups. The writer can then tailor the message to the channel that is consumed by that particular audience. This is true for television and radio.

When we talk about target audience, it is worth mentioning political advertising. Most political advertising is only going to 10-15% of the actual American audience. These ads are marketed to swing voters; those that are just on the borderline of uncertainty. Some people love a particular political candidate or political party no matter what, and some people hate them no matter what. They usually cannot be changed. It is those that you can be effective with that you should seek. In political advertising, it is the swing voters.

PERSUASIVE APPEALS

Another technique to employ in writing commercials is **persuasive appeals**. What desire will the writer activate in the audience member that will motivate them to do what a sponsor wants? Usually, what a writer will want to do is, considering their product or service, use one or two persuasive appeals to try and reach them. A great example here is **safety**. We mentioned this in the beginning of the book; the Brinks security advertisement uses an appeal of safety to sell their home security system. That can be a very effective motivator.

Convenience is another persuasive appeal. Food places often do this; they promise that it is so easy and convenient to order and have delivery. Or, the advertisers might use an appeal to **sex**. For example, I do not know how Swedish supermodels dancing in a fountain is related to Miller Lite; yet I am recalling it just now. Axe body spray uses this appeal as well; Freud says this can be one of the most psychologically motivating factors. In this case, we are sold the idea that we cannot be sexually fulfilled without a product.

In all these examples, some sort of artificial need is created. **Loyalty** is another frequently used appeal. This may come in the form of loyalty to our country or loyalty to our company. **Value-economy** is also used; this is where you stress saving money on a product, good, or service. **Novelty**, or the idea that a good or service is new, different, or unique, is another appeal. If the audience is offered an "exclusive" anything, that is using "**snob-appeal**." **Scarcity** can be used to convey that a product is running out, i.e., "They're going fast. Get yours now!" **Spectacle**, or the idea of ballyhoo or a show, is another appeal. Think of when there is a car sale and they offer food, car washes, movie tickets, and other unrelated benefits.

These appeals are relevant to any type of advertisement, but here, for our purposes, particularly to television and radio.

Motivating Action

In commercial writing, we are not just seeking persuasion; it is about motivating action. Name association and recognition are important. The writer wants the audience to remember the name of the good or service. What is most often used for this are the combination of logos and slogans (**slogos**). Slogos are things like the Nike "swoosh," their logo, and their slogan ("Just do it."). The writer needs to offer something the audience can remember in an attempt to gain name recognition. People have to see an advertisement at least five times before they can remember it. This means the writer should want to repeatedly show a logo within a commercial several times.

Think about McDonald's and the "I'm Lovin' It" campaign we have previously discussed. That was used several times in each commercial. Several years ago, McDonald's was able to teach most Americans the ingredients of a Big Mac with a jingle (Two all-beef patties, special sauce, lettuce, cheese, pickles, and onions on a sesame seed bun). For those *Seinfeld* fans, it is when George decides to use the "By-Mennen," jingle when saying, "Co-Stanza," to be more memorable. Songs, jingles, slogans, and logos are all important in helping an audience remember. Bounty paper towels have come up with a very clever little song to go with their slogan, "The Quilted-Quicker Picker-Upper," and it is catchy enough that when you go to buy paper towels, you will at least see the Bounty slogan and think of it. Meow Mix came up with a rather catchy one a few years ago that was just a "meow," song. I do not even own a cat, and when I walk by Meow Mix in the store, I sing that jingle in my head. Signatures need to play for at least five seconds.

The writer should tell audience members what to do, how they can do it, and when they can do it. Be clear. Use the four structural considerations to build your commercial. Also, quality writing should be always be clear, correct, concise, and complete. Be explicitly clear, particularly in how they can perform the action or behavior we want to invoke.

Organizational Strategies

Once again, use of narrative is an effective organizational strategy. This applies to advertising as well. Audience members like drama. **Problem-solution format** reflects dramatic structure. Here, the product is used as the climax to the problem, which is a form of drama. Think of Jennifer Love Hewitt and ProActiv. She has a problem, which was acne, and her dramatic story, being scared, being worried, was solved by ProActiv.

Situation format is another useful tool. Cell phone commercials use this, where they show a teenager with a flat tire alone at night and they indicate that because she had a Verizon cell-phone, she could call home to dad. It was when cell phones were first coming out; I went out and bought one the next day, thinking of my family driving and something happening. Another example is the OnStar commercials where they put the audience in the POV of a cop chasing a stolen car. The voice over says, "It's OnStar, we found your car and we are shutting down the engine," as the police apprehend the suspect. Here, the audience is put in the situation of, "What if someone stole my car? How would I get it back?"

Spokesperson is another format. This is using a known icon of some sort to sell a product. Sometimes the celebrity will tell us about a problem-solution, like the ProActiv example with Ms. Love-Hewitt. **Product-as-star** might be an option for your commercial. This would be like M&Ms, where the regular and the peanut one walk around and go to parties and get eaten. In this case, the product *is* the spokesperson for the brand. **Comparison format** may also be used if you have a competing dual product, such as the "Coke verses Pepsi" debate. One of the most successful examples is the "Mac vs. PC" advertisements. **Special effects** may be used if they help attract attention to the story and the product to motivate action. Always consider drama first and then use other formatting elements.

STRUCTURAL PRE-RECORDED SPOTS

Many times in the local market an advertiser is getting part of their budget from a national organization. The national organization then provides some content but leaves space in a commercial for local content. Chevy uses this very frequently; they will give national footage to their dealerships who will then add-on or splice-in their own local variations of footage, deals, and on-air talent. Usually, the last five or six seconds will be local footage tagged-on to national footage in a **structural pre-recorded spot**.

The other part of your budget comes from co-op from local advertisers. What a writer has to do is be able to work within those confines. A writer needs to use visual and audio that feature the client's logo, slogan, and information about where, when, and how audience members can act.

INFOMERCIALS

Infomercials are usually half-hour or so commercials that look like regular advertisements, but go much farther in-depth with the product. In *Requiem for a Dream*, we see a sequence where the protagonist's mother is obsessed with an infomercial about losing weight and being healthy. If you get the opportunity to write infomercials and make lots of money: quit your job and go do something that *matters* to the world.

SUMMARY

We have talked about three types of spots, motivating action, organizational strategies, and using voices in advertising. Let me say this again: good writing is good writing. The most important thing is always clarity. We want to be clear to the people that we work with and clear to our target audience. As always, be concise in commercial writing because time is of the essence. We want to be correct and give good information about our products and services. Finally, we want to be complete; tell them everything they need to know in order to be motivated to act. There is no substitute for good writing. Good luck in selling people products they do not need by exploiting their psychological weaknesses.

CHAPTER 16:
PUBLIC RELATIONS AND STORY

Public relations practitioners have changed the world. There is not an area of progress within the last 200 years that didn't involve public relations and effective use of public relations tools. The reason we don't have children working in factories is because of child labor laws, and those came as a result of advocates using public relations methods to change the laws. Abolitionists, before 1860, utilized literature, telegraphs, protests, and other forms of communication to force the nation to look at the policy of slavery. Women's right to vote is also a direct result of women and citizens with affinity toward the women's cause pushing our country to expand suffrage rights to women.

These are examples of effective use of public relations. Public relations is really about empowerment—not only for an individual or a corporation, but for citizens who bond together to try and change something in their neighborhood, state, nation, or world. Effective use of public relations tools can change government policies, especially with the liberal mass media of Westernized democracies. Simply put, public relations grant us the power to change things.

In this chapter we will cover a working definition of public relations, the role of good writing, the role of publics, the stages of public relations writing, the media as a public, communication tools, public relations and advertising, and crisis communication.

DEFINING PUBLIC RELATIONS

Princeton.edu suggests that a definition of public relations is "a promotion intended to create goodwill for a person or institution." While this definition has its limits, public relations may be about a celebrity (prominent people doing stupid things). It may be Lindsay Lohan trying to communicate correctly to the judge that she will go to rehab and that she's not doing drugs anymore, or it may be her PR people or her publicist trying to get that message out. It may be Bill Clinton suggesting to the world that he "did not have sexual relations with that woman," or British Petroleum spewing petroleum goo all over the gulf coast and saying, "It wasn't our fault," or, "We're doing what we can to clean it up," or, "We won't let it happen again." These are all practical examples of public relations at work in the media.

The Public Relations Society of America's national assembly in 1982 suggested that "public relations helps an organization and its publics adapt mutually to each other." While this definition is antiquated in some ways, PR is about organizations or an individual effectively communicating to their publics. Traditionally, public relations professionals disseminated their messages through mass media or media that was generated by the individual or organization. Increasingly, public relations professionals are finding ways to more directly communicate to their publics. In public relations, there is no such thing as a general public. Rather, public relations professionals seek to reach specific publics. They may incorporate traditional media such as personal appearances on television or radio programs or op-ed pieces in magazines and newspapers. Public relations professionals are also reaching their publics through emerging channels such as the Internet via YouTube or social networking sites.

THE ROLE OF GOOD WRITING

Good writing is good writing no matter what the context. Mass media writers have the unique opportunity to take the principles of good writing and apply them across various media, such as straight print, feature print, television news, radio news, and blogging. The principles of good writing in all those areas are also the principles of good writing in public relations.

The focus of public relations writing should be the creation of effective messages. Media releases are one of a number of tools to disseminate the message to particular publics. Media releases alone should not drive a public relations effort. Rather, constructing effective public messages should be the central focus. Media releases are one of the ways to disseminate a message.

When thinking about good writing, it is important to tell a *story*. Writers who consider dramatic principles in public relations writing can better craft engaging public relations messages. Telling a good story particularly applies to public relations, and thus, we need to consider the narrative paradigm and the model of dramatic structure. Even in public relations, we want a protagonist who has a will and want, faces complications, has a realization, and at some climactic moment, either achieves his/her will and want or does not. If we tell a story like that in the public relations context, it grabs attention and keeps an audience engaged even if the story is relatively insignificant to the audience.

Giving a face to the story is an effective public relations tool. If there is a human being in the story, that human being becomes the indicative example of what is being advocated. For example, no one is a better "face" for Apple than Steve Jobs. His struggle to make Apple what it is today tells a great story: starting in the garage with Steve Wozniak, then fighting against the big IBM corporation. At various points he faces complications like "how do we tell good stories with computers?" Jobs responded with Pixar and *Toy Story*. "How do we expand computers?" He gave us the Macintosh. "How can we make it easier?" We now have our iPhones and our iPads. His face provides a great story for Apple, and thus, he becomes a primary dramatic tool for the PR people at Apple.

Public relations writers can learn how to humanize an issue from Oprah Winfrey. Oprah has emphasized how people respond to people in her talk show program. Oprah has taken unusual and dramatic stories and allows normal people to tell those stories. Audiences relate to normal people who appear on Oprah and tell those stories. People also relate to the normal people from the studio audience who respond to guests on her talk show. Effective public relations professionals understand that members of their publics relate to people in a story. This helps create audience identification. Public relations professions should always try to put a face on the issue.

Public relations writing should be clear, correct, complete, and concise. When approaching quality writing, the first consideration is that the writing be clear. As stated all throughout this book, the most important consideration when writing for mass media is clarity. Second, we want to be correct. Make sure that all the dates, spelling of proper names, and overall facts of the story are accurate so that the audience receives the right information. This is not only to ensure a writer's credibility, but also so the writer can report specific information to the public. The third consideration is that the writing should be complete. We want to make sure when we're writing for public relations that we have all the essential ingredients the audience is going to need, such as the release date of the new product.

The other day I bought my fiancé's son Nick the new *Call of Duty: Black Ops* video game. Because of Call of Duty's public relations, I knew what day the game was going to be released, whether I learned it through the TV ads or reviews in magazines. The PR people clearly told me when I can get the product. So, at 1:35 am on Monday night/Tuesday morning, I was at Walmart. Why did I know when the product was going to be released? Because the video game's public relations professionals effectively communicated its message to their desired publics.

The last consideration of quality writing is concision. Every word must tell because in mass media, time is money. When we see the commercial about the release of Black Ops, we are not presented with extraneous information. Its PR professionals want to keep it simple and parsimonious so the audience gets the essential elements.

In addition, the public relations writer should incorporate structural considerations. To consider **unity** means making sure that all pieces of the public relations effort tie together. To consider **pace** means making sure that the press release flows well, and that it does not drag down. To consider **variety** means having all different kinds of information in PR messages. Lastly, **climax** refers to telling a good story.

When writing for public relations, recognize whether the message is informational or persuasive. In public relations, there is always intended result. If you work for Hugh Grant and he got arrested for sleeping with a prostitute, his public relations people wanted his publics to like him again. Lil Wayne just got out of jail, and his PR people are doing the best job they can to inform us that he has never left the music scene. They are trying to persuade us that he is still part of the industry, and are going to make sure we still think he is on the scene.

Although it seems like it is informational, Richard M. Weaver suggested that there is a **sermonic function** to every message. Although the audience is learning the facts, PR people are also trying to persuade the audience of something. PR attempts to persuade more than most other forms of mass media writing. Most often, though, subtle persuasion produces the most favorable results in public relations.

Public Relations and Publics

In public relations, the particular audience an organization is trying to reach is referred to as a **public.** Just like in all other forms of mass media writing, it is important to know the target audiences of messages, both intended and potentially unintended targets.

The Catholic Church is always apologizing, often attempting to convince Catholics to remain Catholics. That is one of their publics. In addition to this particular public, there are other publics for the Catholic Church's public relations efforts such as political officials from various countries, financial organizations, and members and clergy from other denominations. Public relations professionals working on behalf of the Catholic Church are well advised to expand their efforts beyond just preaching to the choir.

In terms of Lil Wayne, other people in the industry, disk jockeys, programmers, and fans of Lil Wayne may be part of his PR group's publics. After the oil spill in the Gulf of Mexico, one of BP's publics was the stockholders of the company, convincing them not to sell. BP should also consider other publics, such as future customers. BP should be talking to my little girl. She is eight. She says, "We don't go to BP. They spewed oil all over the gulf coast Daddy. Don't pull in there." After the spill, there was a BP station that opened in our town where they were selling gas for extremely cheap and there was a line. My little girl said, "They're tricking to trick us, Dad. They're trying to make it seem like they care about us by giving us cheap gas." BP should be thinking about her as a member of one of their publics. BP is a hundred-year-old company that would like to be two hundred years old. Maggie is a member of an important public: future customers.

These are considerations when writing for public relations, but remember that good writing is good writing, no matter the context.

THE STAGES OF PUBLIC RELATIONS WRITING

The stages of public relations writing are a cyclical process. A public relations firm, or the public relations spokespeople for a given entity, will first research to find out its publics, and then figure out how they can reach those publics. If BP wants to appeal to stockholders, they need to take into account the demographic features of the stockholders. What are they reading? What are they watching? This is part of the research phase of public relations.

The second phase is planning. If the people who own stock in BP read *The New York Times* and *The Wall Street Journal*, and BP does not want them to sell the stock, BP can spend large amounts of money putting advertisements in *The Wall Street Journal*, *Fortune* magazine, or *Money* magazine, in order to try and reach the stockholders. BP may decide to keep the advertisements in those publications for the next four months. In public relations, **planning** means building a schedule for communicating the message.

After planning, the next step is **execution**. PR staff engages in communication through outlets such as publications, op-ed pieces, letters to the editor, statements in magazines, press conferences, television commercials, donations to organizations, and any other way they can get their message to the masses. For example, if BP donates $25 million to a center for renewable energy and The Wildlife Fund of Southern Texas, BP's public relations professionals can write a press release about it and have a big press conference when BP officials hand the check over. These efforts help create and support the impression that BP cares about the damage caused by the oil spill.

The fourth and final stage of public relations writing is **evaluation**. How well did the communication attempt work? Was it effective? To figure this out, the PR group might have a debriefing with representative samples of their publics to try and see if their message not only reached the public, but was decoded in a way that benefits the organization.

After evaluation, the process starts all over again. Take that evaluation information and think about the next campaign. When engaged in writing for public relations, think about executing these stages.

THE MEDIA AS A PUBLIC

It is important for a public relations writer to realize that the most important public is **the mass media itself.**

There are mass media gatekeepers with whom public relations professionals must interact. In broadcast media these gatekeepers are media producers and news directors. In the press the gatekeepers are assignment or desk editors.

Public relations professionals must pitch their stories to media gatekeepers. A **pitch** is how public relations professionals get their idea across, or how they sell their story to media personnel. The public relations professional needs to pitch their idea to gatekeepers and reporters in terms the media personnel can understand and connects with. The same idea applies when a writer pitches a feature film or television show, as described in Chapters 18 and 19. If the public relations professional can effectively pitch a story to news media gatekeepers, there is a possibility these gatekeepers will develop a relationship to the story.

A couple years ago I was involved with directing and producing a documentary about Joe Amrine—a man that was on death row with no evidence against him. A couple other guys and I got together and made a documentary about him, and we got it shown from Taiwan to Madrid. Both *The New York Times* and *BBC* covered it.

I can show a documentary to 200 people in, say, Kansas City, but if I can get the television news media there, and they show clips of the documentary on the 5 o'clock news, and I get a newspaper reporter there, and they write a story about us showing the documentary, and I get a radio reporter there who's going to broadcast a radio story of the reactions of people who saw the documentary, how many people do I reach? A public relations professional can reach hundreds of thousands, if not millions. If you can effectively use public relations tools with a consideration of the mass media as one of your publics, you can exponentially increase your available and potential audience. That is how PR is empowering. In terms of our documentary, the Missouri Supreme Court had considered Amrine's case before they decided to turn it down. However, after the story was on the news and on the cover of newspapers in Kansas City, St. Louis, Jefferson City and Columbia, Missouri, the Missouri Supreme Court couldn't ignore it anymore. They reheard the case and ruled in favor of Joe. His life was spared, and public relations played an important role.

COMMUNICATION TOOLS

One very effective public relations tool is using the mass media to transmit a message. Media lists are very important. Media lists include contact information such as email addresses of all the media personnel, or all the phone numbers of the news directors and the assignment directors. This way when a writer sends out a press release, the writer already has all the information about who to send it to. Email is the number 1 way to send media releases in the twenty-first century. Many PR professionals would view delivery of media releases via fax as obsolete. In the case of our documentary about Amrine, the ability to use computers with fax machines was amazing, because we could have all the numbers stored up in a program, craft a press release, and then hit send to group, and within a minute there were some 60 media personnel's fax machines printing up our press release.

Media lists containing contact information are a critical public relations tool. Second to that are media kits, or press kits. An example of a media kit would be a folder, maybe with a logo on the front, which contains a press release, background information, brochures, photographs and fact sheets. For us, we also included a DVD of the documentary. If all of the stories that the other media outlets have written about your business is included, then that helps build credibility.

Media kits provide some kind of physical thing to give reporters and news directors, often containing much more material than they can use. One of the most important things to do in public relations is to make a newsperson's job easy. If all the research is done for them, then that press kit is all they need to write the story. Including our documentary in our media kit was very important because once they have the documentary, then they have footage of the witnesses, jury members and the people involved in the case. Television reporters can put this video footage into their news story without ever leaving the station. Again, remember that one of the most important things you can do as a public relations person is to make a media personnel's jobs easy, and that is exactly what a good press kit does.

The news release, or press release, is another important tool of public relations. The most basic press release is just an inverted pyramid story. The news elements are given right up front in a summary lead: who, what, where, when, and why. In terms of press releases, it is best to have some incident of punctuated equilibrium. That is a complex way of saying: Have an event.

The press conference can be an important part of an event. For example, a press conference could be part of an initial screening of a documentary on a political or social issue. Another example is a press conference as part of the unveiling of a new product or service. The press conference is an important vehicle to promote an event. Press conferences can be an important part of event promotion.

Press conferences can also be part of an image restoration campaign. At a press conference, the accused can speak to news people. For example, the chairman of BP could speak to the press, he could have several experts who speak on the corporation's behalf and could also have someone from the U.S. Wildlife Fund who thanks him for the $15 trillion donation.

Public relations professionals should hold press conferences at a time when reporters are going to be available. Two o'clock is a great time because you can still make the five o'clock news. For the documentary, we sent out a press release 10 days before. Then, we changed it up a little bit, and sent it out 5 days before. Then we changed it up a bit again and sent it out the night before, so that when the news directors arrive in the morning, they have a fax. They're in charge of sending out reporters, so if they actually get the fax and look at it, there is a chance of your story getting on the news—depending on the news day. If somebody whips a shoe at the president, chances are it is going to be a thick news day and might be hard for you to get in. However some news days are slower than others. Always remember the secret behind television news: "If there is no news, they have to make news." So in a slow news day, your press release stands a much better chance.

If a writer knows how to write an inverted pyramid press release, the writer has power. If you have an event in your community, you can broadcast that. It could be the release of your band's album. It could be a protest you are planning about the meal plan at your college. It could be an event that your fraternity has to raise money for muscular dystrophy. If you know how to write a press release, and send that press release to the media, you have power because you potentially focus the attention of the media and the public onto your event. The media might not tell us what to think, but they do often tell us what to think about (agenda setting). Women who wanted to vote, and who effectively communicated that message to the mass media compelled the American public to extend suffrage rights to women. These suffragettes effectively used events such as demonstrations and protests. They were effective in communicating with news gatekeepers and news people covered these events.

A writer also has the choice to use a feature release, which more so follows the dramatic paradigm than the inverted pyramid. It tells a story, and can put a face on the issue. If a writer sends out an inverted pyramid press release 10 days before the event, then maybe it would be good idea to send out a feature release 5 days before the event to offer the media a variety of information.

There is a myriad of other tools for the public relations person. **Media advisories** are like a bulleted memo to the media to remind them what events are happening. **Fact sheets** just give basic facts about an incident, event, or person so the reporters don't have to research those basic facts. **Backgrounders** give some kind of context, and go into more detail about the background of a story.

There are also going to be instances where a writer will need to write speeches for those speaking at a press conference. **Talking points** are the very important points the speaker has to hit. The talking points should be included in the press releases, and everyone who is going to talk to the media is going to try and communicate the same ideas. For speeches, a writer should stick to the talking points, and as a PR staff member, you want to limit who is qualified to talk to the media. Examples of our talking points for the documentary were as follows: "There are no witnesses and no evidence against Joe Amrine. Whether you are for or against the death penalty, nobody wants their tax dollars to be used to kill an innocent person. There is another man against whom there are witnesses and evidence, and he should've been prosecuted for the crime." After that, we can say, "Thank you very much for your time Mr. Reporter. I've got to go now."

Public relations professionals control the message. They do not have to speak any more than they want to, because if media personnel want the story and all the public relations people say are the three good talking points, what is going to be on the news? The three talking points! When the media really needs a statement from you, you control that statement. Do not wander in the speech, and stick to the talking points.

Websites are also critical. Anyone in public relations who does not have a website is not even in the game. The same principles of good writing apply to websites. Be clear, correct, concise, and complete. Tell a story and tell it well.

Video news releases are potentially the future of public relations. A **video news release** is produced by an organization, and looks just like a television news story. The release is given to the television media, and often times the media will take pieces from it and put it in their story. They will take the actualities from experts in the field that were given to them, and they can put them in their story. Several years ago, Saudi Arabia did a little promotional piece that looked like a news story, and the network CBS ran it without even editing it like it was a television news story. Whatever is included in your video news release—charts, actualities, b-roll shots—the media may use to get your message to the public. If a writer knows how to write television news, then the writer knows how to write a really good video news release.

PUBLIC RELATIONS AND ADVERTISING

Public relations and advertising are not the same thing, but there is often an overlap between image projection and marketing. There is a symbiotic relationship between the two, and it is best when the advertising agency and PR staff work in conjunction.

I have always been interested in how social groups and political movements used public relations to get their message across to people. A more recent example of this is the giant link between the Tea Party movement, the media, the public, and elected officials. The Tea Party advocates know how to write a press release. They know how to have an event in their local neighborhood. They know how to get in front of the camera and talk talking points. Thus, they were tremendously successful in the last election. It was because they knew how to use public relations to reach the media, which gets their message across to the public, who pick what officials are elected into our political system.

You can make a difference in your community when you are an effective public relations writer. For instance, imagine you have kids in grade school, and there's a giant pothole out in the middle of the road in front of the school. If you know how to use public relations, you know how to get that hole filled. What you do first is have an event around that hole next Thursday at 3 pm. You send out press releases to all the media to tell them that you're having a little event around the pothole at 3 pm. Then when the event comes, you have all the little kids singing about the pothole. What you do is you get the television media and a photographer for the newspaper at the event, and then have a little kid curl up into the hole. I guarantee you that the image will end up on the front page of the newspaper. Also, the radio guy is there because you sent out press releases 10 days and 5 days before, and it is a really slow news day. If you know how to send out press releases, how to talk to media, and you give media kits to all the reporters there with pictures, facts, and statistics (such as how dangerous potholes are!), I guarantee you that someone in city government will be sending a truck out the next day with some asphalt to shovel into the hole. You could invite the mayor to come to the event and tell everyone how much he cares about potholes. Then you could tell the media, "Well the mayor was invited, but he declined to come because he doesn't care about our kids. Maybe he's got more important things than the safety concerns for our children." This is all public relations. It is about knowing how to speak to the media, who then speak to the public, who invariably gets to elect the officials. All of a sudden, you've made a difference in your community. You've taken power that is yours in a democracy and you've used it for the benefit of you and the people you love and care about. That is the power of public relations.

Crisis Communication

Whenever an organization or institution is attacked, there are various image restoration strategies that they can enact to respond to those attacks. The study of image restoration is ultimately the study of effective strategies. For instance, if Bill Clinton is attacked for having improper sexual relations with one of his interns, there are several things he can do.

He can attack the accusers: "Well, it's just a rightwing conspiracy out to get me!"

He can deny: "I did not have sexual relations with that woman."

He can minimize: "Well it was just a dirty dress and a cigar."

He can engage in corrective action: "I promise to go to sexual rehab and to go to more marriage counseling with Hilary!"

Or, he can engage in mortification: "I'm sorry! I'm sorry!"

What Bill Clinton actually said did not achieve his image goals, because he mortified "I'm sorry!", but afterward, he denied it "But I didn't do it!" Or "I promise I'll do better, but I didn't do it in the first place." This kind of an approach comes off as insincere. Research indicates that what works really well is to mortify, or self-blame, and then follow it up with corrective action.

This is a very important part of public relations. When Mel Gibson was picked up after drinking three bottles of tequila and was bitching on some anti-Semitic rant, he has got some public relations explaining to do. The Catholic Church has been accused of many mistakes, but the organization has sometimes failed to follow mortification with meaningful corrective action. For instance, the Catholic Church has said, "We are so sorry that throughout history women have been treated like second class citizens. It is horrible." However, two weeks later the Pope sat on his big chair, put on his funny hat, grabbed his staff, and said "Women cannot be priests." If an entity apologizes for something, it should engage in some corrective action or else it rings hollow.

In the mid-1990s, Nike was attacked for using child labor, and they did a bunch of public relations to try and respond to that. They tried to enact voluntary codes of conduct and had their PR staff making a bunch of websites saying how much they cared about it. The company made changes. Now, Nike will require no one to work more than 16 hours a day, no one under 12 works for them, and they will pay these people at least $1.10 a day. Thank God for Nike and their progressive, humanistic labor policies. This is an example of image restoration discourse as a part of public relations crisis communication.

We have discussed several ideas in this chapter, including defining public relations, the role of good writing, media as a public, communication tools, public relations and advertising, and crisis communication. Again, good writing is good writing. Good writing is always clear, correct, concise, and complete. Also, it tells a good story. When you are able to do that with public relations, you have power. Effective public relations has changed the world. In a democracy, the conscientious writer should get involved in those kinds of battles for what is right. Once you have the tools and know how to effectively use them, you have power.

CHAPTER 17:
TELEVISION ENTERTAINMENT

As stated before, the goal of this book is not only to teach aspiring writers to effectively write for mass media, but to also teach every reader of this book to be more critical consumers of mass media in general. My hope is that the next time you find yourself lounging around on a couch watching TV, not only will you be entertained by whatever show you are watching, but you will also have a better understanding of the process involved in the writing of that show. In this chapter, we will cover writing for television in more detail, focusing on the topics of **writing episodically**, **rules of television drama**, **proposing a television show**, and **climbing the staff ladder**.

WRITING EPISODICALLY

Most television series are **episodic**, which means the show is released in individual episodes. Each time the viewer sees an episode, they get another glimpse into a little part of the story. Watching a television series is an entirely different experience than watching a feature film because a film requires the viewer to digest the entire story, from start to finish, in one sitting. On the other hand, though a viewer may watch an entire season of *Dexter* in one sitting, most television series viewers will have a week-long gap between each show to digest the episode they just saw. Since almost every television series we see on TV today is released in episodes, it is important for the mass media writer to have a general understanding of the principles behind writing episodically.

Every television series generally includes at least one long narrative, or overall story, that takes more than one episode to tell. The viewers may see more dramaturgical developments to each of these long narratives every week they tune in, but the story may not reach its climax and resolution for a couple of episodes, an entire season or even six seasons into the show. For example, if two characters of a series get engaged—let's just call them Fred and Wilma—the series may tell a long narrative about the planning of the wedding that leads up to the actual wedding three episodes later. In the first episode, Fred might fight with Wilma about the fact that she invited her ex-boyfriend that Fred hates to the wedding. In the second episode, Wilma might have an emotional breakdown about which color napkins to have on the table during the wedding reception. Then in the third episode, Wilma's mother may arrive on the scene and try to take over the planning of the wedding, nearly sabotaging it, until everything comes together in the end and the couple successfully gets married.

ER and *CSI* are examples of series that incorporate these kinds of long narratives. Though the audience may not see the resolution to the long narrative until way down the line, the smaller conflicts that come up and resolve within each episode, along with each character's personality and their interaction with one another, are entertaining enough to keep the audience coming back for more. So as a writer, not only do you have to think about dramatic development episodically, but you also need to keep in mind the longer narrative.

Every television series has at least one series creator, or the guy that came up with the idea for the whole series. Obviously if it were not for the series creator, there would be no series. However, much like making a film, making television drama requires much collaboration. Though the series creator may have come up with the concept, the show would not be able to stay on the air if it were not for the writers. The writers are the guys that come up with the shocking plot twists that keep each episode in a series interesting. Their main goal is to keep the attention of the audience by telling them a good story. In order to come up with each episode, the writers may take the overall theme of a show and discuss it with each other. They might bounce around ideas of how to further develop the theme, brainstorming until they come up with some story that becomes the basis of the next episode.

RULES OF TELEVISION DRAMA

There are some rules a writer must consider when it comes to writing television drama. First of all, an episode **has** to fit the time slot. If the time slot is an hour long, then the show itself will generally be between forty eight to fifty two minutes. In television drama, there is no room for going a little bit over or under the time limit—you have to be **exact**. Millions of dollars may have been put into the production of a show, so make sure to utilize every second you get to tell the story. They must also make sure there is still room left over for the commercial breaks.

A second rule is to make sure the story is finished and submitted on time. When it comes to TV drama, **deadlines are real**. If the script is not submitted by the deadline, then the production crew may not be able to get all the shots they need in time. As a writer, if you fail to meet a deadline in the industry, you are likely to make far more enemies than friends.

Before I go on, I just want to say that writer's block is a myth. While I was teaching at the University of Missouri, I saw Mike Reiss give the best lecture I had ever heard on writer's block. Reiss is a writer who has been involved with many television productions, including *The Tonight Show Starring Johnny Carson, The Simpsons,* and *The Critic.* He asked the rhetorical question, "Have you ever heard of plumbers block?" He went on to say that the plumber has a job to do—undoing the pipes, getting rid of clogs and so on. A plumber does not get the opportunity to call off a job due to a sudden "lack of inspiration." He is expected to work no matter what. According to Reiss, that is exactly what writing for a real television series is like. The writer has to just start typing, even if what they write is bad.

While working for the *Tonight Show*, Reiss said you had to write 60 jokes a day, and that no matter how hard you worked, one out of three jokes bombed. He also added that, though actors may be able to act on drugs, a television series writer cannot write on drugs. But back to the point, writing for a television show is hard work. You must be ready to work twelve hours a day, five to six days a week, without falling victim to the excuse of "writer's block." Having a job as a writer is no different than having a job as a plumber. In both professions, you are paid to do a job, and if you fail at that job, you are fired.

Another rule of writing for television drama is to incorporate a four-act structure, unlike film's three-act structure. Most television drama is aired around commercial breaks, and thus follows a four-act structure. A writer must make sure to include suspenseful cliffhangers at each commercial break. Television dramas on HBO or Showtime do not have to worry about this since they do not have commercial interruptions, but shows like *Grey's Anatomy, ER, Breaking Bad,* and *Mad Men* need cliff hangers to keep the audience's attention through the commercial breaks. Ultimately, and unfortunately, that is what television is all about. Television stations want to retain the attention of their audience so that they can sell the audience to the highest bidder. They say to advertisers, "Hey, we got fifteen million viewers last week and we'll sell them to you for 30 seconds for the low price of one point five million dollars. Deal?" Television is designed to attract us, the viewers, so our attention can be sold for the highest price. Luckily, with the modern marvels of TiVo, DVR, and OnDemand, we viewers do not have to suffer through the ads much anymore. Still, when writing for a TV series, make sure the story is effectively structured around those commercial breaks.

The last thing I want to mention is that every television series fits a franchise. A **franchise**, or **paradigm**, is the organizational sequence that every episode of a series follows. Consider *Law and Order*. Generally in each show, the crime happens, then right after the crime, the cops come and investigate. They think they might have it solved the case before the first commercial break, but after the commercial we come back only to find that their theory was wrong! So they investigate further until they come across a new piece of evidence that leads them to someone who they might think is the perpetrator. Then it goes to commercial, and when it comes back, the story turns to the lawyers and then the prosecutors. They go through the trial and get a conviction, but something else happens that messes them up again! The show goes to another commercial and this time when it comes back, the audience finds out that the perpetrator is someone else. They get this actual bad guy on trial, solve the crime and lock up the criminal—because crime does not pay.

Although there are obviously many more plot twists and surprise developments that happen in each episode, the show follows a similar franchise overall. *CSI* does this as well. Sometimes, a new show might not know which organizational sequence works best at first and may take a season or two to find it. But once they find it, every show will likely follow a very similar structure.

Proposing a Television Show

When writing a proposal for a television show, a writer has got to use the TV format. This means having a cover page with a short description or mini-treatment on it. This synopsis could be fifty-word description that tells the reader the title of the script, the audience it will appeal to, and the day-to-day complications faced by the characters. Next, a proposal is going to require a **pilot**, or the first episode of a series, to test the waters of the public's interest in the show. This is the episode that introduces the audience to the main characters, along with the premise of what the show is going to be about over the course of the season.

Another approach a writer can take is to script a **backdoor pilot**. A backdoor pilot is a movie that introduces the characters of a series before the story is told in episodes. *Variety* magazine defined it as a "pilot episode filmed as a standalone movie so it can be broadcast if not picked up as a series." Before posing the script of a pilot to various mass media networks, you might attach a package about which actors or actresses are potentially interested in being in the show.

Climbing the Staff Ladder

One last thing to keep in as a television writer is your ability to climb the staff ladder. You may start out as a mere writer's assistant, throwing out ideas to the higher-up writers who laugh and tell you how stupid you are, but if you stick around long enough and work hard at improving your craft, you are bound to climb the ladder. You may go from being a writer's assistant, to becoming a staff writer, to becoming the story editor, to becoming the head writer, until one day you get asked to work on a third series as the executive producer. Then, after you have worked on so many series over the course of ten years, you might find yourself at a lunch with a network executive one day where he asks, "Say... do you have any ideas for new TV shows?" Unless you do the executive short cut where you write a successful play, move into film, make a bunch of money and then approach a network executive, chances are you will have to work up that ladder if you ever plan on being more than just a writer's assistant.

There are other ways to break into television entertainment writing, including building a web buzz about short pieces that could be part of future television programs (for example, *South Park* and *It's always Sunny in Philadelphia*). There are probably other ways as well, such as marrying a network executive's daughter, but those avenues could be more thoroughly explored in a course on television writing. Hopefully, this chapter inspires some students to pursue such a course of study.

In this chapter, we covered writing for television in more detail, focusing on the topics of **writing episodically**, **rules of television drama**, **proposing a television show,** and **climbing the staff ladder**. As in all forms of mass media, when writing television entertainment, the writer should tell a good (dramatic) story and tell it well (clear, correct, concise, and complete).

CHAPTER 18:
DOCUMENTARY

Documentary creation is about executing your vision; really, it is about empowerment. When you choose to do a documentary about a particular subject, you are asking your audience to consider that subject. If you have an audience's attention and you tell them what ideas have value, you have power. On a micro-level, you are deciding what they will hear and see. Talking about a social issue is one thing, but showing a starving child crying is another thing entirely. In this way, documentary is uniquely effective in talking about social and political issues. When you watch a documentary, you are *in* the social or political issue. A good documentary writer will craft a text in an empathic way that immediately transports the viewers into the shoes of the protagonist.

In this chapter we discuss the power of visual images, characteristics of documentaries, types of documentaries, drama in documentaries, development of a documentary from treatment to script, research, visual storytelling in documentaries, use of b-roll, logging documentary footage, choices of inclusion and exclusion, narration, dramatic re-creation, and the usefulness of documentaries in public relations. When writers begin to think about writing and creating documentary film, they need to remember to incorporate the dramaturgical approach while also making sure the film is clear, concise, correct, and complete.

POWER OF VISUAL IMAGES

Documentary film and video has a unique power to transport a viewer to another time and place and allow the viewer to become a witness. I did a study way back when I was at Southern Illinois about Martin Luther King and some of his colleagues that were marching in Selma, Alabama. During the march, the police beat the protesters and set attack dogs loose on them. Women and children dressed in their Sunday morning church clothes were attacked by police dogs. The police also used high-pressure water hoses to pummel the protesters into submission. The marchers were brutalized. In my study, I had people read about this event in a newspaper, and then I asked them how they felt about it. Their reaction was strong: 7 out of 10 people were "outraged." Then, I showed them actual footage of the cops injuring and accosting kids, women, and innocent citizens through the use of attack dogs and water hoses. These marchers were only defending their constitutional right to vote. The outrage experienced by the people in the study was off the scale: 10 out of 10 reported feelings of outrage. The point is seeing can be more emotionally involving than reading. That is why when we create a documentary, we get the chance to put our audience in the moment.

You have probably heard of the fat, rich guy that never lets the truth get in the way of a good joke—Michael Moore. I think there is a place for him in our democracy, but let it be noted that we have a wide range of voices. In a democracy, you get several options on how to interpret information. The realignment of the margins moves the middle. The extremes on either end of an issue affect the position of the mean. For example, when Martin Luther King, Jr. first appeared on the national scene, people called him a "radical." Then, Malcolm X gained prominence and MLK became a "moderate"; suddenly, the public loved him. What was considered to be "extreme" was modified, and the overall perspective of things was redefined. When MLK was around, he *was* radical, but in comparison to Malcolm X, he was desirable and peaceful. After Malcolm X, we named street signs and parks and schools after MLK. We need the Michael Moores of the world so that what we perceive as "radical" can be seen in a new light.

In America, Frank Capra released a series entitled *Why We Fight,* which aimed to motivate the American people to take part in the fighting of World War II. This series may just sound like a load of propaganda, but when it all boils down, the only difference between propaganda and free expression is whether or not the viewer agrees with the perspective they experience. One man's propaganda is another's self-expression.

Scripting a documentary is a more recursive process than scripting a television program or dramatic film, because documentaries are usually restricted to what actually happened, as captured on videotape, instead of what can be dramatically created or re-created. In television production, a script is usually completed first, and shooting schedules are then generated based around the shots in that script. In documentary production however, the initial script is more like a wishlist of scenes and shots. Footage is gathered with the understanding that additional footage might be needed, and the shots on the wishlist are slowly whittled down. Simply put, the makers of a documentary cannot plan on getting the exact footage that they want, but rather they must work with the footage they get. As Walters (1994) suggested, "In the true documentary, in contrast to programs that are re-creations, the sequences cannot be scripted in detail in advance; they can only be loosely planned" (p. 449). Footage of what actually happened is gathered, while only the best selections make it to the finished film.

CHARACTERISTICS OF DOCUMENTARIES

Documentaries are beautiful in the sense that it allows an audience to see the world through a **documentary point of view**. The writer of a documentary gets to choose a point of view, and then go into detail about the world as it appears through that perspective. It is important to recognize that point of view is not the same as an editorial opinion. Point of view is the perspective through which the audience experiences a story, while an editorial opinion is simply someone else's opinion about an issue. For example, the point of view in Errol Morris's 2003 documentary *The Fog of War* details major wartime decisions during the Cuban Missile Crisis and the Vietnam War through the eyes of then Secretary of Defense Robert S. McNamara. The film seeks to provide lessons of war from a man who had the insights and first-hand knowledge of these twentieth-century wars. Other points of view could have been through the eyes of a soldier or the Vietnam resistance, McNamara was likely the POV employed because Morris was trying to tell a relevant story that spoke to the events in Iraq and Afghanistan in 2003.

Another important element of documentary creation is **audience involvement**; we want our audience to be engaged in the story we are telling them. The best way to get people interested in any topic or issue is to incorporate *drama*. Tell a good story. By taking a dramaturgical approach, the audience becomes involved with the conflicts they see on the screen. *King of Kong: Fistful of Quarters* is a documentary about a guy who is trying to break the world record for the high score in Donkey Kong. Though I could not care less about who holds the Donkey Kong world record, I watched this documentary and became involved in it because it told a good dramatic story.

Documentaries have the power to capture events *as they are happening*. When I was at NYU, I tried to make several different films with actors, but after I saw *Pulp Fiction*, I wanted to quit. I knew that I would never find a way to make people act as real as they did when acting for Quentin Tarantino. Then, I found documentary. In documentary, you do not have to get people to act. You just turn on the camera and they act as they would in real life—because it *is* real life.

When working on a documentary, you want to get shots of events as they are happening. A student of mine actually ended up getting a job with MTV's *True Life* and helped shoot an episode called, "I'm broke." At one point during the shooting, the woman they were filming broke down in tears. So, instead of zooming in to capture the personal moment, he zoomed out to allow the woman to maintain some privacy. MTV fired him for that. Although I may not morally agree with MTV's decision, the story does emphasize the point that you want to get the shots *as they are happening.* Then, once you have gathered a nice collection of all sorts of shots, you get to choose which story you want to tell.

TYPES OF DOCUMENTARIES

There are several types of documentaries, much like there are genres for major motion pictures. One type is the **sports documentary**. Sports documentaries show the inside perspective of an athlete's life and struggles. ESPN does a very good job with these. I once saw a documentary about high school football culture in Texas. I have no interest in this subject whatsoever, but the documentary told a very interesting story. *Hoop Dreams* is a great documentary about two gentlemen who play basketball in the Chicago area and their attempts to make it to professional basketball. *When We Were Kings* is a documentary of the 1974 heavyweight championship bout in Zaire between George Foreman and Muhammad Ali. What a great *story* that one is. I am not a fan of boxing, but getting the chance to get inside the mind of a boxer is a thrilling experience, especially when Muhammad Ali is the protagonist. A documentary with a good story can make its audience appreciate more of what the protagonist of the story went through to achieve their will and want.

Next on the list is the **political documentary**. One popular example of a political documentary would be Michael Moore's *Fahrenheit 9-11*, which is about the attack on the World Trade Center in 2001. Another example would be Ed Murrow and Fred Friendly's *Harvest of Shame*, which is about migrant workers in the south in the early 1960s. These kinds of documentaries carry the potential to change a political system or social issue.

Another kind of documentary focuses on event or process. A recent worldwide example of this is Michael Jackson's *This is It*. It was about Jackson's creative process and how he rehearsed for his upcoming tour prior to his death.

Nature documentaries focus on life in the natural world. Jacques Cousteau was the first person to really get into this area. Cousteau invented the equipment used to dive underwater, and he made excellent nature documentaries. Recent examples of this kind of documentary would be *The March of the Penguins,* or *Planet Earth.*

Slice-of-life documentaries, as the name implies, are documentaries that give the audience some insight into someone else's every-day life. One of the first, most notable examples of this was the PBS documentary *An American Family,* which was created by Alan and Susan Raymond and aired in 1973. The 12-hour documentary series followed the daily life of an American family for seven months. A more recent example is the MTV series *True Life,* which follows subjects as they go through phases of their lives. Programs that are edited in a manipulative way to primarily entertain reflect an effort to capture the appeal of slice-of-life documentaries, but are not documentaries. Examples of these are *John and Kate Plus Eight, The Real World,* and *Jersey Shore.* Although I cannot say that I agree with MTV finding a bunch of borderline crazy people and putting them together in a house with eighty cameras filming 24 hours a day, *The Real World* has been successful in proving that people are interested in these kinds of quasi-documentary programs.

Although these are the main genres documentaries fall into, it is not uncommon to find a documentary that is a hybrid of multiple genres. For example, Al Gore's *An Inconvenient Truth* discusses political, social, and natural issues all within the same film. A documentary like this has the power to shift status quo assumptions about what is really an issue and what is not, along with increasing the public's awareness of the issues that really matter.

The popularity of documentaries has flourished since the invention of cable television. As soon as the amount of television channels began to increase, the number of documentaries aired on a regular basis increased as well. The History Channel and the Discovery Channel are examples of networks that play a lot of documentaries, as well as ESPN, which, as noted previously, plays sports documentaries. Also, the proliferation of technology is making the process of filming a documentary easier and easier by the year. In our day and age, almost anyone with a little camera and Microsoft Windows Movie Maker can make a documentary.

DRAMA AND DOCUMENTARIES

You must think dramatically when writing a documentary. Always consider your protagonist and their will or want. They will have complications that lead to a resolution in a climax. It is the same for documentary as for any other form of storytelling. You also need to make sure your documentary abides by the structural considerations: unity, variety, pace, and climax.

FROM TREATMENT TO SCRIPT

As stated earlier, documentary writing is a recursive process, meaning the writer makes more of a wishlist than an exact list of shots. After coming up with the wishlist, the next step is to write a short treatment of what you want to produce. A **treatment** is a synopsis of your idea for the film. Here is an example of a short proposal treatment:

> **"Picture This: A Fight to Save Joe"**
> A Righteous Production
> This riveting documentary, narrated by Danny Glover, draws viewers into the public battle to stop the execution of Joe Amrine, a Missouri man on death row for 17 years for a prison murder, despite there being neither witnesses nor evidence against him. This documentary traces advocate efforts to save Joe's life; the production and exhibition of Unreasonable Doubt: The Joe Amrine Story (a video documentary about Joe's case, trial, and torturous limbo); the public relations battle to attract attention to Joe's plight; and the precedent-setting Supreme Court case that resulted from the admirable efforts of an excellent and conscientious defense team. Influenced by "Thin Blue Line" (Errol Morris) with *cinema verite* qualities of "Bowling for Columbine," the startling and inspiring end of this documentary reveals the empowering potential of video, courageous legal representation, and the truth.

On your treatment, give a dramaturgical model summary identifying the protagonist and his or her will or want. Make sure that the pages are numbered, and that you include the latest draft date somewhere on the treatment. Use single-column page format to write out your story. You do not have to go into extreme detail; just make sure you get down the basic structure of the story. (See Final Project Treatment Example in the Appendix.)

When you are writing a wishlist for a documentary, ask yourself, "What shots do I wish I could get?" Then, go out and try to get them. Label the footage you gather as it appears in your storyline so that it is easier to find when you are ready to edit together the film. Once the wish list is made and all the possible shots have been gathered and edited together, watch the final product and make another wishlist of shots that can help bring the piece together better. In film, you write and you shoot. In documentary, you write, you shoot, you re-write, you re-shoot, you re-write and then you re-shoot until finally you tell the story the way you want it to be told.

Research

Like any other kind of writing, documentary writing requires you to do research. You will need to know more information than what will be included in the final version of the film so that you can choose the most effective way to tell the story. It is very important to figure out where the visual resources you need for the film are located. In terms of my documentary, Joe Amrine was about to be executed and two other prisoners admitted that they bore false witness against Amrine. When I finally found the tapes of those men recanting their testimony that implicated Amrine in the prison murder, the documentary came to life. I had to find those tapes and get permission to use them in my documentary. I searched all over to find out if there were photos of the murder location, or even press releases about the murder. Once I found enough visual resources, the documentary began to take shape, and I began to wonder how I could tell this story in the best way possible.

Before drafting the script for my documentary, further research was necessary. Sean O'Brien, Amrine's attorney, sent me a number of legal documents. I now had access to transcripts of depositions from other people involved in the trial, such as the prosecutor, additional witnesses, jurors, and O'Brien's legal motions. I then conducted an extensive media search about the case and found archived articles from local newspapers on the murder, trial, and sentencing. I also found a short piece about the trial published in *Newsweek* ("They're on Death Row," 2000), which was important because it featured a photograph of Amrine. I believed that a shot of the article in the documentary would add to our credibility, for if *Newsweek* had raised questions about the case, the general public, other activists, media personnel, and government officials might be inclined to think our position had merit.

In the pre-production stage, we also had to make arrangements to use whatever video footage was available and relevant to the case. For example, Jim Theabuat, a filmmaker in Kansas City, had footage of the Jefferson City Correctional Center, the prison facility where the murder happened, and footage of the Potosi State Correctional Center, the prison in which Amrine was being held. Theabuat even had footage of the room in which Amrine was to be executed. We solicited his help and he offered us the footage for inclusion in the documentary.

Visual Storytelling and Documentary Writing

One of the communicative powers of video is its ability to juxtapose images and sound. When a collection of shots are arranged in a deliberate and artful way, the result is a cumulative meaning and effect that transcends the individual images and sounds. In editing documentary, particularly in reality shows like *The Real World*, viewers never know if the two shots that are spliced together are from the same conversation or even the same day. Editing is very important because of this reason; the audience will fill in gaps if you miss them.

We used a computer-editing system to capture and label good shots that conveyed important information. The best shots were then slotted into the script using the label of the captured video clip. This labeling process makes editing relatively easy because the file names of the clips in the computer are the same names that are written into the script. Further development of the script then gives rise to what other shots are needed. In this case, after logging between 20-30 percent of the footage we had gathered, I crafted a general developmental plan for the documentary and placed the name of the captured video clips into the appropriate places in the script. As shots were slotted into the script, we became aware of additional shots and interviews that were needed. This necessitated further pre-production work, including conducting additional research (e.g., gathering interview contact information) and making arrangements for further interviews and shooting plans. Thus, the process was continually recursive.

USE OF B-ROLL

We also had a variety of b-roll shots written into the script that had yet to be filmed. **B-roll shots**, also called **inserts** or **cut-aways**, is video that can be used under a voice-over to help increase the visual variety within the story. Some of our b-roll shots included locations, maps and a few dramatic re-creations of actions. In the editing process, we would cut to these shots to visually reinforce the words being spoken, as well as provide some variety. Without those b-roll shots, the documentary would be constantly cutting to boring footage of talking heads from interviews.

LOGGING AND WRITING

When making a documentary, it is very important to pay attention to logging sheets. **Logging sheets** identify what footage or images are on the tapes that you shot. After you gather the footage you want, go through minute-by-minute, or even every 30 seconds, and write a logging sheet describing what happens throughout the footage. Above the descriptions, you will write dialogue or important soundbites. This way, you can put notes next to the good shots that you will want to use. You can also make a **Sound on Tape List** that has all the soundbites you would like to include. Time stamps can help you to identify what point in the tape that your SOT or shot comes from.

CHOICE OF INCLUSION AND EXCLUSION

When gathering shots for your documentary, make sure you get as much as you possibly can—always shoot more footage than you need. Documentaries *document* things as they happen. This can, unfortunately, lead to some legal issues.

While shooting my documentary, I was also working full-time as a college professor. One day, I got a call that the Supreme Court was hearing Joe's case. However, I had to teach class that day and decided not to go and shoot. That trial ended up being the trial where they overturned his death sentence. Considering how much of an impact that trial had on my documentary, I should have been there to film it. Fortunately for me, a local TV network did get footage. However, when I asked them for the footage, they said they would have to talk to their legal team. This bothered me, as I had been letting them use *my* footage for several months, so I told them I would have to talk to my legal team and see if I needed to sue them for not paying me. They responded, "Come on in, we'll give you that footage!"

The night they announced that Joe was being released from prison, I was in Normal, Illinois, and Joe was in Columbia, Missouri. I got in my car and drove all the way there through the night. I needed that money shot of my protagonist walking out of prison. Even cooler than that, afterward I drove Joe from Columbia to Kansas City, Missouri, where his family was. I was able to get footage of him getting out of the van and walking toward his family. I needed that shot; there is no way I could have ever re-created that moment in my documentary. I just had to be there. Like I said before, documentaries *document* events as they happen. As a maker of a documentary film, you need to make it a priority to *be there* to capture those powerful glimpses of reality.

WRITING NARRATION

There are some other things to consider when making a documentary. Try to use soundbites when you can; they help break up the amount of narration and add variety. Also, **try to minimize your narration**. In *Saving Joe Amrine*, Danny Glover did the final voice-over narration, however I had my colleague Dr. Lippert doing scratch tracks of that narration dozens of times. **Scratch-tracks**, in terms of narration, are when you record run-throughs of the narration to make sure it sounds alright when read.

One issue to consider with narration is that, if you are not careful, the voice-over may come off sounding like the all-knowing voice of God. When scripting a narration, make sure that the voice-over does not simply give the audience the answer, or that it is simply telling the audience how to feel about the situation. We want the audience to decide for themselves what the message is through the use of carefully selected soundbites and images. We want the audience to hear both sides of the story, and to come to a conclusion all by themselves.

DRAMATIC RE-CREATION

Dramatic re-creation has the potential to spark ethical issues. Some documentaries include footage of a dramatic interpretation of an event that the documentary maker did not actually witness—I would recommend that you avoid using these as much as possible.

There has been some controversy over the inclusion of dramatic re-creation in documentary (see, e.g., Walters, 1994), and out of this controversy arose cinéma vérité. **Cinéma vérité** is a style of documentary film making that emphasizes the use of actualities instead of interpretation; it places value on footage that captures reality, rather than footage that captures a *representation* of reality. This new style of documentary making has lessened the use of director reconstructions in our current day and age (Bruzzi, 2006). In view of this controversy, we decided to keep such re-creations to a minimum in our documentary—including only two small clips of re-created events. The first clip was of a weapon we crafted that met the exact specifications of the murder weapon as described in court documents. We included a shot of this re-creation when the weapon was mentioned. The second clip involved dramatically re-creating prison officials destroying the original testimony from the witnesses. These two instances did not distort the narrative in any way, but added valuable visualizations to two important aspects of the case.

DOCUMENTARY VIDEO AND PUBLIC RELATIONS

Once you finally have your documentary completed, it may be in your best interest to offer your footage to a local television network. TV networks love to use footage that they did not have to leave the studio to get. Many times, like in the documentary I worked on, you will have footage of many different people discussing the topic your documentary is about. By giving them access to all that footage, you are giving the media all the soundbites and footage they need to run a story. If you make a documentary, you might reach 500 or 1,000 people if you are lucky. However, if a television news program runs a story about your documentary, hundreds of thousands of people can potentially be exposed to your story. By capturing the attention of mass media outlets, you can vastly widen your viewer audience. A simple documentary film can be an effective catalyst to get a story heard. That is where documentary can be a part of effective public relations.

In this chapter we discussed the power of visual images, characteristics of documentaries, types of documentaries, drama in documentaries, development of a documentary from treatment to script, research, visual storytelling in documentaries, use of b-roll, logging documentary footage, choices of inclusion and exclusion, narration, dramatic re-creation, and the usefulness of documentaries in public relations. When writers write documentary film, they need to incorporate the dramaturgical approach while also making sure the film is clear, concise, correct, and complete.

CHAPTER 19:
FEATURE FILM WRITING

In the beginning, God created drama. Somehow, it is a universal notion that we understand how stories work and how they affect audience emotions. Thus, we continue to dissect drama. Whether we are film writers or television writers, aficionados or couch potatoes, we need to understand how to not only write, but **critically consume** films.

In this chapter we explore writing feature films. In order to cultivate critical consumption insight and prepare future dramatists, we discuss principles of drama, setting, genre, character, story design, and types of plots. The feature film writer needs to think as a dramatist, and, thus, needs to study the components of effective storytelling.

PRINCIPLES OF DRAMA

It is necessary to abstractly consider the elements of a good story when considering writing feature films, as with any other writing forms the mass media writer may encounter. It is, again, helpful to consider the dramatic model when writing feature films. First, in drama, there is a protagonist. A **protagonist** is a character who is driven by a goal. This is the person that makes decisions and acts in ways that move the story forward. The protagonist is a main character who, because of their choices resulting from their goal, actively moves the drama forward. Thus, the protagonist is motivated throughout the drama by a **will/want**, which is what the protagonist desires to achieve. The overall will/want is what the main character is trying to achieve whether it be external or subconscious. Sometimes there is an explicit, eternal and/or conscious will/want and sometimes it is more implicit, internal, and/or subconscious. The will/want often manifests through conflict. Flaws in the protagonist often contribute to the conflict. Drama is driven by the over-arching **dramatic question**, which is, "Will the protagonist achieve their will/want?"

The **realization** is the point at which the main character comprehends what they have to do to achieve their goals. A series of complications are another major component of an effective story. **Complications** are roadblocks to achieving the will/want. There is a point of **climax** toward the end of effective drama, or the point at which the tension related to the dramatic question is most acute. Finally, effective stories have a **resolution**. Resolution, or denouement, is the point at which things return to normalcy, albeit sometimes changed. Action falls, and some sort of stasis resumes. Writers must consider these dramatic principles when crafting effective stories.

As writers use the dramatic model to craft effective stories, however, they must be careful to avoid clichés. Too many movies are nothing but replicas of other movies. Some writers do not understand why a story is effective or ineffective, because they have not adequately studied the principles of solid drama. The problem here, according to Robert McKee, author of *Story: Substance, Structure, Style, and the Principles of Screenwriting*, is that writers do not know the setting and background information of their story in-depth. This is why, when approaching writing for feature film, we need to start with the film's setting. McKee's iteration of dramatic concepts is an important source of many of the ideas outlined in this chapter.

SETTING

Setting is the location and/or time period of the story. Thoroughly understanding a story's setting helps present the writer with all possible options and limitations of a story. Writing is about choices; in order to write well, the writer must make good choices. When the writer has stronger grasp of their setting, the more options they have for making strong dramaturgical choices.

Setting can be thought of in terms of a four-dimensional landscape. The first of these dimensions is a story's **period**, or the time frame in which the story takes place. In the recent television series *Breaking Bad*, the story takes place in present-day. It is about the trials and tribulations of a chemistry teacher who begins to cook and sell crystal meth. In contrast, the period that the television series *Young Victoria* takes place in is the early 1800s. This series talks about the English aristocracy and Queen Victoria's life. Obviously, the periods in which both of these shows take place are not the same, and thus, they both uniquely influence the resulting dramatic action in each show.

Duration is the second dimension of setting. When we say duration in film writing, we are referring to the period of time over which we follow the character in their story. In a film like *Nixon*, the story encompasses Nixon's entire life—from his birth to the end of his presidency. However, in a film like *Memento*, the entire story happens over only a few days. In the television show *24*, as its name suggests, each episode is supposed to represent one hour in a 24-hour period.

The third dimension of setting is **location**. Location is where the story literally takes place. For example, the location of the setting might be the streets of Miami, like in *Scarface*, or it might be in a galaxy far, far away, like in *Star Wars*. Location tells us where, geographically, the drama is located.

The fourth dimension of setting is the **level of conflict**. The level of conflict is where on the scale of human endeavor the story lies. Think of the comedy *Dude, Where's My Car?* The ultimate conflict that takes place is very low on the level of human conflict and endeavor when compared to *Schindler's List*, which is about good and evil on some level that is historically epic. In other words, where on the hierarchy of human struggle does the story reside? If I tell you a story about not being able to find my office keys for the last few days, people might consider that story's level of conflict to be low. However, if you tell a story about the starvation in the world or genocide in Rwanda, people might consider the level of conflict to be high on the scale of human endeavors. Often times, films or stories occur on several levels of conflict at once. *Up in the Air* is originally about one man's quest to accumulate material wealth, but by the end of the film, he realizes that material goods are not what make him happy. Thus, the level of conflict is raised because the story grows to address an overlying or greater idea. What separates cookie-cutter, unsatisfying movies from true drama is the ability to tell a good story and work within some overlying psychosocial issue. When choosing a setting for your story, always consider the four dimensions of setting: period, duration, location, and level of conflict.

We now turn from setting to the relationship between setting and structure. A story must obey **internal laws of probability**. The story must follow the rules of the universe the writer has created. For example, imagine that the duration of a story is only supposed to be a few days, and the generally clean-shaven main character suddenly appears with a full beard. Using the internal laws of probability of that story, we can determine that the main character is in disguise, he contracted some sort of super-fast-hair-growing virus, or the writer is being inconsistent with duration. In *Young Victoria*, Queen Victoria cannot pull out her BlackBerry and text a friend. *Breaking Bad* provides a very good example of internal probability. This story takes place in a town near a desert. The desert becomes very important to the story when the main character and his partner use an old Winnebago to drive to an abandoned spot in the desert and cook crystal meth. They have no water, and the battery dies. In a story like this, the location largely affects the story structure, the drama and the choices the main character is able to make. Your story must obey its internal laws of probability. These conventions, chosen by the writer, dictate every subsequent aspect of the story we have mentioned, from setting to conflict.

In his book, McKee talks about what he calls the **principle of creative limitations**. The principle of creative limitations says that the smaller the world a writer chooses to write about, the more knowledgeable of that world a writer can be. Good dramas generally have writers who know their story's world inside out, and thus, have a thorough understanding of the elements that might affect their drama. In *Pulp Fiction*, it is apparent that the writer, Quentin Tarantino, knows things about those characters that we as the audience may never see within the film. When writing the story, Tarantino had to know more about the characters than would appear in the finished film. Tarantino had to know enough to be able to make choices.

When writing the award-winning *Up in the Air*, the author of the novel (Walter Kirn), and eventually the writer of the screenplay (Jason Reitman), had to know more about the world of high-class travel than they would ever explicitly say in the film. They had to know that flying 10 million miles is almost an urban legend in the travel business. They had to know that once you reach that many miles, you get your name painted on the side of a plane, dinner with the captain, a special flying card, etc. They needed to know these things about the main character's world so that these events could affect the story structure and dramatic action. The writers had never been in this fictitious world, but the result is that the film feels very real. The minutiae in the choices the writers make are what create a "real" fictional world. If you create a world that is believable, you can break the war on clichés and create a story that seems completely true. However, in order to create this narrative fidelity, a writer's first step is to do **research**.

Research Methods

Some of the concepts on research discussed in Chapter 3 on the writing process are worth mentioning and applying to feature film writing. The first type of research is from **memory**. Think to yourself, "Have I ever been in this situation?" In *Up in the Air*, the writers had to think, "Have I ever waited in an airport? Have I ever gotten drunk in a hotel bar?" This can inform your writing. Memory is a primary source of research.

The second type of research is asking, **"what if?"** Here is where the writer asks herself, "What if I lived my entire life traveling on an airplane? What would it be like? What kind of shoes would I wear?" This can help a writer imagine specific elements of the setting that can be used in the drama.

This leads to the third level of research: **fact**. Here is where the writer may ask people who travel frequently what kind of shoes they wear, or what type of luggage they would want.

You might even want to talk to people who run airport security or counters at the airlines. I am specifically considering the scene where George Clooney's character talks about the different types of people who go through airport security; families, tourist groups, old people ("They have more metal in their bodies then we will ever carry around."), etc. While telling this aspect of the story, the writers could have gotten this information through talking to people that have done a lot of traveling.

To reiterate the main point, writers have to know more about their stories than they will ever actually use. By knowing more than the mere necessities, a writer can make creative choices about what to include or exclude in a story. This is how a writer can break clichés. Good drama loses its appeal when it lacks authenticity, and so to give it fidelity, a writer must make good choices.

GENRE

In writing film and television, we must think about other elements that affect setting. **Genre** is the type of story. Like setting, genre also affects the structure of the story and the choices the writer makes, another element that affects how the action unfolds. Stories within a genre share elements that can be used to categorize those stories. There are many types of genres: love stories, epics, war films, maturation plots, crimes, social dramas, action-adventures, docu-dramas, teen comedies, redemption stories, etc. Some of the best stories are those that incorporate **redemption stories**. Here, the main character or characters must learn a lesson to redeem their character. *Slumdog Millionaire* is an example of a film with a moving redemption sub-plot.

There are now even hybrid genres like the "mockumentary," a film made to look like a documentary that is really a comedy. *The Office*, both the British and American versions, take mockumentary to a television level, but one of the most popular film examples would be Rob Reiner's *This is Spinal Tap*. Some of these genres come from theater and literature, like the musical or the tragic drama, but some are new. Science fiction, animation, and art film are all newer genres.

The important part about genre is that you must understand the relationship between genre and structure. Roles, events, values, and issues that compose a given genre must be mastered before a writer can write in that genre. When the audience walks into the theater, they have expectations about what your film will be according to its genre. When I first saw the preview for *Seven* with Brad Pitt and Morgan Freeman, I thought it was a love story. Let me say: while *Seven* is a great film, it might not be the best movie to take a date to. Very good writers will know the rules of the genre and then start to break them. *Punch Drunk Love* is another example of a film that breaks the generic conventions of the love story genre in order to tell a good story. Genre will influence your choices. Horror films, for example, have certain conventions. At one point, the good guys will usually separate, go through hard times, scream a bunch, be found by the bad guy and then get picked off one at a time until the protagonist either overcomes the killer or dies. However, we do have freedom within genres.

I once wrote a film about a haunted theater. Before I started writing it, I wanted to find other films within this genre. First, I watched *Poltergeist*, and minute-by-minute, I broke down the action in order to understand the generic conventions of the genre. Then, I watched *The Shining*, which is about a haunted hotel, and I did the same thing. I then found an Italian film called *Demons* about demons that take over a theater, and I watched and broke-down that story. After this, I briefly understood the parameters I had to work with. It helped me understand the different foundations underlying the horror genre, and thus helped guide me through the making of unique choices. By identifying genre parameters, writers can better understand their choices and decide which options to utilize.

Within the action-adventure genre, the main character, often a hero or heroine, must be at the mercy of the villain at some point in the film. Then when the heroine is trapped by the villain, the villain delivers... can you guess it? A monologue! The villain has to have a monologue once he catches the hero. There is always a point in which that exact monologue is the opportunity the hero is looking for to escape. Even in *The Good, the Bad, and the Ugly*, a famous spaghetti western, there is a point where the main character is in the bath tub when he is caught by the villain. The hero uses the opportunity to shoot the villain with a gun hidden under the bath bubbles. Likewise, in *The Incredibles*, the villain is about to give away the key to his plot and then suddenly stops, claiming that he has seen the way all villain-hero movies end, refusing to give up his secret until the hero is at last dead.

Writers can also mix genres. Some films are several genres in one story, and that can be helpful in the circle of opportunities as well. However, you are not promised a good story in doing this. *Funny People*, a film by Judd Apatow starring Adam Sandler, was some sort of mix between a comedy, a drama, and a death-experience plot that really did not blend very well. The film did not know what genre it wanted to be, and the end result dragged on with very little climax. Apatow also wrote *The 40-Year Old Virgin* and *Superbad*, two of the best recent comedies, but *Funny People* did not seem to know enough about any of the genres to make the blended story work well. The bottom line is that the dramatist needs to learn to work within generic conventions so they can carefully and decisively break them. It takes so long to write a good story that you must love the work. Pick a genre that you enjoy, because writing requires the skill of endurance. If you like what genre you work in, you will be able to better master the genre.

Just as jazz musicians need to first know musical theory before they can break conventions and create jazz, writers need to understand what is expected of a genre before they can determine how to make their story stand out from the rest. When writers play with genre conventions, they tell good stories. Once writers recognize generic conventions, they know how to break the common pattern and surprise the audience.

It is important to note that the writer will not always get exactly what they want out of the finished film or show. In particular, if the writer options the story, then they have very little control over the finished product. Tarantino wrote the screenplay for *Natural Born Killers*; however, he had no control over the final product of the film. He ended up extremely unhappy with the final film and asked that his name be taken off the story. What was written and what was shot told two completely different stories. At that point in time, the film was out of his hands.

Advertising can also throw off a writer's vision. Have you ever seen a film where the preview is nothing like the film? Again, *Seven* sold itself as a kind of love story, when, actually, it was kind of a pre-cursor to the *Saw* series. Sometimes advertisers take liberties in selling a story that does not reflect the writer's vision. The only way the writer is guaranteed that the final product will match their vision is if they are also the director; but even then, the producer or the studio still has the power to make changes and take creative control. This is why you want to make sure you at least attempt to work with people who share a similar vision. Filmmaking is a collaborative effort; many people go into the creation of a finished film. As a writer, you can try to work with others that share your vision, but understand that it may not happen.

CHARACTER

In writing film, we must understand the difference between character and characterization. **Character** is defined by the choices made by the main character under pressure. In contrast, **characterization** is the sum of the traits of the character, such as how old they are or what their educational background is. Real character is defined by choices made and actions taken under pressure. Like McKee says, "The difference between a good choice and a bad choice is a not choice at all. We want competing good choices or competing bad choices." In *The Empire Strikes Back*, Luke Skywalker faces a dilemma: go with his father and rule the universe, or commit suicide. This is one of the many ultimatums that reveal his true character. Luke ends up attempting to commit suicide and lives, but since he did not know he was going to live, the choice he made tells us about his character.

Character unveils gradually over the course of a story. Ultimately, our goal is to create dramatic dilemmas that reveal the true character of the protagonist. A **character arch** is how the character comes to know themselves throughout the dramatic complications. In *Star Wars*, when we meet Luke, he is really quite cowardly as he is whining about picking up power converters. However, when he meets Obi-Wan after his aunt and uncle die, he gets sucked into a dramatic dilemma which ultimately results in him choosing to blow up the Death Star or not. Luke's character changes throughout the story in the character arch. The function of structure is to put the character in the situations that will teach the character to grow. Therefore, the climax is not only the point at which the dramatic tension is highest, but also the moment at which the pressure on the main character is so great that their truest character is revealed. Choices are structured with the most acute choices occurring in the climax. The last act is critical, which is why we always save the best for last.

Aristotle and the ancient Greeks debated about whether the plot is more important than the character, or vice versa. The whole point of structure is to increase the pressure on the main character so that they will make choices. Likewise, their choices determine structure. It is an artificial dichotomy; they are the same thing. Structure influences character development, and character development decides structure.

The meaning of a story should come out of its structure. Generally, the meaning of a story is found either in the dialogue, in a soliloquy by the main character or the structure of the drama itself. The story should have a universal moral, and thus, the main message is going to be in the structure.

The second part of this chapter will cover the dramatic breakdown of film, although many of the dramatic principles also apply to television writing. We will focus on the concepts of terminology, story design, archplot, miniplot, antiplot, the story triangle, formal differences within the story triangle, and the politics of story design.

STORY DESIGN

Drama is a series of events that has story values. **Story events**, or major plot points, are when major things happen that can change the direction of the drama. As we look at a whole story, we see units of dramatic development, along with leads. **Leads** are a change in dynamics of a given scene. A **sequence** is a series of scenes put together that are some element of a unit. Most films have a **three-act structure**, contrary to most television dramas that are found in four because of commercial breaks. The consolidation of all the leads within the scenes, all the scenes within the sequences and all the sequences within the acts, ultimately form the story of a film.

In the traditional three-act structure, the writer sets up the story, establishes the major will or want, and posits the first major plot point in the first act (approximately 18 to 28 minutes long). A **plot point,** or **inciting incident,** is an event that changes the direction of the story. For example, in *The Social Network*, the inciting incident occurs when Zuckerberg creates Facebook. The most important plot points are story events. In the second act (from approximately 25 minutes into the film to 70 to 90 minutes into a film), the protagonist faces the bulk of the complications or obstacles. There is usually another major plot point at the end of the second act, and often the protagonist achieves a conscious will or want, only to discover the achievement of this conscious will or want does not offer true satisfaction, but that there is a subconscious desire that has yet to be pursued. In the third act (usually the last third or fourth of the film), the protagonist either achieves or fails to achieve the will or want in a climax, and then the story is resolved. This three-act structure is found in most feature films, although a few films follow other structures, such as one-act structures (*Mean Streets*), two-act structures (*Full Metal Jacket*), four-act structures or five act structures. Nevertheless, the three-act structure provides a way to understand and craft traditional arch-plot dramas.

Whenever we think about a film, we need to remember to think in terms of drama. Again, the **protagonist** is someone that makes the decisions and moves the story forward through the decisions they make. In terms of the movie *Up in the Air*, George Clooney's character is the protagonist who has a will and want—something he desires. In good drama, we have an apparent will and want which is what the main character believes they consciously desire. Usually in good drama, the protagonist realizes somewhere before the second or third act that what they thought they wanted is not really what they need. It is similar to when you were a child and wanted a toy for Christmas. You really wanted that Transformer, and if you could get that Transformer your whole life would be complete. Then Christmas finally comes and you get the crappy plastic Transformer that falls apart two hours after you get it, and you realize that your life was not going to be changed by the Transformer like you thought it would be. Often times in drama, the main character thinks they want something and they work toward getting it, only to realize how hollow of a goal it is when they get it at the end of the second act. For example, after Dorothy finds herself over the rainbow in *Wizard of Oz*, she finds the experience terrifying. Dorothy changes her mind and declares, "There's no place like home."

When the main character has a will and want, this desire usually leads to an inevitable major dramatic question that is either answered in the affirmative or negative. The will and want of George Clooney's character is to accumulate ten million miles. The first complication to this will and want, or **plot point**, usually happens about twenty minutes into the film. In terms of *Up in the Air*, the first plot point is that he is going to be grounded, and it looks like his job may end. Suddenly, our dramatic premise is set up.

Always think back to the dramatic model and the four structural considerations. **Unity** is the way that everything ends up together in a whole. **Pace** is the rate at which the drama unfolds. **Variety** is when things change up in order to keep our interest while the story moves forward. **Climax** is the point at which the tension relation to the dramatic question is most acute. The dramatist should always consider these structural considerations when crafting their story.

TYPES OF PLOTS

When McKee talks about plot, he defines it as a verb rather than a noun. It is to navigate through the possibilities, and to choose the correct path. Writing is all about making choices. The writer is making decisions about what is going to happen to the main character. The reason that the story triangle exists is because there is an absolute archplot, an absolute miniplot, and an absolute antiplot. Often times stories are somewhere inside that triangle rather than being one definitive plot type.

An **archplot** is the classic design where a protagonist actively struggles against the forces of antagonism to pursue a desire through consistent time, with consistent causality, in a fictional reality that culminates in an absolute and irreversible change. In the film *The Hangover*, around the twenty-minute mark, the plot the characters find themselves in is that their friend Doug is gone. From that point on, they struggle against the forces of antagonism to try and find their friend Doug before his wedding in two days. Another example of an archplot is the film *Rudy*. In this film, the protagonist, Rudy, is struggling against the antagonistic force of getting to play on Notre Dame's football team.

Different from an archplot, a **miniplot** is more internal. A miniplot often features a character who is struggling against him or herself to achieve something. An example of this would be in the film *Crazy Heart* where Jeff Bridges' character struggles internally with his alcoholism and his relationship with his family. **Antiplot** is a way to expose the conventions related to an archplot. An example of this would be the film *Adaption*, because it shows us the conventions as they work in a regular plot. Another example would be *Monty Python and the Holy Grail*, in which King Arthur is arrested at the end by modern day cops. *Psycho* is another movie that plays with conventions in the sense that it starts the story with a protagonist. The audience followed the protagonist for thirty-five minutes. Then, suddenly and unexpectedly, the protagonist is stabbed to death. The shock value is so powerful because it turns convention on its head.

One formal difference is that stories can have either a **closed ending** or an **open ending**. In most conventional dramas, we have closed endings. An example would be when Rudy finally gets to play for Notre Dame. In antiplots or miniplots, it is more likely that there will be some questions that are answered, but some that are not. In our day and age, open endings sometimes mean a sequel is in store, though some films just leave the audience wondering what happens next. For example, *No Country for Old Men* and *There Will Be Blood* are films that end with some plot themes open. This allows room for an artistic experience as the consciousness of the audience members fills in the blanks.

Another difference is the concept of an **external** or an **internal** conflict. In the film *Clash of the Titans*, Peruses has to fight against external forces to get the head of Medusa and kill the dragon in order to save his love. An internal conflict is when a character is struggling with their own self-conscious fears, doubts and demons, such as in *Black Swan*, *A Beautiful Mind*, or *Shutter Island*.

Stories can have **single** or **multiple protagonists**. Traditionally in archplots, we have a single character that fights against a number of antagonists, but increasingly we see more ensemble-like dramas such as *Syriana*, *Crash Traffic*, *Love Actually*, or *The Lord of the Rings*, that tend to be more miniplots with multiple characters.

Another difference within the story triangle is an **active protagonist** versus a **passive protagonist**. Most protagonists want to do something to make something happen. Tony Montana from *Scarface* wants to get the money to get the power to get the women, and he will do whatever he has to do to achieve that. In more internal or antiplot dramas, we often have characters that just want to be left alone. An example of a passive protagonist is the main character in Scorsese's *After Hours*, Adam Sandler's character in *Punch Drunk Love,* or the Dude in *Big Lebowski*. The rare instance of the Dude actively doing something is when he went to the other Lebowski to try and get the other Lebowski to pay for the damaged rug. In the rest of the film *The Big Lebowski* the Dude is passive in that people seem to do things to him that move the story forward. (The rug really brought the room together.) The passive protagonist merely wants things to remain the same, but circumstances threaten their status quo.

Stories can have plots that are either **linear** or **nonlinear.** Films that have a starting point and go through time chronologically as it would happen in reality are considered linear. Sometimes, films will break that convention and tell a story in a non-chronological way. Examples of nonlinear films include *Memento* or *Twenty One Grams*. The stories are told in a non-sequential order, yet somehow the story is brought together by the end.

Causality versus coincidence is also a demarcation point between plot types. In traditional archplot drama, somebody does something because of something else that happened, and often times the main character takes this action hoping for a desired result only to find that the opposite happens. This normally starts a chain of doing something for a desired end and then something else happens. In miniplots or antiplots, major plot points often occur just by coincidence. Examples of movies that rely on coincidence are *Punch Drunk Love*, *The Big Lebowski,* and *Burn After Reading*. In *Burn After Reading*, McDermott's character and Clooney's character meet through single ads online, yet their stories are completely intertwined. It is as if there is an element of causality, yet two of the protagonists meet by total coincidence.

Consistent versus inconsistent plot is another characteristic dichotomy of plot types. Examples of movies with an inconsistent plot would be *Donnie Darko* and *Mulholland Drive*. They all incorporate an inconsistent reality that are like levels of a dream, and are often hard to completely comprehend. Inconsistent plots are much more common in an antiplot-based story.

Is the protagonist seeking **Change** or attempting to maintain **Stasis**. In most classic drama, the protagonist is fighting to change things. In *Schindler's List*, the desire is to save the people. In *The Lord of the Rings*, the desire is to destroy the ring. Rocky wants to be the champion, and Rudy, a lower-middle-class kid from Joliet, wants to play football for Notre Dame. All the protagonists change the world they live in.

There are few more basic areas of consideration when beginning to understand how to write a good feature film. First, the central message of the film should be revealed in the overall story, not in pedantic dialogue from the characters. When individual members of the audience understand the message at the cognitive and emotive levels, it creates meaningful, sometimes profound, artistic experiences, or epiphanies. A visual imagery system, or the use of particular pictorial motifs with symbolic meaning value, can be incorporated to reinforce the central theme of the plot of a story. Sub-plots can also add support or provide idiomatic juxtaposition to the central theme.

Consistent with this is the idea that character dialogue should be indirect, as is conversation in real life. Dialogue should be natural, and not too on-the-nose. Often, there is subtext to many conversations. If the writer does not create room for actors to animate meanings between the spoken lines, the actors may invent a subtext the writer never intended.

In addition, the dramatist must aim at creating dramatic gaps on the micro- and macro levels. A dramatic gap is the difference of what a character (and the audience) expects what will result from an action and what actually occurs. The gap, then, is between what is subjectively anticipated and what objectively occurs. This is the locus of the beginning of dramatic situations. Significant dramatic gaps create major plot points between acts and small gaps that create beat shifts within scenes.

The bottom line is that, as a writer, we need to know the classical form before we break the rules. As with generic conventions, writers need to master the classical form before they can venture away from it. On the other hand, writers should adhere to script format conventions, which are explained in Chapter 13. The script may start as a synopsis (50 words to a couple of pages) of an idea, be developed into a detailed outline, before the writer builds a treatment, which is a scene-by scene narrative description of the entire story and may run from 5 to 80 pages. Use of note cards each containing the details of particular scenes can also be a useful tool in this process.

As writers, we need to believe in what we write. You will spend so much time in front of that blinking curser on the white screen that you had better choose to write about a subject you care about. Since you will spend a lot of time researching and writing, you have to make sure your heart is in it. In this chapter we explored writing feature films. Thus, we discussed principles of drama, setting, genre, character, story design, and types of plots. A good story is a good story, whether from the time of *Antigone* and *Oedipus Rex* to today. By breaking down drama and dramatic characteristics, you will know what makes a good story good, whether you are seeing it on the big screen or writing it yourself. Aspiring writers should dare to dream about where their writing can take them. When Quentin Tarantino wrote his first script, he was working at a video store. When Oliver Stone wrote the academy-award winning *Platoon*, he was driving a taxi. They dared to dream, as should all aspiring writers. Quality writing, consideration of structural considerations, and story-telling craft can open many doors for a committed and willing communicator. The voyage of a thousand miles begins with one step.

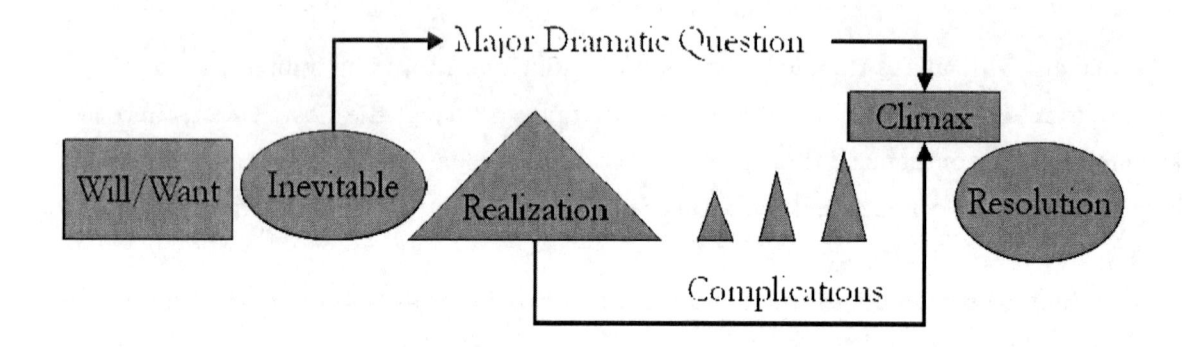

CHAPTER 20: SOCIAL MEDIA

Every journey, be it a small one or one of a thousand miles, starts with one individual step. Buddha suggested this, although it was also used in the stop-motion Christmas classic *Santa Claus is Coming to Town*: put one foot in front of the other, and soon you'll be walking out the door. When you started this text, you may have known very little about media writing; this might even have been your first college writing class. But hopefully, throughout this text, you have embarked on the journey of becoming a better writer. Our journey is now almost complete, but not before we understand writing. Our journey has nearly run its course, but not before we learn to write for developing technologies and social networking.

As we begin to discuss how new media evolves with technology, it is helpful to review the basics of good writing. Today, the question on the minds of every corporation is: How can we monetize advancements and present our messages through mobile phones, websites, tweets, and other status updates? It should come as no surprise that, ultimately, these corporations are seeking to make a profit using new forms of mass media. But what does this mean to you?

What it means is that when you are able to apply the basic considerations of good writing and storytelling for new forms of social media, you will have skills that will be profitable and valuable in the marketplace. Mobile communication is going to continue to grow, and in the meantime, the entire mindset of how Americans consume news media is changing along side. We are moving from an information age to a conceptualization age. At this point, I cannot help but to think about Neil Postman's book *Amusing Ourselves to Death*, where he essentially prophesized that not only are mediums of communication changing, but that these changes are also altering the way we think and view the world It could be said, then, that part of this shift may be teaching us to write more concisely, as that is what writing for web requires. Last year, web advertisement surpassed the budget for traditional advertisement for the first time in media history. What that should tell you is that media is changing, and you as a writer need to be prepared to change with it.

The publishing model has also changed. Books have changed. What used to be pamphlets are now antiquated. What used to be a media release is now anachronistic. Your audiences now want web and mobile offerings of all the content they have come to know.

WRITING FOR THE WEB

At this point in our media history, the Internet is ubiquitous and inescapable. When we consider writing for new media, we must consider Internet and web publication first. Companies frequently market products through the Internet; however, the web also hosts content sites for any imaginable interest. Content sites are those that offer bulk information and media. However you also have text-setup outlets online such as Norton or Microsoft Support. These software sites send instant update notification through Internet browsers and smart phones. Most of the time they do both. You need to be prepared as a writer in this technological world to write for the interface of such ideas. The web undergoes constant change—it used to be only HTML text. Now it is mostly Java text, which enables more simple access and design. Despite these changes, quality writing is quality writing, and we need to always adhere to the basic principles of good writing.

WRITING FOR SOCIAL MEDIA

Social media are those forms that allow people to gather together electronically. How many of us logged onto Facebook in the last five days? Who did *not* log on? If you did not log on, good for you. The rest of us are addicted to it. Although none of us seem to be resistant to Facebook, believe it or not, most corporations are. Facebook, Twitter, and YouTube allow users to gather together electronically as communities of people. People used to only gather socially in the traditional face-to-face sense, and now we can do so at any point in time with anyone in the world digitally. Social media empowers those desiring to gather together online, and facilitates the ways in which we can do this. Though they were initially apprehensive about social networking, many corporations are now making the push to incorporate these media into their daily public relations efforts. You may not like the "like" button, but the point is one-way communication in the mass media is dying, if not dead already. There are entire careers now for people whose sole responsibility is to run the social networking accounts for companies and individuals. An ISU alum and former Writing for the Mass Media instructor, now runs State Farm's social networking accounts. That's all he does. And they pay him a small ransom to do so.

Word-of-mouth advertising is still very important to audiences, and this is reflected in social media. Interactions about companies, products, events, albums, or films are shared thousands of times per minute online between friends. We still trust our friends, even if we do not trust corporations. A good example of this is expectant or new mothers. It is common for mothers to search on Google for a good or service in which they may be interested, and blogs related to motherhood are numerous. Recently, several corporations were caught paying fake bloggers to hype products. Social networking allows this interaction and sharing to occur. Also, social media is now taking a front-row spot in crisis-management utility. Using the web, a celebrity, company, or product producer can attempt to repair their image almost instantly after the scandal occurs. Customers and audiences can also interact and share information instantaneously, which is also a powerful downside to social media. This is why businesses are increasingly committed to the use of social networking. It has gotten to the point where the social networking pages of companies and celebrities act almost as a kind of advertisement for the entity itself. After all, where would Charlie Sheen be without his Facebook page? Increasingly, social networking is becoming our link to popular culture such as music, television programs, and films.

Much like television audiences, which are not decreasing in numbers but rather, fractionalizing into audiences with more specified needs, social networking and writing for the web are increasingly segmented as well. Therefore, who we reach as mass media writers becomes about *quality* of the audience (how interested they are in what I have to offer) versus *quantity* of the audience (how many people I am reaching). The upside is that you as an audience member get to join in the fun. For example, if you are my friend through social networking and I communicate about a film, you can then share that film with me, which directly effects whether I go see that film or not. This is a wonderful example of how traditional media forms (motion pictures, advertisement) can be supported with new media forms such as social networking (Facebook, Twitter). You may have smaller audiences, but they are audiences that will build in their own suggestions, their own sharing, and their own culture of advertising the idea.

When you are writing for social media, you are writing for your audience to build and create their own fun. Of course, it is always about *telling a good story*. It is about authentic connection. It should feel like "the real thing" when we are using social media to connect. Therefore, if you use social media to write for a corporation or organization, you should still seek to keep a human face on the project.

WRITING FOR TWITTER

Given the fundamental purpose of Twitter and its media characteristics, writing for this media must be of the utmost brevity. You only have 140 characters. The Senior Software

Officer for *The New York Times* suggests that sites like Twitter help news organizations find out *who* is consuming their news and what they want from their consumption. At the most basic level, Twitter is a marketing tool that helps users keep abreast of what friends and interesting parties are doing. For news organizations, Twitter is a resource for publishing work, finding what people are interested in, to communicate with other journalists, and to find story ideas. *The New York Times, The Sentinel, The L.A. Times, The Patagonian,* are all using Twitter to post their news headlines on sports, traffic, business, etc. Audiences can read these updates via smart phone, instant message, or social media sharing. So, why would a news organization that you work for want you to use Twitter? Because Twitter communication is easy, it is free, and it does not take much time to create.

WRITING FOR MOBILE COMMUNICATION

This leads us up to the discussion on writing for mobile consumption. Even though the United States is three years behind the rest of the world in this area, 2011 was a watershed year for mobile communications. As the electronic marketplace becomes more prominent the only way to reach the millennial generation is through mobile devices. There were more smart phones in 2011 than there were regular cell phones and traditional phones. Very soon there will be more PC activity on mobile devices than on actual PCs. In 2010 there were more Google searches on mobile phones than on personal computers. Mobile devices are becoming a major mass media outlet. Regardless of the media outlet, we should tell a good story, engage in effective practices of quality writing, and reflect structural consideration.

STORYTELLING AND QUALITY WRITING

The first big concern is that no matter what we are writing for the web, we have to tell a good story. Initially this causes us to consider our audience. We must know who we are trying to reach. We have to make the audience care. One way to achieve that is by personalizing a story or putting a human face on the subject. Whatever medium on the web, be it Twitter, Facebook, or Mobisodes we want to tell a good story. To connect with people, you must create content that moves them. Even if it's the caveman telling the story of how he brought the antelope back to the cave, he wants to tell a good story. When we want to share a Twitter post about new software that enables us to do our work more effectively, we want to tell a good story. Writers must connect to the audience in an engaging way, which goes back to the principles of effective storytelling.

The key is developing empathy. Why does the audience care about the people involved in this story? This concept applies to new media just as it does traditional media. It is storytelling ability that will allow you to survive and thrive in the new media with consideration of particular aspects of each other individual platform. In the final analysis, it is about the story. Whether it's a cave painting, making a silent film, putting on a play, or posting a message on Facebook or Twitter, we want to tell a good story and have that story reflect some truth. Always craft your story with a protagonist that has a will or want, who faces complication and at some moment either succeeds or doesn't, with a return to some kind of stasis or resolution. Another big key is to reflect quality writing in whatever you write and as always the most important consideration when writing for mass media is **clarity**.

CLARITY

We need to be clear no matter what we are writing. When it comes to web pages we must consider what is best for the audience, not the designers of the web page. In talking about clarity for web pages, a very important consideration is ease of navigation. Your page must be easy to navigate with an accessible options menu and links to other pages. It should also be very easy to get back to that home page, because nothing is more frustrating than following links and then you are unable to navigate back to the home page. A sitemap may also be a good option to ensure clarity. There can be flash and graphic effects, but the most important consideration for a web page is always going to be the content or the message.

Expressed in earlier chapters, we talked about theoretical considerations in mass media; the message is premier no matter what medium we are using. When writing for the web page, the same considerations we talked about for other mediums apply. We have to make action sequences clear. We want to avoid jargon by using everyday language. Avoid nomenclature that is used by a specialized audience. We steer clear of this by using familiar words that are understood by a large general audience. We should use abbreviations sparingly when we write for the web because abbreviations cans be confusing. We don't to assume the audience knows what the abbreviations mean; rather, we want to make it clear what the abbreviations stands for. We want to employ active voice and descriptive writing, as we would in any kind of mass media. Mostly we want to apply those same principles of clarity to writing for web pages.

Clarity can be achieved by keeping what we write simple. Include only one or two ideas per short paragraph on a web page. Choose common words over more difficult ones. Even if technical and more sophisticated language is appropriate we are going to want to define that language for a more general audience. Write for a lower reading comprehension level that you would expect your readers to have. That will make your web page more inclusive. Be clear by shaping your text for online reading. The text that works best on the web is text that gets to the point fast and makes it easy for the reader to pick out key information.

Online reading is a different experience that is different from reading text in print. Part of that is because it is physically different. For most, online reading takes a little longer, or at least feels that way, because the computer screen displays the text at a lower resolution, with less detail and sharpness as the printed page making the letters fuzzy or harder to read. Maybe some people feel their eyes tire faster reading text on screen than from paper, and to that extent, we must make an effort to be even clearer.

The principles of clarity must apply to web pages, social media, and all web content. Whether you are using Twitter at a news organization, advertising agency, or public relations firm, you must consider clarity. Effective writing requires participation and discipline regardless of the medium. With Twitter only allowing 140 characters you must really be clear. It might even be good practice to keep the message under 140 characters to be concise and to keep it simple for the audience. For search purposes use key words in your tweets so there is a record and others will be able to go back and find your messages. Do not over abbreviate. For link tweets, wherein which we want others to visit links posted, effective summarization gives people a reason to re-tweet. Summarization technique is hard to reduce to a formula so when replying, make it easy for the receiver to identify the conversation stream.

When we tweet, punctuate for clarity not just to follow general punctuation rules, because some of those rules aren't as important when we are tweeting. The same observation can be made about AP style rules. AP style rules can help with brevity but can sometimes confuse. The most important consideration is that we are being clear in that form. Use abbreviations only if you are sure the audience will understand them, because clarity is clarity no matter what we are writing. Always consider what is easiest for the audience to understand, and how to make the message clear. Clarity is the first consideration for effective writing for mass media.

CONCISION

The second consideration is the message should be concise. All new media demands that we be concise. For instance, on the web, it's helpful for the audience if we use direct, declarative language. We use short words, short sentences, short paragraphs, and short pages because the audience has a very short attention span. We need a lead with a link to the rest of the story. The lead should often be the climax to the story, and we need to write that in a way that compels the audience to read the rest of the story. When we get the audience to click the link to learn more, we need to tell them a really good story that culminates into the climax that was the initial link. In that initial link, we should try to incorporate the protagonist, their will or want, their realization, the complications they face, and whether they were able to achieve their will or want, answering the major dramatic question. This dramatic model applies to websites, as it does every kind of writing. By limiting the number of words on a web page, as well as the amount of prose text on a navigation page, we are able to better attract the audience to want to know more about the story.

Concision also plays a role in social media, because we don't have much space when we are posting. We want to think about how we tell the audience the essential information, and do it in a brief way. Twitter must be concise. The Twitter writer has only 140 characters. That is usually between 10 and 15 words, so we want to get to the point with the story. By thinking about subjects and verbs, we get to the essentials of a sentence. Even if you ask my 6-year-old boy Woody, "According to White, what do we have to have in every sentence?" Woody will respond, "A verb and a noun." We always want to think about including a verb and a noun, as well as some kind of action. Emphasize the verbs. Make them active and descriptive. Remember that "to be" verbs can be understood without being written sometimes, and that you can drop the articles "a," "an," and "the" from the sentences.

When considering the importance of concision, we also need to think about mobile communication. The news director at the NBC affiliate in Chicago said that the future is mobisodes—mobile episodes. People will be watching television shows, receiving announcements, and watching commercials on their cell phones. Whatever we write for mobile phones, the content has to be shorter and more concise. The way our brains process information is changing, and so the way we write needs to be more concise for mobile delivery.

COMPLETENESS

The third consideration of good writing is that our message be complete. The key to this in the web sphere, or any other new social media, is to include links. In a web page, what we want to do is allow people to link to the video footage and other resources of a particular story. On Facebook, when you decide to write a status about your favorite band, you also get to include a link to their music video, live footage from their latest concert, or a web page where your friends can download their music. Links are what help "complete" messages in new media. Also, it can be really convenient to provide an internal search engine for the web site. So we want to make sure that the audience has enough information to give them an idea of the story, and then we need to provide links to all the information about the story. This is how we can be assured that a story is complete when told through new media.

CORRECTNESS

The fourth characteristic of quality writing is that the writing is correct. In order to assure this, you need to write, revise, re-write, revise, re-write, and revise again. If you write a tweet for your organization, it might be the only thing from your organization that somebody looks at. You want to make every word count, and that is going to take you proofreading your work. Typographical and spelling errors will send people away from your page. They will think you are a *doofus* in the social networking realm if you can't spell. There are emoticons that now enable us to speak to each other more briefly, but we want to use those selectively. When we are using language, we want to be able to spell and use proper punctuation, so proofread your work. Everything you post to the web, or send to people's mobile phones, or tweet, or post a social network, proofread it. It's the same idea discussed throughout this entire book, and it applies to social media and the web as well. If you're sending out a tweet or a post on a social networking site that really matters and is going to reach a lot of people, what I would do is type it on Microsoft Word first, revise it, re-write it, revise it, re-write it, then copy and paste it into the tweet or post, and finally send it. Write the message out and scrutinize it beforehand. That's what's going to separate you from the rest of the writers and come off as professional.

STRUCTURAL CONSIDERATIONS

We've talked about the importance of telling a good story and quality writing, so the last area to cover is structural considerations.

UNITY

The first consideration is unity. Do all the small pieces add up to something as a whole? In this case, what you want to do is consider all the small pieces of a campaign, for instance. Everything that you send out via twitter, social networks, web pages, or mobisodes, does it all fit together? Consider the whole campaign. Likewise, think about all the links from your page. Do all of them add up to some kind of whole? When you consider the sitemap of your web site, are all the pieces connected somehow? Do they create some kind of holistic picture? Yahoo has done some eye-tracking studies of people when they go to a web page, and that there's a general pattern of how people browse a web page. There's a triangular area in the upper left corner of a web page where most people's eyes go first. What we want to do is consider the whole, and then consider what the most salient part of that whole is.

VARIETY

The second structural consideration is variety. The big thing about new media is that it integrates text, pictures, and video. Sixty-six percent of online users watched a video clip last week. So what we as mass media writers want to do is provide a variety of content and information for our readers by incorporating text, pictures, and video. We want to keep the audience interested.

PACE

The third structural consideration is pace, and is probably one of the most important. Web moves fast. People want it to move fast. To that extent we have to be cognizant of our file sizes. We don't want people to have to wait too long to upload or download things. So wherever we can decrease those file sizes, we need to optimize that so people can continue to navigate quickly. Pace likewise reflects that we need to put the most important information at the beginning of our headlines, paragraphs, or sentences. Do not waste time leading up to the point. Make your point.

CLIMAX

The last structural consideration, the one we end up on after considering everything else, is climax. Climax is all about the story. Are we telling a good story through our page design? We want to get to the point, and getting to that point is about sharing the climax with our audience.

In conclusion, I want to say that there's one thing that separates new media from old traditional media, and that is that it is more of a two-way communication process. This reflects consideration of a transactional model of communication. Remember, with Twitter, we can be talking to individual users and we shouldn't be afraid of them. Whenever we're writing for new media, we need to have respect for the audience—and that's true with traditional media too. As a writer of a web page or social media or mobisodes, we should realize that it's possible to have more interaction with our audience. There's the possibility for feedback like there is in face-to-face communication. The bottom line here is that media is going to change, but good quality writing is always going to be good quality writing. No matter what medium you use, tell a good dramatic story that reflects quality writing principles, while being cognizant of structural considerations.

APPENDIX

GRADING CRITERIA AND EVALUATION GUIDELINES FOR ASSIGNMENTS 1-4	222
ASSOCIATED PRESS STYLEBOOK (AP) EXERCISE ONE	226
ASSIGNMENT 1: (STRAIGHT PRINT) NEWS STORY OR PRESS RELEASE	227
STRAIGHT PRINT NEWS STORY FACTS	228
STRAIGHT PRINT NEWS STORY EXAMPLE	229
STRAIGHT PRINT NEWS EXERCISE	230
STRAIGHT PRINT MEDIA RELEASE EXAMPLE	231
ASSOCIATED PRESS STYLEBOOK (AP) EXERCISE TWO	232
ASSIGNMENT 2: (FEATURE PRINT) NEWS STORY OR PRESS RELEASE	236
FEATURE PRINT NEWS STORY EXAMPLE	237
BREAKING DOWN THE ELEMENTS OF A DRAMATIC FEATURE PRINT STORY EX.	241
CRITICAL READING AND TAKE-AWAY MESSAGES (IN-CLASS EXERCISE)	242
EXTRA CREDIT OPTION: OPINION PRINT PIECE	243
OPINIONS WRITING (IN-CLASS EXERCISE)	244
ASSIGNMENT 3: STRAIGHT RADIO NEWS STORY	246
STRAIGHT RADIO STORY EXAMPLE	249
INTERVIEW (IN-CLASS EXERCISE)	252
RADIO PUBLIC SERVICE ANNOUNCEMENT (IN-CLASS EXERCISE)	253
ASSIGNMENT 4: STRAIGHT-TELEVISION NEWS STORY/VIDEO PRESS RELEASE	254
STRAIGHT TELEVISION NEWS EXAMPLE	257
TELEVISION NEWS (IN-CLASS EXERCISE)	259
EZNEWS TUTORIAL	260
ASSIGNMENT 5: TELEVISION ANNOUNCEMENT (COMMERICAL OR PSA)	262
TELEVISION ANNOUNCEMENT EXAMPLE	264
TELEVISION ANNOUNCEMENT (IN-CLASS EXERCISE)	270
FILM SCRIPT: PULP FICTION EXAMPLE (IN-CLASS EXERCISE)	271
FINAL PROJECT	272
FINAL PROJECT OPTION 1: RADIO, TELEVISION, OR FILM SCRIPT	273
FINAL PROJECT OPTION 2: DOCUMENTARY SCRIPT	275
FINAL PROJECT OPTION 3: PUBLIC RELATIONS CAMPAIGN	277
FINAL PROJECT OPTION 4: TWO 100-POINT ASSIGNMENTS	278
FINAL PROJECT OPTION 5: SHORT ISSUE FILM	279
FINAL PROJECT OPTION 6: PROPOSE YOUR OWN FINAL PROJECT	283
FINAL PROJECT FILM SCRIPT TREATMENT EXAMPLE	284

The things we care the most about are those into which we put the most effort.

The things we care the most about are those into which we put the most effort.

Assignments 1-4
Guidelines

A

Paper follows directions for the assignment and has zero formatting issues. Paper is free of writing errors and the paper uses the proper writing style for the assignment. Sentences are clear, concise, and complete. Organization of the piece follows journalistic styles appropriate for its purpose and the lead grabs the audience's attention. Paper includes references cited correctly and avoids misappropriation using five or more sources.

B

Paper follows directions for the assignment and has less than one formatting issue. Paper has less than two major writing errors and the paper uses the proper writing style for the assignment. More than one sentence is not clear, concise, and complete. Organization of the piece follows journalistic styles appropriate for its purpose and the lead grabs the audience's attention. Paper includes references cited correctly and avoids misappropriation using more than three sources.

C

Paper follows directions for the assignment; however, the paper has three or more formatting issues. Paper has less than five major writing errors and there is evidence of using the proper writing style for the assignment. Paper uses the proper organizational pattern; however, the lead does not catch the audience's attention. Paper includes references, but references are not cited correctly.

D

Paper does not follow format or directions. Paper has more than six major writing errors and it is evident that the paper was not proofread. Sentences are not fully developed. Organization of the piece does not follow the journalistic styles appropriate for its purpose. Paper does not include references and/or actuality when appropriate.

Writing Error Tip Sheet

This list is in no way comprehensive. Please keep in mind that EACH error will be deducted regardless if the same error is made throughout the paper. Please proofread all assignments to prevent losing points. Late work will be penalized as outlined in the syllabus.

Minor (-4):

- Awkward sentence structure: Sentences should be clear
- Minor clarity issues

Major (-8):

- Spelling errors
- Grammatical errors
- Punctuation errors (improper use of comma, semicolon, etc.)
- Run-on sentences (A sentence with two or more independent clauses.)
- Sentence fragments/incomplete sentences (A complete sentence has a noun and a verb.)
- Inaccurate information (i.e. wrong date, city, or other crucial information)
- Inappropriate overall structure (chronological when inverted pyramid is requested, most pertinent information not in the lead, or subjective/opinionated in a straight news story.)
- Verb tense (not using past tense when needed or mixing tenses throughout story.)
- Form issues (indentations, one sentence paragraphs, actuality form.)
- Major clarity issues

Significant (-16):

- Misspelled proper names (John Lenin instead of John Lennon.)
- Misuse of people, places, or things.

Class Participation Points

In order to assess your participation during the course of the Mass Media Writing course, you will be required to compose an argument justifying your grade in this aspect of the course. Participation consists of 100 total points in the course.

The **first paragraph** should consist of how you have participated in the lecture component of the course. The **second paragraph** should consist of how you have participated in the lab component of the course. The **third paragraph** should consist of outside of class contributions that have been attempted such as the discussing of a project with an instructor (please note that emailing an instructor or asking for assignment clarification does not count as participation). The **fourth paragraph** should include a conclusion along with the alpha and number grade assigned by you. This assignment is to be typed in 12-pt Times New Roman font and should be 1-2 pages. Handwritten assignments will not be accepted. Be sure to include specific examples along with general trends in your rationale. **This is due the last day of regularly scheduled class**.

Grading Criteria and Evaluation Guidelines for Assignments 1-4

Format
    Paper follows given assignment page requirements
    Paper is typed double-spaced
    Paper uses an acceptable 12-point font
    Paper includes section number
    Paper includes slug
    Paper signals the end of the story or more copy at the bottom of the page
        (i.e. ### or –more--)
    Paper uses appropriate script format for broadcast stories
        (i.e. radio and television news scripts)

Writing
    Paper is free of grammatical errors
    Paper has been proofread for errors
        (i.e. redundancy, typing mistakes, spelling)
    Paper uses proper punctuation
    Paper uses proper verb tense
    Paper uses proper writing style
        (i.e. print, broadcast, AP guidelines)
    Paper includes phonetic spelling when appropriate
    Sentence structure is varied
    Transitions are used when appropriate

Organization
    Paper has a proper lead
        (i.e. comprehensive, delayed, straight, feature, etc.)
    Paper uses proper organizational pattern
        (i.e. inverted pyramid, narrative, action-reaction, effect-cause, etc.)
    Paper includes actuality for radio broadcast story on separate page
    Paper is broken into logical paragraphs

References (for assignments #3 & #4)
    Reference page has at least three sources
    Sources are varied
        (i.e. not all from the same web site, newspaper, etc.)
    Sources follow APA style
    Reference page cites actuality source
    Reference page cites eyewitness reporting

Overall Impression
    Paper follows guidelines for assignment
    Ideas flow logically together

Associated Press Stylebook (AP) Exercise One

Directions: Answer the following questions about the AP Stylebook.

1. What are the contents of the AP Stylebook?

2. Under what heading can you find information about writing a street address?

3. If you were unsure about how a question mark fits in the middle of a sentence, how can the stylebook help?

4. If you were writing a story about terrorists and some of the names were Arabic, what kind of information in the stylebook would be useful?

5. If you were writing about the pope, what information does the stylebook provide?

Assignment 1: (Straight Print) News Story or Press Release

Format: Hard news style, breaking news.

Technical Details: Include your name, course, section number, release date, and a two- to three-word slug in the upper left corner of your assignment. This assignment should be between one and two pages. Indent paragraph breaks. If your story continues past one page (which it could), be sure to include the following at the bottom of the first and subsequent pages: -- more --. At the end of the story, include the following: ### or --30-- to make it clear that it is the end of the story.

- For additional examples and a further, in-depth discussion of the Inverted pyramid, please review Yopp & McAdams pp. 152-160. In addition, this paper is evaluated with a level of rigor unfamiliar to many students. Any and ALL grammatical or misuse of AP style error leads to an eight-point deduction. Please consider that if just one error occurs in every paragraph of an eight-paragraph story, your final score will be a 36. Please be mindful while proofreading.
- Consider neutral attribution denotes an attempt at objective reporting—ALWAYS use "said" for attribution in print news (not "suggested," "cried," or "added."

THESE THREE EXAMPLES ARE CONSIDERED WRONG:

1. Lou Reed exclaimed, "There's always next time."
2. The note said the kidnappers would be waiting at the Bates Motel.
3. "I really don't care for the shrimp scampi," stated John.
   - Please note: For attribution, "said" is preferred when someone is quoted. "Stated" is the preferred use from a written source.
   - Please avoid "stated" unless you are quoting from documents.
   - Print attributions should be past tense in print.
   - Don't (do not) use contractions in print unless it is a direct quote.

Assignment:

Write a news story or a press release using inverted pyramid style and organization. Include a comprehensive lead and organize material in descending order of importance. Do not write in narrative form or chronological order. Be sure your story is free of grammar, punctuation, spelling, and style errors.
You have two topical options for this assignment.
1) Write a straight news story or press release about a hypothetical event of your choice. This could be an imaginary news event, a corporate announcement of new goods or services, a press conference to react to accusations against an organization, the release of a film or music product, or any other organizational event about which you would like to write. [Do not misappropriate from other sources.]

OR

2) Write a story that reflects the scenario on page 27. It is not necessary to include all information, but rather include the information you decide is most important. You should rewrite the sentences and follow AP style. The specific facts given may not be in appropriate AP form. You can also add information if you wish to help your story flow and move the action along. Refer to facts on page 27.

Straight Print News Story Facts

- September 3rd, Thursday 2009 at 9:14 P.M. (EST).
- Hillary Clinton (Secretary of State) was leaving Copley Hall at Georgetown University.
- She gave a speech to undergraduate students.
- Exited main entrance, shots were fired.
- Hillary Clinton was not shot, was admitted to GWU Hospital for contusions and released at 11:07 PM (EST).
- Two secret service agents shot.
- Agent Timothy Kuznesky, 27, dead on arrival.
- Agent Ron Paulener, 31, in intensive care at George Washington University Hospital.
- Paulener expected to recover.
- According to Al Jazeera, Jordanian-born terrorist leader Abu Musab al-Baruni, claimed responsibility for the attempted assassination.
- Al-Baruni sent a video to Al Jazeera at 11:03 P.M. (EST)
- Al-Baruni (translated from Arabic by Department of Defense translators: "Death to America! We must unite in retaliation to the American siege of Syria, Iraq and Afghanistan."
- Whereabouts of al-Baruni unknown; last known whereabouts: Sulaimany, Iraq, where he lead rally August 15, 2009.
- Three shooters were detained, more are being sought out in connection to assassination.
- No statements have been given by Hillary Clinton.
- White House Press Secretary, Robert Gibbs, gave a briefing at 9:35 PM (EST).
- "All airports, train stations, metros and all major highways have been closed off in the Washington, D.C. area. We are under high alert and doing everything possible to get the situation controlled."
- Vice President Joseph Biden joined Gibbs at briefing: "We will take action against our attackers. We will win this war against terror. This will not defeat us but will only heighten our efforts."
- President Obama has not addressed the nation and has not been available for comment.
- The President's trip to Beijing has been cancelled.
- Third attack on American soil by terrorist networks in the last three weeks.
- Osama bin Laden nor al-Baruni did not claim responsibility for the previous attacks in San Francisco and Miami.
- Next briefing schedule for 10 A.M. (EST); carried by all major networks.
- According to Homeland Security Advisory System, threat level is red or severe, meaning severe risk of terrorist attacks. Has been at same level for six weeks.

Straight Print News Story Example

First Last Name
Com 161-Section #
Release Date of Assignment
Bin Laden Captured

WASHINGTON D.C. – The U.S. Army captured Osama bin Laden and two top al-Qaeda leaders Thursday morning in northern Pakistan.

Bin Laden's capture comes three weeks before the 10th anniversary of 9/11.

"It's been a long time coming," said Army Gen. David Petraeus. "But we finally got the son of a bitch."

Petraeus said soldiers from the 140 Airborne found bin Laden and Ayman al-Zawahiri huddled over the recently deceased Atiyah Abd Al Rahman in the Swat district of the North-West Frontier Province in Pakistan. The cause of Rahman's death is still unknown, but Petraeus said cannibalism may have occurred.

"It was one hell of a sight," said Petraeus. "His left leg was severed and it appeared as though they were trying to start a fire."

Since 2009, State Department intelligence has identified Zawahiri as the primary organizer of al-Qaeda, leaving bin Laden's role in the organization as a figurehead. Rahman was another leading al-Qaeda official and a member of the Libyan Islamic Fighting Group.

"It feels good to accomplish a decade-long objective," said President Obama while speaking at a children's hospital in Peoria, Illinois. "However, we must remember that our soldiers will have to continue their hard work as we continue to bring peace to the region."

--more--

Meanwhile, thousands of citizens flooded the streets of New York City to celebrate the capture.

"I'm so proud of my service members," said Ben Slack, a Marines Corps veteran. "I think they should skip the trial and go straight to execution."

Obama said he planned to meet Petraeus late Friday to discuss the situation.

###

Example courtesy of Brian Seay.

Straight Print News (In-Class Exercise)

The inverted pyramid style requires reporters to organize facts from most to least important. They also need to develop summary leads that include the most important elements of a story (who, what, where, when, why and how). Using the list of facts below, complete the following:

1) Organize the facts from most to least important.

2) Write a summary lead that would appear in a straight hard news style story for a national newspaper (e.g., *The New York Times*).

- Since 2009, State Department intelligence has identified Zawahiri as the primary organizer of al-Qaeda, leaving bin Laden's role in the organization as a figurehead.
- Obama said he planned to meet Petraeus late Friday to discuss the situation.
- The U.S. Army found them in northern Pakistan.
- Thousands of citizens flooded the streets of New York City to celebrate the capture.
- Army General David Petraeus said soldiers from the 140 Airborne found bin Laden and Ayman al-Zawahiri huddled over the recently deceased Atiyah Abd Al Rahman in the Swat district of the North-West Frontier Province in Pakistan.
- Rahman was another leading al-Qaeda official and a member of the Libyan Islamic Fighting Group.
- The capture comes three weeks prior to the 10th anniversary of 9/11.
- Osama bin Laden and two top al-Qaeda leaders were captured Thursday morning. The cause of Rahman's death is still unknown, but Petraeus said cannibalism may have occurred.

This exercise is courtesy of Brian Seay.

Straight Print Media Release Example

First Last Name
Com 161-Section #
Release Date of Assignment
(There is no slug in a press release; however, you should have your company name at the top of the press and/or news release similar to this example. In addition, you will also title your press and/or news release in bold similar to this example.)

Monday, Sept. 7, 2009   Contact: Anna Wall

For Immediate Release   Phone: (309) 242-0763

Email: Amwall@ilstu.edu

Illinois State will hold Relay for Life

NORMAL, Ill. - Hundreds of ISU students will gather on the quad for the sixth-annual Relay for Life against cancer, Friday at 6 p.m.

This free event is held to increase awareness and raise money for the fight against cancer. So far more than 200 teams have raised $60,000. When the event concludes Saturday morning student organizers hope to reach the goal of $80,000, topping the $75,000 raised in 2008.

The community is invited to watch or participate with the students and cancer survivors. Participants will walk around the quad for 12 hours. Teams will be walking at different times. During off times, teams will participate in activities to raise money.

These activities include face painting, games, sports competitions and a drag show. All proceeds go directly to the American Cancer Society.

National Relay For Life Co-chair Richie Lawry said, "Money raised through Relay for

Life has two purposes; to fund cancer research and to provide, at no charge, a variety of cancer related programs and services to patients and those affected by cancer."

Cancer survivors will speak at the opening ceremony. Survivors and their families will walk the first lap around the quad with torches while the others cheer them on.

The Luminaria candlelight ceremony will begin at 10 p.m. to commemorate the people lost to cancer and honor survivors. The closing ceremonies will be held Saturday at 6 a.m. where organizers will announce the total amount of money raised.

The quad is located in the middle of the ISU campus, which is accessible through the Bone Student Center parking lot at 100 N. University St. In the case of rain the event will be held in Redbird Arena located at 700 W. College Ave.

For more information about this event, or to sign a team up please contact John Smith at (309) 245-8675.

This example is courtesy of Anna Wall.

Associated Press Stylebook (AP) Exercise Two

Directions: Using the AP Style Guide, correct the following sentences.

Numerals

1. 98 people were injured during a baseball riot.

2. Ashley, six, was found safe in her tree-house.

3. The 1st time Mary saw the dead body, she jumped.

4. That was the 28th showing of the film.

5. The lotto prize was for $60,000,000,000,000.

6. Only three hundred people participated in the walk.

7. The 2-year-old child was found in a garbage dump 3 days later.

8. The stock market rose 2.3% after a rough day of trading yesterday.

9. The Walmart stock was down 2/3 points compared to last year's earnings.

10. The bullet wound was .04 inches wide.

Date and Time

1. Jane Doe was born on September 13, 2000 at 3:01 PM.

___

2. The hurricane season began in Aug.

___

3. Amber left the hospital Wed.

___

4. The alarm sounded at exactly 12:00 a.m.

___

5. The season premiere of "Lost" will air at 7:00 p.m. Thursday night.

___

6. The White Sox won the game after playing 35 min. in extra innings.

___

7. The Halloween party in Oct. 2000 ended in tragedy for one family.

___

8. Holly was first sent to court duty in September, 2001.

___

9. The summer Olympics in Greece were memorable, said Jessica Heart, a volunteer from the U.S.

___

10. Jerry Stone, an environmentalist, blames the depletion of the ozone layer for the absence of the Fall and Spring seasons.

___

Names and Titles

1. Illinois Senator Jane Doe led a cooking demonstration at the County Oaks retirement home.

2. The President was debriefed about the restoration.

3. The senator, Jane Doe, received a letter of recognition from Jon Adams, the Owner.

4. Doctor Henry Jones saved Anna's life.

5. The president quoted a passage from the "Bible."

6. Brittany Spears' Toxic is currently at the top of the music charts.

7. Kirsten Dunst played the role of a disturbed teenager in Crazy/Beautiful.

8. "Microsoft Excel" was the top selling software program for two years at Best Buy stores.

9. The leader of the Catholic church in Chicago, Cardinal Brophy, met with mayor Daley Friday.

10. Also part of the ceremony, Reverend Jesse Jackson gave a brief statement.

Addresses

1. Marilyn, originally from Tenn., now lives at 848 Lincoln Avenue, Ill. 60354.

2. Roseanne was born in Denver, CO.

3. The perpetrator was found at seven Elmwood Court.

4. The walk began at Monroe St. and ended at Adams St.

5. Donations can be sent to 100 North Vernon Avenue, Normal, Ill. 61761.

6. Resumes should be sent to PO Box 340, Bloomington, IN. 60007.

7. The tornado touched down in the State of Kan. early in the morning Saturday.

8. The new school will be built on Raab Rd.

9. Police searched down Linden and Vernon Ave.

10. The other student was from Bloomington, IN.

Assignment 2: (Feature Print) News Story or Press Release

For this assignment, you will write a 2-3 pages feature article on a topic of your choice. You can write the story on the topic for which you wrote for Assignment #1, or another topic. Keep in mind that the topic should be interesting to your audience. For this assignment, assume members of your target audience are students at ISU (This does not necessarily mean you are writing for *The Vidette*). Follow the same technical details as in Assignment #1.

Write the story utilizing a narrative form rather than an inverted pyramid form. Tell a compelling story, not just provide soft information. We would advise that you craft an effective lead and use the dramatic model we have discussed in class as an organizational scheme for this assignment. You will want to personalize an issue by focusing on an individual or a small group of people.

Please refer to the example provided in the packet.

Revise and rewrite.

Be mindful of the grammatical rules and stylistic considerations addressed by McHale and AP Stylebook.

A feature story, or feature press release, typically tells a story about people and examines details beyond the initial "who," "what" and "where." The "why" and the "how" typically are most prominent. We strongly encourage using the dramatic model as a paradigm.

Feature Print News Story Example

9-11-08

Olympic Boxing

A young man sits in his corner. He is soaked in blood and sweat, literally beaten unrecognizable. He is in pain, but he does not show it. When most people would have thrown in the towel, this young man waits for that last bell. He knows this is the last opportunity to fulfill his dream.

Jose "The Real Deal" Villireal, sits in his corner, waiting for the last round of his final Olympic qualifying match. He has been working his whole life for this opportunity, and he will not let it slip away.

"The only thing I've ever wanted to be is a boxer," said the 26 year-old Normal native. "Ever since I saw Rocky beat Apollo in 'Rocky II' I knew I had chance to make it in the boxing world."

Similar to Rocky, Villireal, did not have an easy path toward success.

"My family didn't have a lot of money, so it was hard for me to get good training, and my high school didn't have a boxing team," said Villireal, a graduate of Normal West High School. "I just had to make due with what I had."

Although Villireal lacked formal training, he found a way to hone his skills.

"I am what's known as a backyard boxer," said Villireal. "I was able to save up enough money to buy a couple pairs of gloves, and my friends and I would just have fights in my driveway."

After beating all his friends in his driveway, Villireal took his first step toward becoming a real boxer.

"In 1999 I went to Wisconsin to fight in the Golden Gloves Tournament," said Villireal, who finished second in the tournament. "I ended up doing really well, and it opened up my eyes to what I could really do with my hands."

Not only did it open up his eyes, but he also drew attention from college scouts.

"The first time I saw him fight he was unpolished, but he had a lot of power and I could tell that he was going to be something special," said Tony Dushack, head boxing coach at the University of Northern Michigan. "I decided to take a chance on him and offer him a scholarship."

The University of Northern Michigan is a school known for its boxing program. The college is one of four schools in the country that participates in the National College Boxing Program. The program is designed to get amateur boxers ready for Olympic trials, and Villireal was excited about his new opportunities.

"It was just an honor to know that somebody believed in me, and I wasn't going to let them down," said Villireal. "My freshman year in college was probably the hardest year of my life. I was going up against some of the best boxers in the country every day."

In the face of adversity, Villireal discovered the most important characteristic of a boxer, determination.

"Jose was determined to be the best. He really learned how fought with a chip on his shoulder," said Dushack. "Once he learned he couldn't knock everyone out with one punch and how to control his punches, he really started to assert himself into the boxing world."

Villireal fought his way throughout college and finished his career with an amateur record of 24-5-2 with 12 knockouts. However, his record wasn't his greatest accomplishment in college.

"I graduated with a degree in chemistry," said Villireal. "I love boxing, but I know it isn't going to last forever. When my boxing career is over, I can always fall back on chemistry, but right now I am focused on the Olympics."

After College, Villireal started training harder than ever.

"After I graduated, I stayed in Michigan and I focused all of my time to boxing," said Villireal. "Coach Dushack was determined to get me an invitation to the Olympic qualifiers."

Villireal was invited to Atlanta to tryout for an opportunity to participate in the 2008 Olympics in Beijing.

"I was invited, along with 50 other heavy weights from around the country to fight for five spots on the team," said Villireal.

After winning his first two fights with ease, Villireal found himself fighting for his life in his third and final match.

The bell rang and Villireal came out swinging. Two men were standing in the middle of the ring, both fighting for the same dream. Villireal finally connected with a right and his opponent fell to the mat. With that punch "The Real Deal's" dream became a reality.

"When they raised my hand, I knew I was heading to China to represent my country," said Villireal. "I just hope I can go, fight with pride and bring home the gold."

-30-

Breaking Down the Elements of a Dramatic Feature Print Story

When writing a feature print story using the dramatic method, it is important to include all of the dramatic elements as well as news value for the audience. Read the feature print example and then briefly identify the dramatic elements in that story by answering the questions below.

1. Who is the protagonist and how much of their life does this feature cover?

2. What is the protagonist's will or want?

3. What is the dramatic question in the story? In which paragraph is it located?

4. What obstacles does the protagonist face in achieving their will or want?

5. What happens at the climax of the story? In what paragraph is the climax?

6. What do you think is the resolution at the end of the story?

7. Describe the news value for the audience.

8. Who might be a good audience for this feature, or why is this an important story to write? Do you think this feature would have the same impact on the audience if it were written using the inverted pyramid rather than the dramatic model? Why or why not?

Critical Reading and Take-Away Messages (In-Class Exercise)

Whenever we read a news story, we read it from the perspective of our own social, gender-based and cultural filters. It is important to be aware of how those filters affect the way that we process information. Use the following questions to examine your ability to be a critical consumer of mass media.

1. Do you think that you are reading this story through a social filter? If so, how does that filter affect your perception of the story and of the protagonist's experience? If not, why not?

2. How might someone from a different culture or social background read this story through a different social filter?

Extra Credit Option: Opinion Print Piece

For extra credit, you can write a 1-2 page opinion piece. The subject can be any current issue or topic. You should include an intriguing lead that includes a thesis statement and a preview. The piece should also contain two to four well-reasoned and evidenced arguments that support your position. End with a conclusion that ties the piece together. Citing outside sources for information that bolster your position will increase the quality of your piece. I also encourage you to submit it as a letter to the editor in the *Daily Vidette*, the *Indy*, or *The Pantagraph*.

Revise and rewrite.

You can earn a maximum of 10 points if your piece is published as a letter to the editor. If it is not published, you can earn a maximum of 5 points.

Opinion Writing (In-Class Exercise)

Goals:

- You will better understand how to build and support an argument.
- You will become more critical consumers of opinion writing as they learn to recognize what claims others are making and what evidence is provided for those claims.
- You will better understand their own opinions and thus, will be able to more effectively articulate those opinions.

Bring the following items to class with you:

- An example editorial or opinion article (preferably from a source other than the school newspaper)
- Topic ideas for your own opinion pieces

Procedure:

1. Introduction

    a. Briefly discuss the purpose of opinion writing.
        - To present your viewpoint on a particular topic
        - To persuade others to agree with you

    b. Using evidence and reasoning to construct quality arguments is central to persuading others.

2. Three key parts of an argument (derived from Toulmin's Argument Model)

    a. Claim – your main statement or assertion, the point you are trying to make

    b. Evidence – the proof used to substantiate your claim

    c. Warrant – links the claim and evidence together; explains how the evidence proves your claim; demonstrates that making the mental leap from one to the other is rational

3. Go through an example together as a class.

    - Example: As cameras scanned the flooded New Orleans streets in the days after Hurricane Katrina, viewers saw thousands of suffering individuals, many of whom were black. Who came to their rescue? No one, they report. The government response was clearly inadequate under a president who does not care about black Americans.

> ➢ Claim: George Bush does not care about black Americans.

> ➢ (Ask yourself: What evidence is there for this claim?) Evidence: The government response to Hurricane Katrina was inadequate.

> ➢ (Ask yourself: How is the government's response to the hurricane tied to the president's feelings toward black Americans?) Warrant: Many of the hurricane victims were black.

- Warn you that oftentimes their evidence will become another claim. For example, you may need to provide evidence to support the claim that "the government response to Hurricane Katrina was inadequate."

4. Apply concepts to the example opinion or editorial articles that you brought to class.

   a. Get into groups.

   b. Identify the claim(s), evidence, and warrant(s) in each of your examples.

5. Apply concepts to your topic ideas.

   a. Working in the same groups, choose one of your topic ideas.

   b. Develop the claim, evidence, and warrant for the chosen topic.

Assignment 3: Straight Radio News Story

Using three to five print sources (your original could be a newspaper article on an existing story) and at least one other non-print source (most likely an interview); create a 60-second radio news story. This story should be "hard" news and relevant to your audience. Your resources should provide enough information to create a 60-second radio news story. You may also consider writing your hard news story from information on a press and/or news release. Keep in mind:

- Your original story gives you a base for your story. Your other sources should update, enhance, and provide new information for your radio broadcast.

- Your print stories should be based on **statewide and/or national news**. Your interview and other sources should provide a **local angle**.

- Your broadcast should address any questions left unanswered that your audience would like to know. Expand and clarify these points.

- Three sources is the minimum (average) and five would be preferred.

Things to consider:

- After finding the same information in at least three separate sources, it becomes common knowledge. This does not mean it is okay to copy direct quotes from the sources, but rather take what you know and put it into your own words.

- Do not assume that your audience has prior knowledge of your story (unless it has been a MAJOR news event, e.g., Michael Jackson case, tsunami). It is up to you to inform your audience of the news as if they had no background information.
- Follow the format (include slug, sound bites, etc.)
- Make sure your story demonstrates good aural style.
- Use your interview as actuality material, to give the story a local perspective.
- Read your script aloud to yourself and others. Get feedback. Is it clear, concise, and 60 seconds?
- Remember when timing to include the time taken for your actuality.
- Proofread, proofread, and proofread.
- Do not forget to list your sources (use any style, but be consistent) and attach them to your news story.
- Please note that your actuality may not necessarily time to 15 seconds like the example. Please time your actuality and adjust accordingly.
- Additionally, an actuality longer than 15 seconds in a 60-second news story is about the maximum length.
- If the story is over 61 seconds or under 59, this is considered a major error and 16 points will be deducted.
- Whenever in doubt, use phonetic spelling especially with proper nouns. Questionable pronunciations without phonetic spelling will be subject to an eight-point deduction per omission.

- Your **entire** story should time to 60 seconds. This includes your actuality.

- Each line of copy equals approximately four seconds. A half-line would equal two seconds.

- Broadcast writing is primarily present tense.

Straight Radio Story Example

First Last Name
Com 161-Section #
September 24, 2005 – 5 p.m. **(This is the recorded date and time of your story.)**
Contraception

Today New Yorkers contemplate (CON-tum-plate) life without trans fat. City officials announced Wednesday, the artery-clogging ingredient may be banned from over twenty thousand city restaurants. Trans fats are common in fried (FRIDE) fast foods. Chicago considers a ban as well. The city halted the sale of foie gras (FWAH-GRAW)...a goose liver delicacy (DELL-a-kussy)...and approved non-smoking legislation (LEJ-us-lay-shun). The town of Normal...which will also ban smoking...may likely follow Chicago's health-conscious lead. I-S-U professor of nutrition doctor Robert Cullen (KULL-in) explains the danger these fats pose.

> START: DR. CULLEN
>
> TIME: 17
>
> OUT: "...DEVELOPING HEART DISEASE."

A ban in Normal would mean fast food chains and I-S-U cafeterias (kaff-uh-TEERY-uhs) would need to find healthy alternatives. Some local restaurants, like Wendy's, have voluntarily removed trans fat from their menus.

Rec Date 10/2

Tot Time 1:00

Trans Fat Actuality

October 2, 2006

Dr. Robert Cullen

:17

"Well…trans fats are…are now very much linked to the development of heart disease…so it's a risk factor…just like eating saturated fat or dietary cholesterol. If you're eating foods that have any of those types of fats…including trans fats…that increases your risk of developing heart disease."

Rec Date 10/2

Tot Time :17

References

Caruso, D. B. (2006, September 27). NYC weighs ban on artificial trans fats. *Associated Press*.

Frieden chews the fat [Editorial]. (2006, October 1). *Daily News* (New York), p. 34.

Morales, N. (Reporter). (2006, September 29). *The Today Show* [Television broadcast]. New York: National Broadcasting Co. Inc.

Schmeltzer, J., & Washburn, G. (2006, June 29). Burke seeks trans fat ban for Chicago restaurants. *Chicago Tribune*, business and financial news.

Example courtesy of Griffin Hammond.

Interview (In-Class Exercise)

For each general news topic listed below come up with at least one person that you would want to interview in order to get a local angle for the story. Also, come up with at least three questions that you would ask that individual about the topic.

Feature story interviews are typically easier than hard news stories with typically more difficult questions. As such, interviewees in these types of stories are far less apt to give answers without prompting than a source in a feature story. This exercise consists of your lab instructor acting as a persona of your choice during a press conference for each topic listed. Take a few moments to write down questions (with possible follow-ups) to ask the interviewee. Remember, the more specific and informed question that you ask, the more specific and informed answer you will receive.

1. State legislators are set to discuss cutting the funding for drug rehab centers.

    Interviewee:

    Question 1:

    Question 2:

    Question 3:

2. The United States Supreme Court overturned a Federal District Court ruling that even if a defendant received a fair trial, actual innocence is grounds to release them.

    Interviewee:

    Question 1:

    Question 2:

    Question 3:

Radio Public Service Announcement (In-Class Exercise)

(As a group of five to six students, you will need to access a press release from a non-profit agency on the web [i.e., Farm Aid or Working Bikes].)

A non-profit agency has sent a press release to your newsroom and is asking for a 20-second radio announcement about their event or service. After reading the press release carefully, answer the following questions and decide what is the most important information my audience needs to know.

1. Who is my target audience?

2. What persuasive appeals will I use?

3. Who will my talent be and what sound effects will I include?

Write your announcement keeping the agency and your audience in mind. Also, decide who in your group will present the announcement to the class.

From: McHale, J.P. (2011) *Mass Media Writing Course Packet: Com 161.* John P. McHale; ISU PIP Printing. Except by Vicky Tsoumbakopoulos.

Assignment 4: Straight-Television News Story or Video Press Release

This story or video press release should be 60 seconds. We will allow you to use the same subject matter from your radio news story, but if your story has evolved, please include new, updated information. You must use a VO/SOT (voice over/sound on tape) approach (in which an anchor delivers the story with video b-roll and actualities) rather than a package approach (in which a reporter delivers a pre-recorded story with video b-roll and actualities). Keep in mind that the addition of visual elements may influence the appropriateness of the dialogue (so do not just cut and paste). You will use EZNews as the formatting standard. Things to consider:

- Use at least three outside sources such as newspaper articles, web pages from credible news sources, etc. DO NOT MISAPPROPRIATE! Please submit a reference page with your story. This may have to be in a separate document such as a Microsoft Word file.

- Assume you and your camera crew got the shots you need to visually tell and enhance your story. This does not always happen in the real world, but the chance that you will have good shots will increase if you write and re-write the story throughout pre-production, during shooting, and in post-production.

- In later applications, you will find that various personnel will contribute to writing (or designing) the television news story as it appears on the air, including researchers, reporters, camera people, producers, editors, and directors. The intent of this assignment is for you to assume all the writing responsibility. For this assignment, you will use these considerations:

- Do you have adequate visual variety to maintain audience attention? Are you using a variety of b-roll shot? Do you use a "Two-shot" and have one anchor lead into the story for the other? Do you then feature an "Anchor On Cam"? Are you showing the anchor with an "over-the shoulder" graphic? How can you use still-stored maps or photos for maximum benefit? Would graphics of CG (computer-generated) fonts help you clarify ideas for the audience?

- Your grade will be based on the effectiveness and specificity of your b-roll directions and shot choice. (Bad example: Shot of hospital. Good example: Outside medium shot of front entrance of Bromenn Hospital with outpatient leaving in wheelchair with family.)

- Visual elements should work with copy to give your message without being too redundant. **(Write to video)**

- When you denote "VO" (voice over) in EZNews, use the space to the right (but still in the left column) to identify what the audience would see (i.e., 'Shot of Gov. Ryan at a ribbon cutting ceremony'). As we grade the assignment, we will ask ourselves, "What will the audience see as they hear this VO?"

- Use at least one actuality to add a local angle or update the story in some way. The actuality you use should come from an interview that you conduct, not a quote from your sources. For example, you could interview a professor that teaches in a field related to the subject matter of your story. Use computer generated font to identify the source and title of your actuality.

- Use an appropriate lead and an appropriate close.
- Make sure it is clear to your audience, technical staff, and talent. Use phonetic breakdown for names that are difficult to pronounce.
- Include total time at the end of the story like the example.

We will go through a tutorial of EZNews and we will discuss additional specific aspects of the assignment in the following week. Please start planning for topic preparation and research.

Television News Example 1/2

Lawton kid napping [VO/SOT]   (Comm 161 Media Writing sec 5)   Script

ERT:0:37/SOT:0:23/TRT:1:00   Pg 1

(Ben / 1shot)

        Normal Police are searching for two unidentified men believed to be responsible for last night's kidnapping.

Take VO [Wide Shot of the Lawton residence then zoom to the broken front door]
Locator - CG#: $$$$
Lawton Residence
This Morning
(Take at:0:00)
Deko

        Little Cindy Lou Lawton of Normal, age seven, was taken from her home after the two men kicked down the front door. Police Chief Brian Duggins says the men's primary goal behind the home invasion was kidnapping.

Take SOT Runs.. 0:15 ..culprits to justice"
"This was not an attempted robbery. This was a kidnapping pure and simple. We believe we have identified the men responsible for this horrific act, and we are going to do everything in our power to bring the culprits to justice."
Locator - CG#: $$$$
Police Chief Brian Duggins
Normal Police Station
(Take at:0:00)
Deko
Continue VO [Panning shot of the Lawton family living room. The Lawton family is sitting on couches and chairs. Go to a close up of Mr. Lawton embracing his wife.]

        The Lawton family is hoping for the safe return of their only child.

Printed by blslack, on Thursday, December 10, 2009 06:51:50 PM

Lawton kid napping [VO/SOT]　　(Comm 161 Media Writing sec 5)　　Script

ERT:0:37/SOT:0:23/TRT:1:00　　Pg 2

Take SOT Runs.. 0:08 ..to come home."

"Cindy is the light of my life and I just want her back. She is probably scared and just wants to come home."
Locator - CG#: $$$$
Mindy Lawton
Mother
(Take at:0:00)
Deko
Take Full Screen SS (Mug Shot)
　Full screen picture of Cindy Lou Lawton

　　　　　　　　　　　　　　Cindy Lou Lawton has blond hair and blue eyes. She is four feet tall and weighs 55 pounds. She was last seen wearing a red dress with pig tails in her hair.

(Ben / B-O-C)
Locator - CG#: $$$$
Normal Police
309-543-7891
(Take at:0:00)
Deko

　　　　　　　　　　　　　　If you have any information on the where abouts of Little Cindy Lou, please contact the authorities at 309-543-7891.

Printed by blslack, on Thursday, December 10, 2009 06:51:50 PM

Television News (In-Class Exercise)

For each scenario below, you are given a general statement about a national news event that has taken place and a direct quote from a local individual. Use the direct quote to determine the point of view and local angle that the story will take. Briefly, describe the possible facts and information that you would want to find in order to develop a TV news story. Additionally, describe the b-roll footage that you would incorporate into the story.

1. General story topic: The number of soldiers killed in Iraq in the last month has reached 100.

    Direct Quote from a mother of one of the local soldiers that was killed. "He always wanted to fight for his country, even if it meant dying. You expect bad news everyday, but it is still a shock when the news arrives."

2. General story topic: A severe drought across most of the Midwestern states has led to shortages in vegetables.

    Direct Quote from a local farmer.
    "I lost at least 90% of my crops this year. I've lived through droughts before, but I don't remember a year where the rain has been this scarce."

EZNews Tutorial

The best way to learn EZNews is to work with it and explore options as you go. With that it mind, there are some preliminary issues to consider:

Opening a file
- Select the course and your section number from the drop down menu.
- Create a file from the File menu: <New>
- Then you must find the file you created and highlight it.
- Select the form you prefer to use for the file. <VOSOT>
- Now you are ready to work within the document.

EZNews Command Icons (Instructions)
ANC: (Anchor): Identifies when the anchor is "on-cam": You have several options:
1-shot: is not an option in EZNews, but you will likely want to type it in manually.
BOC (Back on Camera): a 1-shot when returning from VO, for instance from a 2-shot
Other cameras
- **ANC** (anchor): SOT text
- **OTS** (over-the-shoulder box or graphic) is one ACH option. If you use this, you should then go to the OTS icon to **define** what is in the box/graphic.
- **SS**: (Still Store) Static Graphic: Full screen
- **VO** (voice over): Include a description of the shot of the right (although it will still be on left side in split screen.
- **SOT** (sound on tape): show video with audio: Usually for actualities.
- **PKG** (package): Extended pre-recorded piece.
- **NS** (non-scripted event): Used for "anchor banter."
- **BNP** CG: 1 line: Banner, story subject, etc.
- **LOC** (CG Locator): Tells crew where clip is. This is usually a number.
- **NAM** (CG name): A name is superimposed on the screen.
- **2TAL** (CG names two people): Two names are superimposed on screen.
- **FS** (full screen): CG full screen: 3 lines
- **FS** (full screen): CG full screen: 5 lines
- **FS** (full screen): CG full screen: 7 lines
- **VOS** (voice over sports)
- **2TM** (CG scoreboard 2 teams)
- **4TM** (CG scoreboard 4 teams)
- **Sky cam** (rare camera angle, but is sometimes used at the end of a newscast).

Printing a File

Due to our current licensing arrangement, you have to take several steps to print a file in the split page format required.

Your script must be highlighted in yellow on the bottom of the screen to print, even if it appears in the window at the top/right of the screen.

Go to Print Set-up in the File drop menu: Select Letter form

In the <File> drop menu, choose <Print...>Open the menu off of <Selected Scripts> and choose <Standard>

If you have saved your story in your home on EZ News, then you will have to follow a different procedure to print. Here are the steps:
File
Print > Selected Scripts As > Standard
Choose Format to Use
ISU Show Print
OK

Assignment 5: Television Announcement (Commercial or PSA)

Write a thirty-second television announcement. This can be a public service announcement or commercial. You must use a storyboard format with approximately ten to twelve frames, although there can be exceptions depending on the message. Below each frame, provide the aural copy (including dialogue, music, sound effects) and visual cues (shot information, other directions, and transitions [e.g., cut, dissolve, fade, pan, wipe]) after each frame. Type all information under each picture cell. Make sure the shot information/description under each cell matches the illustration of each cell.

Make sure the storyboard format is clear. We recommend two cells per page. Do not forget to number your cells and include total time. Refrain from over-crowding, turning in rough drafts, and improper subject matter. Make sure this is a realistic announcement that you may actually see on television.

The quality of your art is not graded. Stick figures are acceptable. Use color if necessary. It is important, however, that the pictures match the video descriptions. Consider using logos and slogans. Also, consider showing the product or representation of the service. Visual variety is highly encouraged. Using a slogan and a logo can be an effective way to end a television announcement.

You have **two options** for this assignment:

1. Create an original commercial for an **existing** public service agency or commercial product or service. The commercial or PSA cannot be for a fictional product or organization. Assignments of this nature will not be accepted.

2. Write an announcement that promotes involvement in the Special Olympics. You can use information from the web site but DO NOT PLAGIARIZE. Use the following facts:

- Date of function.
- Financial and time contributions wanted.
- 309-888-2551; contact information in Normal
- Create your own slogan
- www.ilso.org

Feel free to add other hypothetical facts for your spot. For either option, make sure your spot is clear to both the audience and the people who would potentially produce the piece. Consider your preferred target audience and carefully select persuasive appeals that would appeal to that audience.

Television Announcement PSA Example Television Example 1/6

PAGE 1

FADE IN:

SHOT 1

MWS- LIVING ROOM: YOUNG MAN- BRIAN- LYING ON THE COUCH WATCHING TV. HE STARES AHEAD.

(SOT)(NAT SOUND): REALITY TV JOKES AND CANNED LAUGH TRACK...MORE BAD JOKES...

BRIAN SIGHS WITH BOREDOM.

CUT TO:

SHOT 2

MWS –BEDROOM, FROM TV: YOUNG WOMAN- KRISTI- SITTING ON THE BED WATCHING TV, BORED.

(SOT)(NAT SOUND): SAPPY ROMANCE DIALOGUE, ...

SWEEPING SYMPHONY UNDER.

KRISTI THROWS HANDS UP AND SIGHS

CUT TO:

264 Mass Media Writing: Telling a Good Story Well

Television Example 2/6

PAGE 2

SHOT 3

MWS- OFFICE: YOUNG MAN- MIKE- SITTING AT DESK, READING A BOOK.

(SOT)(NAT SOUND): CLOCK TICKING

MWS: MIKE SIGHS AND TURNS THE PAGE. HE SHUTS BOOK IN FRUSTRATION, IT FALLS TO THE FLOOR.

(SOT)(NAT SOUND): BOOK 'THUDS' ON FLOOR

CUT TO:

SHOT 4

CU- OFFICE: MIKE TURNS TO HIS COMPUTER SCREEN.

ANNOUNCER (VO)(MALE VOICE): Do you have a story to tell?...

(SOT)(NAT SOUND): CLOCK TICKING

CUT TO:

Mass Media Writing: Telling a Good Story Well

265

Television Example 3/6

PAGE 3

SHOT 5

ECU, VERY SLOW ZOOM: BLINKING CURSOR ON COMPUTER SCREEN

(SOT)(NAT SOUND): CLOCK TICKING

CUT TO:

SHOT 6

ECU: THE KEYBORAD OF THE COMPUTER, MIKE'S FINGERTIPS HOVER JUST ABOVE THE KEYS

ANNOUNCER (VO): ...Tell it......

(SOT): MUSIC, FULL, MAJOR-SCALE, UPLIFTING, *The Polyphonic Spree's* "Reach for the Sun," OR *Fischerspooner's* "Everything to Gain," OR similar.

ECU: YOUNG MAN 2 BEGINS TO TYPE FERVENTLY

CUT TO:

266   Mass Media Writing: Telling a Good Story Well

Television Example 4/6

PAGE 4

SHOT 7

MCU- BEDROOM: FAST PANORAMIC AROUND KRISTI, SITTING IN BED, SMILING, WRITING FERVENTLY IN A NOTEBOOK.

(MUSIC): CONTINUES

WIPE TO:

SHOT 8

MCU- LIVING ROOM: FAST CONTINUING PANORAMIC AROUND BRIAN, SITTING UPRIGHT ON COUCH, TYPING FERVENTLY ON LAPTOP AND SMILING.

(MUSIC): CONTINUES

DIP TO SILVER:

Mass Media Writing: Telling a Good Story Well   267

Television Example

PAGE 5

SHOT 9a

WHITE SCREEN

(MUSIC): DOWN UNDER VO

ANNOUNCER (VO): ...Writing is power....

(CG): "WRITING IS POWER"

SHOT 10b

WHITE SCREEN

FADE IN: (CG) LIBRARY OF CONGRESS LOGO

ANNOUNCER (VO): Tell us your story.

(MUSIC): CONTINUES UNDER

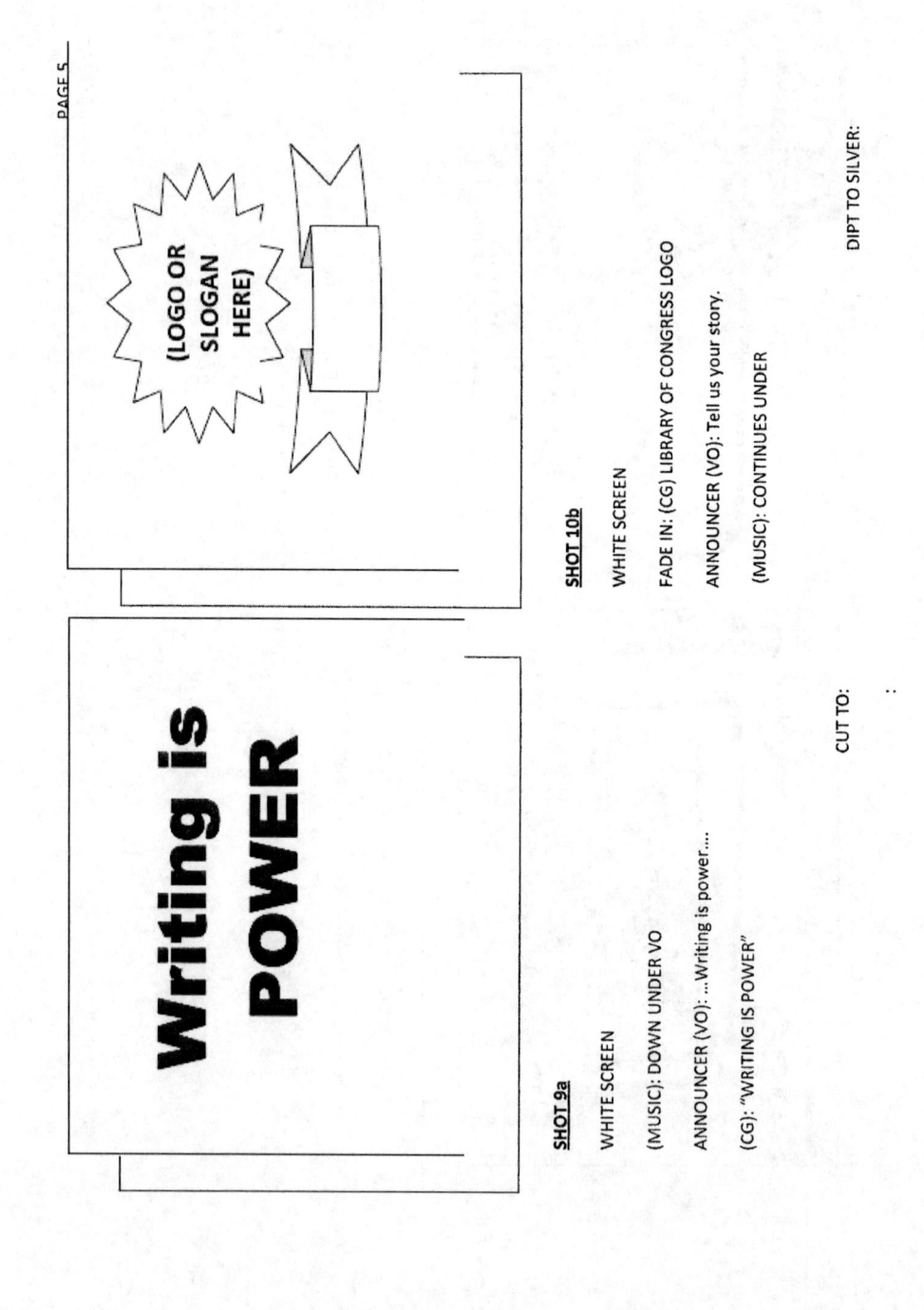

CUT TO:

DIPT TO SILVER:

Television Example 6/6

PAGE 6

www.loc.gov/ MemoryProject

SHOT 10c

WHITE SCREEN

FADE OUT (CG): LOC LOGO

ANNOUNCER (VO): ...Find out how with the American Memory Project at L-O-C.gov.

(MUSIC): FADES OUT

FADE IN (CG): www.loc.gov/memoryproject

FADE OUT

Television Announcement (In-Class Exercise)

Create a storyboard from an existing commercial. A good example of a basic commercial is this Monster commercial: http://www.youtube.com/watch?v=s4__xxmPwJI (or search YouTube under Monster commercial).

You will notice the commercial incorporates, music, NAT sound, some camera movement, and the Monster logo at the end.

Film Script: Pulp Fiction example (In-Class Exercise)

Looking at the script for "Pulp Fiction" as you watch the film is a great opportunity to study single column script format and handling visuals. Quentin Tarantino and Roger Avary won the 1996 Academy Award for Best Writing, Screenplay Written Directly for the Screen for this script. Please pardon the use of profanity and violence, but sometimes the best art can make us uncomfortable.

To get to the "Pulp Fiction" script, go to Google, search for 'Pulp Fiction script.' Start with Scene 2, and start the film at the end of the opening credits. Please notice:

1) Standards for single column scripts are exemplified in the Pulp Fiction script.

2) The use of various camera angles, camera movements, and editing choices creates unique impressions in the audience. These can be suggested in a strong script.

Final Project

For the final assignment, you will have the freedom to choose your own emphasis from several options. We have done many assignments in this course. You may choose to write a variety of projects for your final project. This is a way to provide the opportunity to hone the writing skills, which may best serve you in the future.

Regardless of the final project option you choose, everyone must complete a treatment. The treatment will be 2-5 pages. It will provide a rough overview and should give the reader the "big picture" of your script. You will find "treatment" details and requirements for each option.

You will also need to write a grade defense. This will be a one-paragraph description where you tell us what grade you feel you deserve and then provide evidence (participation, grades earned, attendance, events attended) for your grade.

In total, you will turn in three things for your final project:
-The final project
-The 2- to 5-page treatment
-The grade defense

Final Project Option 1: Radio, Television, or Film Script

For this option, you must present 10 to 15 minutes of a script (meaning 10-15 pages when considering the basic rule of 1 minute: 1 page). You can write a script for an episode of your favorite television program, propose a pilot episode of a new television series, draft a radio documentary report, or you could write a portion of a feature film. These options may be in any genre that you choose.

The partial script can be the first 10-15 pages of what could be a final script. It could also be the first several pages, several pages from the middle of the dramatic program, and the last several pages.

If you choose to write a film or television program proposal, we would prefer that you utilize single column script form. A good *free* program available online for long form script-writing is Celtx. You can go to www.celtx.com and download the program. The program is pretty intuitive, but here are some general guidelines (remember, you can always Google your favorite film or TV script and use that as a reference):

Start with "Scene Heading." If you do this, it will type in all caps for the setting of your scene (i.e. "INT. GRIFFIN'S BEDROOM - NIGHT").

After you hit Return, it will automatically shift to "Action" mode, where you type things that happen in the scene (i.e., "Griffin types an e-mail."). This is in normal non-caps text.

Then, you may want some dialogue, so hit the "Character" button. This will automatically indent to the center of the page and go to all caps for the name of the character who is speaking (i.e., "AMY").

Hit enter, and it switches to "Dialog" mode, which is slightly indented and in non-caps (i.e., "Griffin, would you get off the damn computer already?!").

If you hit enter again, it will go back to Character mode, so that you can seamlessly write dialogue.

That should be all you really need to know about it. There are a few other features, but this should be enough to get everyone started.

Here are a few quick screenwriting tips:

1) The first time you introduce a character's name, it is in all caps (i.e., "Suddenly, NICK walked in the door.").

2) Also, sound effects are in all caps (i.e., "The door bell RANG.").

3) In dialogue, if a character is speaking but not seen, write "(V.O.)" next to their name to denote "voice over."

1) In scene headings, use "INT." or "EXT." to denote an indoor or outdoor scene. You need a new heading every time the action moves to a different location.

The scriptwriting examples are courtesy of Griffin Hammond.

The treatment should begin with a paragraph that provides a thumbnail sketch of the entire project (introduction). The rest of the treatment should tell the whole story (not just what is covered in your partial script). If your treatment is for a dramatic film or program, try to keep discussion of character background and back-story to a minimum. If you are writing a treatment for a pre-existing program, assume your target audience is producers of the program.

The treatment for any of the script options should specifically describe the dramatic model and address each area within a separate paragraph (e.g., Protagonist, Will/Want, Dramatic Question, Realization, Complications (Progressive), Climax, Resolution). You should also include a conclusion paragraph. This treatment should also be 2-5 pages.

Final Project Option 2: Documentary Script

You will need to turn in 10-15 pages of script. The partial script can be the first 10-15 pages of what could be a final script. It could also be the first several pages, several pages from the middle of the dramatic program, or the last several pages.

For the script, you may use single script form or split page form. For example, you could prepare a three-part "special news report." The topic may be anything you choose, but it should be something one might legitimately expect to find on the 10:00 p.m. news broadcast on a local TV station. Each segment should be planned to last between 4 and 5 minutes. One segment (probably the first, but not necessarily) is to be completely scripted; the other two may be prepared in outline form (the treatment stage).

GUIDELINES:

Assume you got whatever shots you deem useful. The shots descriptions in the script function as a wishlist, of sorts.

If writing an investigative report, for the scripted segment: Provide an anchor lead-in to the report, and a tag at the end that teases the upcoming segments.

Make sure there is adequate description of the visual content. What are the viewers going to be seeing at all times?

Line up the audio with the visuals in a split-column script.

If sound bites are used in a news format, the leads to the bites must appear in the script and outcues. (The full content of the bites themselves should be placed on a separate page appended to the end of your script.)

Pay particular attention to the sequential development of the material, and to the use of appropriate and adequate transitions, so that the audience will know at all times where the story is headed.

If you are treating it as news, follow the appropriate layout form for television news writing. For the outlined segments: Write out the anchor lead and the tag/tease completely.

Provide a sequential outline for the story and a general description of the visual material, which will be used in each program element.

Overall, if writing news report: Make sure that there is an obvious and logical division of the overall story into the three segments, but at the same time each segment must stand on its own.

This assignment is an attempt to approximate the preparation of documentary material, but without the opportunity to collect actual video and audio material from which to cull and edit your story. In that sense it is less than a true documentary. Nevertheless, you should try, to the extent possible, to follow documentary principles. Let the real scenes and the real people tell the story as much as you can. Minimize your narration, but provide enough so that the audience can follow the progress of the story.

Consider particularly the structural principles of variety and pacing. Do not just do one long interview in each segment, but rearrange your material to get contrasting visuals and ideas in each segment.

For the treatment, give us some background information. What audience were you writing this story for? Is this a second day story? Did you use the dramatic model? If so, break down the dramatic model for us. If you did not use the dramatic model, what organizational structure did you use and why did this story warrant it? How did this class help you to choose/write these stories? Why was documentary the necessary means to tell this story? Etc...

Final Project Option 3: Public Relations Campaign

If you choose to propose a campaign, you will need to present TWO different pieces. For instance, if you did a campaign about a new product or service, you could include an inverted pyramid press release, a feature press release, a video press release, a radio story, and or a television spot. You could even do two 15-second "bumper" spots. "Bumper" spots are two announcements that run at the beginning and the end of a commercial break that complement one another.

If you consult outside sources, please include a reference page.

Please turn in a simple statement of what your project might be to your lab instructor approximately a month before the due date. This is simply a way for you to think about your proposal in advance, and a way for your lab instructor to give some feedback before you put in the bulk of your work for the final project.

During the last lab meeting, you will present your proposal to the rest of the class, as if presenting a pitch for your project. This presentation should be between 30 and 60 seconds. Please do not go any longer than this, because we could run out of time and not get to everyone's proposal.

If you choose this option, the treatment should be similar to a cover letter and will describe the overall campaign and describe, **in detail**, each of the individual pieces of your mass media campaign, why you chose them, and why they are the most effective choices.

The public relations project treatment should include the following: The first paragraph of the treatment should discuss the organization and the event/product being promoted. It should also preview both of the items contained within the press kit. Each subsequent paragraph should discuss these individual item, who the intended publics are, and where they would be taken for distribution with regards to local media. **A single slogan should unite the entire campaign.**

Final Project Option 4: Two 100-Point Assignments

Thus far, we have done a straight print news story, a feature story, a radio story, a television story, and a storyboard. This option allows you to choose any combination of TWO of these stories (e.g., 2 radio stories, or a straight print news story and a storyboard). You will be expected to follow the same criteria outlined in the previous assignments.

For the treatment, give us some background information. What audience were you writing this story for? Is this a second day story? Did you use the dramatic model? If so, break down the dramatic model for us. If you did not use the dramatic model, what organizational structure did you use and why did this story warrant it? How did this class help you to choose/write these stories? Etc...

Final Project Option 5: Short Issue Film/Public Service Announcement

As part of ISU Documentary Project's work with FILM YOUR ISSUE, we are attempting to organize Communication students to help produce a short issue film on those issues ISU students and faculty have deemed important enough to invest time and energy. This is a great way to promote and celebrate these activities. More information may be found on the ISU webpage a-z under American Democracy Project. These short films will help publicize these important contributions to ISU and the larger community.

The objective is to craft a 30 to 60 second short issue film/public service announcement (PSA-video) that illuminates an issue within our society, America, or globally, that touches hearts or changes lives. The style and content of your short film/PSA should attempt to focus on an organization doing work recognized by the ISU American Democracy Project. Any approach is welcome. Consider using honesty, humor, or seriousness. We encourage raw, open, honest expression, as well as inventive cinematic and creative approach. We are not looking for generic, polite "well-intentioned" brief films. We want a dynamic take on an issue, and cinematic style that progresses the idea you are presenting.

You may work on this project in a group. You should create a storyboard of your video project prior to filming. You will need to submit a working script (to keep your group on track), and a final script. This is Writing for Mass Media. We must write scripts.

(Dr. McHale says...) **Because this is designed to serve as a public service announcement, the piece should attract attention and motivate action. Include enough information to make this easy for those interested (i.e. web address, telephone number, info about contact person). Consider using graphics, logos, and/or on-screen font. The spot must not just inform, but persuade viewers to do something.**

Make your own rules. Break the rules. We want uncensored, unzipped, and truthful. You can use bold or rude comedy or searing harsh truth, you can be flashy or minimalist. Obviously, no pornography, nudity, overt swearing that violates FCC standards—you want your short film/public service announcement to be appropriate for broadcast.

- Length—"Issue films" should be no less than 30 seconds and no more than 60 seconds in length. The short digital films can be live action or animated. Keep in mind that TV-10 runs well produced public service announcements that are exactly 30 or 60 seconds in length.
- Personnel—Roles of writers/researchers, producer, director, editor, videographers, public relations liaison, technical liaison, and several others roles have to be filled in each team, likely several

roles for each contributor. As a group, you will be responsible for marshalling equipment and computer resources necessary to create your short issue film. Elect a team leader to keep your group on track and decide each person's role. The following jobs should be considered:

ROLES:

Researchers/Producers/Director: You need to start NOW. Who are the contact people for your chosen issue/organization? [See ISU American Democracy Project Webpage (off ISU webpage "A-Z"). The organization for which you are producing the piece needs to be contacted by contacted ASAP. When can your selected organization sit down for an interview on camera? Do they have existing footage you may use? [Any videotape made of the group's activities? Do they have still photos [extremely useful]? This person would likely be your team leader.

Editors: this person/s should own their own computer editing system and be familiar with editing video.

Videographers: this person/s should own or be able to borrow a camera from friends, family, or other departments.

Writers: Work on the treatment, and work with the producer and director to formulate the idea for the storyboard.

Public Relations Liaison: Build a press kit for the organization emphasizing the promo.

You will need to turn in a sheet on the LAST DAY OF LECTURE on which you evaluate the work/effort/and willingness to consider others' opinions of all the members of your group. Please evaluate their performance on a scale from 1-100.

These additional steps will help you finish your short issue film on schedule.
Please communicate with your instructor regarding:
1) your topic
2) your strategy
3) how you will attract attention
4) what action are you attempting to motivate and how you will motive.
5) your production schedule (see details below)
These five steps should be cleared with your lab instructor prior to filming.

After approval, you should create a treatment of your 30 or 60-second advocacy piece. In addition, create a storyboard from your script to communicate your ideas (for a shot wish list).

Please assign team roles. You also have a **Technical Liaison**. You may contact Brian Seay and/or Dr. Brent Simonds for technical advisement. You may find their email addresses on the ISU Homepage [Find People or Communication page]

<u>Documentary Project Example Production Schedule</u>
Rough Draft Due (one week before final due)
    a) Treatment
    b) Crew List
    c) Production Schedule
Final Production Schedule Due (two weeks before final due)
    a) Treatment
    b) Crew List
    c) Production Schedule (include exact dates, times, and locations)
    d) Location description (consider pros/cons of your location, e.g., sound, lighting, permission)
    e) Storyboard
    f) Shot wish list
    g) Include any Project Meeting dates, who attended, and discussion (Producer report)

We will test screen your video prior to uploading to any web site.
Last day of lab: Your Final Short Issue Film should be submitted to FYI.
You will need to make sure that you have a copy of a rough cut that can be played on the last day of lecture (DVD).

Grading Criteria:
<u>Overall impact</u>: dynamic/ persuasive / informational/ emotionally moving / focused message
<u>Originality</u>: concepts / ideas / format
<u>Cinematic Style</u>: camera angles/ editing/ acting/ direction/ lighting, etc.
<u>Structural Considerations:</u>
1) Does the short issue film have unity?
2) Variety?
3) An appropriate pace?
4) Is there a climax? (Were principles of drama utilized in the piece? Did it tell a story?
5) Does the piece Attract Attention?
6) Does the piece motivate action?

Format for uploading MUST BE CORRECT: (Brian Seay, Dr. Brent Simonds)
Live-action, animation, or a combination of both. Windows media file only.

Video resolution 320 by 240 250k bitrate.
Audio: stereo 2 pass CBR 48K.
The piece must be uploaded to filmyourissue.com before a grade will be issued.

For more information, visit the FYI - Film Your Issue web site. FYI will only accept digital submissions via email/Internet. FYI web page will provide instructions how to upload.

The treatment for this video project will specifically describe the dramatic model and address each area within a separate paragraph. (e.g., Protagonist, Will/Want, Dramatic Question, Realization, Complications (Progressive), Climax, Resolution) assuming you use the dramatic model (which would probably be a good way to organize this video – hint, hint). You should also include an introduction and conclusion paragraph. This treatment should also be 2-5 pages.

Final Project Option 6: Propose Your Own Final Project

You may have an idea for a final project that does not fit within the parameters of the five options listed above, but may be worthy of a final Media Writing project. If you feel you have an idea, be sure to pitch it to your lab instructor at least one month prior to the final project due date (as per the syllabus). Guidelines, details (for the treatment and assignment), and expectations will be discussed on a case-by-case basis.

Final Project FILM SCRIPT Treatment Example

Treatment for Sleeping Charlotte

By Kristi Zimmerman

December 2009

Synopsis:

This two hour romantic comedy is primarily a story about internal growth. It takes place in a midsized town in Wisconsin. The protagonist, Charlotte, suffers from a severe narcoleptic disorder. Her will and want is to be completely self sufficient. Complications to reach her goal revolve around her disorder and a blog she begins that becomes popular nationwide. During the climax, Charlotte is offered a high-paying job as a professional blogger. She declines and decides write a book, achieving self-sufficiency.

Act 1:

All major characters are introduced including Charlotte, her mother, Peg, her love interest, William, her best friend, Laura, and William's lover and boss, Kim. It is uncovered that Charlotte's illness is so intense it has crippled her social and working life. At twenty-six years old, she is unable to hold a well-paying job or live on her own. She does not have a license, boyfriend or many friends but she *does* have multiple degrees from the local university, paid for by various grants offered as a result of her rare disability. Doctors have not offered much medical assistance because the cause of her rare disorder is unknown. Effective treatment is unavailable, making it so difficult for her to control that she must "fall proof" every aspect of her life: baths instead of showers, helmets, the padding of every jagged edge in the house, etc.

She lives at home with her mother and works at the local library, which is the only job she's been able to maintain. A scene includes a montage of every job she's attempted: an assistant at a bakery, a Laundromat clerk, a custodian at a high school, and a representative at a call center. Each flashback includes a comical sleeping mishap that leads to her dismissal from the job.

Charlotte never smiles and hides her mouth when she talks because she has broken teeth (from falling). She wears a football helmet to protect her head when she falls and carries a pumpkin around with her everywhere she goes. Her mother advises her to carry it as a child so that she can maintain focus and not fall asleep during the day. The strategy is in vain but Charlotte gets very dependent on going everywhere with a pumpkin or watermelon (depending on the season) in hand. This is the first story CHARLOTTE blogs about in Act II.

Charlotte meets William, an advertising salesman, when he comes into the library to do research on a particular project relating to blogging on the internet. Charlotte becomes interested in both William and blogging after this meeting.

Plot Point 1:

Charlotte decides to start a blog about living with her disorder. The blog is anecdotal in quality and maintains a self-deprecating humor that, unbeknownst to Charlotte, begins attracting thousands of faithful readers nationwide.

Act 2:

Charlotte's blog becomes exponentially popular. She begins receiving emails from fans that encourage her to continue her humorous anecdotes. Many indicate that they relate to her embarrassing stories resulting from her infliction as they too have medical conditions that do not support a self-sufficient or "normal" lifestyle. She is flattered and completely in awe over the support she receives, but she is even more touched by the fact that her words and stories are giving people hope. She finally feels she has found her niche, and begins considering how the blog could potentially be her key to self-sufficiency.

Recalling her initial meeting with William dozens of times over in her head, she suddenly remembers him mentioning his occupation as an advertising salesman. After some research, Charlotte decides to contact William to assist her with advertising on her blog. Advertisements would pull in a bit of an income that would enable her to revamp her blog and do some of her own advertising to gain additional readers.

William and Charlotte meet to discuss her blog. Charlotte is stepping out of her comfort zone for this meeting, because it requires her to talk to William and "pitch" her own entrepreneurial opportunity. She covers her mouth while talking and is very nervous during their meeting, but there is something endearing about her that William finds himself attracted to. William agrees to help her find advertising and enthusiastically supports her idea.

As the two work together, it is disclosed that William has an unstable and secretive relationship with his boss, Kim. He does not tell Charlotte about this relationship. He begins to become fearful of disclosing this information because he finds himself falling for Charlotte and concerned it will ruin their friendship.

Charlotte's popularity rises and she becomes an overnight star in her community. Advertising on her website is substantial and she begins "guest blogging" on other sites as well. She is finally receiving a steady income and, after speaking with Laura about it, decides to quit her job at the library so she can focus on her blog.

Charlotte is ranked in the top 10 best blogs relating to dealing with disease. Her name appears in magazines, newspapers, and internet articles throughout the nation. She eventually is asked to be a guest on a popular morning talk show in New York and reluctantly accepts. She is fearful of being on national television because of her timid and introverted personality, but knows that it is something she needs to do to achieve her objective because the press coverage will be huge for her business. In the meantime, her relationship with William grows deeper and deeper and she realizes she has fallen in love with him.

Two weeks before Charlotte's debut on national television, she discovers William's relationship with Kim. Kim takes it upon herself to disclose the relationship to Charlotte in a rage of jealousy by coming into the library on Charlotte's last day of work. Charlotte is decorating the library for a Christmas party when Kim breaks the news about the secret relationship. Charlotte does not believe it at first, but Kim provides proof with images of a vacation she went on with William weeks before.

Plot Point 2:

Charlotte discovers the relationship between William and his boss. She is completely devastated and falls to despair. She stops blogging and will not see or talk to anyone. William makes multiple attempts to see her and talk to her but Charlotte refuses. He sends gifts (a new laptop to blog on) and messages to no avail.

Climax:

Charlotte's mother has a conversation with her about her despair the night before the talk show. Charlotte has not packed and indicates she will not be going on the show. After a touching scene between the mother and daughter, Charlotte is convinced to go on the popular talk show. She flies in the next day, and during the show another guest offers her a job as a blogger / journalist in L.A. This offer will monetarily allow Charlotte to live self-sufficiently. The position offers dental benefits to fix her broken teeth as well as medical treatment to subside her narcoleptic symptoms. She surprisingly declines the offer. Charlotte knows she can accomplish these things on her own by writing a book - something she has always wanted to accomplish on her own. She can then stay close to her mother and help support her as she builds her income. She smiles on the program, showing her teeth for the first time. William is impressed as he watches from home.

Conclusion:

Charlotte returns to Wisconsin and immediately begins writing her book. She makes amends with William but does not go back to him. Her pre-existing fame sells her thousands of copies, earning her enough money to do everything she dreamed: self sufficiently.

Meaning/Purpose:

This is a story that faces the dramatic influences overnight fame can have on someone who never really expected or wanted it to begin with. It also reminds us to be grateful for the simple things - a family, a home and a job. These small facets of life are often taken for granted, and for someone like Charlotte, they are the small details that build her vision of "happily ever after."

Example courtesy of Kristi Zimmerman.

BIBLIOGRAPHY

Bruzzi, S. (2006). *New Documentary.* New York: Talyor & Francis.

Giddens, A. (1993). *New Rules of Sociological Method* (2nd ed.). Stanford: Stanford University Press.

King, S. (2000). *On Writing: A Memoir of the Craft.* New York: Simon & Schuster.

McKee, R. (1997). *Story: Substance, Structure, Style, and the Principles of Screenwriting.* New York: HarperCollins.

Sandman, P. M., Rubin, D. M., Sachsman, D. B. (1982). *Media: An Introductory Analysis of American Mass Communications* (3rd ed.). Englewood Cliffs, NJ: Prentice-Hall.

Strunk Jr., W., White, E. B. (1918). *The Elements of Style.* New York: Longman. http://www.cs.vu.nl/~jms/doc/elos.pdf

Tarantino, Q. (1993). *Pulp Fiction.* Film script draft. Movie-Page.com. http://www.godamongdirectors.com/scripts/pulp.shtml

Thompson, H. (1999). *Hell's Angels: A Strange and Terrible Saga.* (Later printing edition) New York: Modern Library.

Walters, R. L. (1994). *Broadcast Writing: Principles and Practice.* New Style: McGraw-Hill, Inc.

Weaver, R. M., Johannesen, R. L. (1985). *Language is Sermonic: Richard M. Weaver on the Nature of Rhetoric.* Baton Rouge: LSU Press.

Yopp, J. J., McAdams, K. C. (2007). *Reaching Audiences: A Guide to Media Writing.* (4th ed.) Boston: Pearson.

INDEX

1-shot, 153, 154, 260
2-shot, 154, 260
2TAL, 154

A Clockwork Orange, 56
abbreviations, 57, 60, 63, 64, 65, 110, 118, 130, 132, 215
acoustical setting, 118
active voice, 44, 45, 50, 52, 70, 105, 107, 116, 215
actual message, 9, 11, 12, 17, 22, 50
active protagonist, 207
actualities, 31, 33, 102, 114, 116, 117, 176, 194, 254, 260
addresses, 60, 61, 63, 65, 110, 173, 235, 281
advertising, 2, 11, 13, 15, 16, 46, 68, 81, 83, 86, 98, 154, 157-165, 167, 176, 178, 203, 212, 216, 285; aural elements, 160; branding, 158-160; considerations 161-162; format, 160; functions, 157-158; infomercials, 165; motivating action, 163; organization, 163-164; persuasive appeals, 162-163; pre-recorded spots, 164; types, 158
affective leads, 148
Affleck, Ben, 26, 49
Amrine, Joe, xii, 172-173, 175, 190, 191, 193
Amusing Ourselves to Death, 211
ANC, 149, 257-260
anecdotal leads, 92, 149
angle on, 123, 135
angle, 6, 24, 88, 115, 122, 123, 133, 135, 136, 148, 149, 246, 252, 255, 259, 260, 271, 281
antiplot, 204, 206-208
antithesis, 80
Apatow, Judd, 202
archplot, 204, 206, 207
artificial need, 82-86, 162
artificial sound, 118
Associated Press Stylebook, 86, 221, 226, 232; abbreviations, 60-65; addresses, 60, 61, 63, 65; as a reference resource, 61-65; dates, 60, 62-63, 65; money, 60, 61, 65; names, 60, 63; numbers, 61; punctuation, 64-65; roman numerals, 64; statistics, 62; times, 63; titles, 64-65; titles of works, 64
attribution, 30, 47, 48, 50, 58, 71, 101, 107, 108, 110, 112, 116, 148, 227
audience, 1, 4, 7, 9, 11, 12, 13-14, 15
audience involvement, 187

b-roll shots, 192
backdoor pilots, 182
backgrounders, 175
BOC, 149, 257-260
boom, 106, 125
branding, 158-160
Bridges, Jeff, 207
brights, 94
broadcast media, 68, 101-112; attribution, 107, 108, 110, 112, 116, 148; format, 106-107; format writing guidelines, 107-109; gatekeeping, 111; leads, 107; style, 104-106; writing considerations, 107-109

camera, vii, 6, 20, 29, 32, 75, 76, 106, 122-125, 131-133, 135, 138, 140, 141, 150, 151, 153, 176, 187, 189, 244, 254, 260, 270, 271, 280; angle, 123; directions, 132; distance, 122-123; movement, 124-125
Capra, Frank, 186
causality, 206, 208
Celtx, 141, 273
channel, 6, 9, 12-14, 20, 22, 86, 107, 111, 113, 157, 162, 168, 189
character, 203-204
character arch, 204
characteristics of good writing, 18-20
characterization, 203
chronological format, 90, 91, 139
cinéma vérité, 190, 194
clarity, viii, 10, 11, 18, 19, 22, 34, 37, 40, 41, 44-46, 50, 55, 58, 59, 63, 96, 102, 104, 105, 109, 111, 121, 129, 131, 136, 138, 152, 165, 169, 215, 223
climax, 2, 4, 7, 21, 52, 67, 69, 72, , 73, 89, 90, 92, 93, 102, 103, 107, 111, 113, 114, 119, 121, 147, 150, 156, 157, 164, 170, 179, 189, 197, 202, 204, 205, 217, 219, 241, 274, 281, 284
Clooney, George, 201, 205, 206, 208
close-shot, 122, 123
close-up, 123, 124, 126, 136
closed ending, 207
coincidence, 208
commercials, 1, 6, 16, 21, 24, 53, 117, 119, 121, 123, 129, 132, 133, 145, 157-165, 171, 217
Communication Process, 9-22
comparison format, 164
completeness, 46, 51, 96, 112, 218
complication, 2, 4, 5, 21, 89, 90, 92, 93, 95, 103, 107, 114, 121, 146, 147, 150, 168, 169, 182, 189, 197, 204, 205, 215, 217, 274, 282, 284
compositional style, 39, 49, 65
concept formulation, 23-24
concision, 36, 51, 53, 54, 96, 102, 112, 169, 217
consistent plot, 208
convenience, 162
convergence, vii, 12, 20, 111
copyright, 98-99
correctness, 46, 51, 96, 106, 112, 218
crisis communication, 167, 177-178
culture of consumerism, 82-86
cut, 125, 137
cut-aways, 192

Damon, Matt, 26, 50
dates, 60, 62, 65, 135, 169, 281
deadlines, viii, ix, 23, 30, 104, 180
decoding, 17, 18, 49
defocusing, 125
delayed identification leads, 192
descriptive leads, 92, 149
dialectic process, 80
dialogue, 9, 21, 58, 118, 130, 134, 135, 139, 140, 141, 160, 192, 204, 209, 254, 262, 273
DiCaprio, Leonardo, 77
diffused message, 11
direct address leads, 93, 149

Mass Media Writing: Telling a Good Story Well 291

disaster story, 149
dissolve, 125, 140, 162
distance, 118, 122, 123
documentary, viii, 19, 24, 37, 76, 80, 98, 99, 121, 134, 146, 152, 172, 173, 175, 185-195, 201, 221, 273, 275, 279, 281; b-roll, 185, 192, 254; characteristics, 187-188; drama, 189; dramatic re-creation, 194; logging, 192-193; public relations, 194-195; research, 191; storytelling, 191-192; treatment to script, 190; types, 188-189; writing narration, 193-194
documentary point of view, 185-186
dolly, 124
doublespeak, 59, 106
drafting, 23, 35, 38, 191
drama, 1-279
Dramatic Model, 1-8, 3, 89, 90, 114, 149, 156, 197, 206, 217, 236, 241, 274, 276, 278, 282
dramatic principles, 5, 89, 168, 198, 204
dramatic re-creation, 185, 192, 194, 195
duration, 198, 199

E-Z NEWS, 153, 260-261
editing, viii, xi, 36, 44, 54, 56, 58, 67; effect and cause sequence, 149, 150
emic knowledge, 29
encoding, 17-18
episodic, 179, 180, 183
ethics, 55, 75-86, 145, 154-155; ethics in advertising, 81-86; ethical reference to a group, 81; journalistic ethics, 75
etic knowledge, 29
external conflict, 207
eye-level shot, 123

Facebook, 205, 212-213, 214, 215, 218
fact sheets, 13, 173, 175
fade-in, 125
fade-out, 125
false advertising, 98
favoring, 135, 141
feature film, viii, x, 1, 7, 14, 24, 51, 109, 126, 129, 133, 172, 179, 197-210, 273; character, 203-204; dramatic principles, 197-198; genre, 201-203; research, 200-201; setting, 198-200; story design, 205-206; types of plots, 206-209
feature lead, 92-93
feature print, 87-96; narrative approach, 89-90; organizational styles, 90-92; types of print stories, 93-96
feature story (television), 149-150
feedback, 9, 14-15, 22, 101, 102, 104, 220, 247, 277
film editing, 124, 126-127, 134, 161, 176, 192, 271, 280, 281; controlling tension, 127
Final Draft, 141
first amendment law, 97
follow-up, viii, 95, 252
franchise, 181-182
free speech, 78, 97-98
Freeman, Morgan, 201

gatekeeping, 111, 115, 116
genre, 51, 68, 188, 189, 197, 201-203, 273

Giddens, Anthony, 77, 289
Glover, Danny, 37, 190, 193
Gore, Al, 189
grammar, 33, 34, 35, 36, 39, 44-46
graph, 48
gratification functions, 85, 145, 155

high-angle shot, 123
historical stories, 94
hour glass format, 90, 91

impact leads, 148
impact, 115
implied consent, 31
inconsistent plot, 208
indecency, 97
information gathering, 23, 26
infomercials, 165
inserts, 192
intended message, 11, 12, 16, 17, 18, 22, 50
interference, 9, 10-12, 76
internal conflict, 207
internal laws of probability, 199
interviewing, 30-34, 117, 161
inverted pyramid, 14, 35, 48, 51, 52, 67-73, 87, 91, 92, 96, 104, 174, 175, 223, 225, 227, 230, 236, 241, 277
investigative story, 149

journalistic ethics, 75
juxtaposition, 118, 119, 121, 126, 127, 209

King Jr., Martin Luther, 185, 186
King, Stephen, 39, 40, 43, 45, 49, 52, 57
Kubrick, Stanley, 56

leads, 69-70
lebenswelt, 75, 76, 79, 81, 86
legal issues, 97-100
level of conflict, 199
libel, 97, 98, 100
linear plot, 208
listing, 23, 35, 38
live news, 150, 151
LOC, 149, 257-260
location, 87, 88, 94, 116, 117, 123, 126, 132, 135, 146, 151, 157, 191, 192, 198, 199, 274, 281
location stories, 94
logging, 185, 192-193, 195
logging sheets, 192
logos, 163, 262, 279
long-shot, 122, 123, 127
low-angle shot, 123
loyalty, 162

magnitude, 103, 115
Malcolm X, 186

map format, 90, 91-92
master scene, 133, 135
McKee, Robert, 7, 8, 26, 142, 198, 200, 203, 206
media advisories, 175
medium-shot, 122, 255
message types, 16-17
method of transition, 140, 141
mini climax, 27
mini complications, 27
miniplot, 204, 206, 207, 208
misappropriation, 99, 100, 222
mobile communication, 211, 214, 217,
money, 19, 193
Moore, Michael, 19, 186, 188
music as sound, 119

NAM, 149, 154, 257-260
names, 19, 43, 44, 58, 60, 63, 65, 107, 108, 109, 110, 134, 138, 139, 154, 169, 223, 226, 234, 256, 260
narration, 151, 152, 153, 160, 161, 185, 193-194, 195, 276
narrative/news value hybrid format, 90, 149, 150
natural sound, 118, 151, 153, 161
nature documentary, 188
news peg and nut graph format, 90, 91
news values, 14, 15, 68, 69, 89, 90, 92, 94, 103, 113, 115, 119, 147, 149, 150
news writing computer programs, 145, 153, 155
nonlinear plot, 208
novelty, 162
numbers, 20, 60, 61, 62, 63, 65, 110, 118, 135, 136, 137, 138, 152, 173, 213

obituary, 95
objectivity, 76-80
obscenity, 97
observation, 28-29, 30, 31
off-mike, 118 [AP is wrong; it should be off-mic]
off-the-record information, 32
online research, 27-28
on-mike, 118
open ending, 207
opinion pieces, 55, 95-96, 149, 243
oral style, 101, 104-106, 108
OTS, 153, 257-260
over the shoulder shot, 136, 153, 255, 260

pace, 10, 24, 72, 110, 116, 137, 155, 187, 198
package (PKG), 151, 154, 182, 254, 260
panning, 124, 125
paradigm, ix, 58, 87, 89, 126, 127, 149, 168, 175, 181, 236
parallelism, 54
parenthetic directions, 139
participant observation, 29
passive protagonist, 207
period, 198
personality stories, 93
persuasive appeals, 162, 163, 253, 263
pilots, 182, 273
pitch (acoustic), 118; pitch, 172, 182, 190, 277, 283, 286
Pitt, Brad, 38, 201
plagiarism, 99-100

planning, 23, 34, 38, 171, 175
plot point, 205, 206, 208, 209, 285, 287
plot types, 206-207
poetic function, 126, 127
point of view, 24, 136
polishing, 38
political documentary, 188
Postman, Neil, 211
preliminary page, 134
principle of creative limitations, 200
print stories, 87, 90, 93, 96, 246
problem-solution format, 163-164
product placement, 159
product-as-star, 164
promo, 154, 158
protagonist, 2, 3, 5, 7, 89, 90, 93, 103, 107, 114, 121, 147, 150, 165, 168, 185, 188, 189, 190, 193, 197, 202, 204-217, 241, 242, 275, 282, 284
public relations, viii, ix, 13, 32, 33, 51, 60, 65, 68, 98, 167-178, 185, 190, 194, 195, 212, 216, 221, 277, 279, 280; crisis communication, 177; stages of writing, 171-172
public service announcement (PSA), 116, 158, 221, 253, 262, 279
publics, 167-178; media as a public, 172-173
Pulp Fiction, 187, 200, 221, 271
punctuation, 11, 46-48, 60, 64-65, 105, 108, 117, 130, 216, 218, 223, 225, 228
purposes of communication, 15-16, 21, 106, 161, 213, 222, 244; to entertain, 16, 161; to inform, 21, 161; to persuade, 16, 161

question leads, 92, 148
quotation leads, 93
quotations, 33, 34, 43, 64, 70, 71, 72; direct and indirect 70-71

radio news, 113-119, 160, 168, 221, 246, 254; handling sound, 118-119; leads, 113; news values, 115-116; research, 116-117; script mechanics, 117-118; story organization, 113-114; style, 116
Rashomon Effect, 28
realization, 3-4, 22, 89, 90, 103, 107, 114, 147, 150, 168, 197, 217, 274, 282
recorded news, 151, 154
redemption plots, 4, 15, 201
Reiner, Rob, 201
Reiss, Mike, 181
research, 24-36, 38, 51, 68, 81, 94, 99, 103, 113, 116, 119, 171, 173, 175, 177, 185, 191, 192, 200, 209
research strategies, 25-34; facts, 26; imagination, 26; memory, 26; observation, 28-30
residual message, 17, 95
resolution, 4, 89, 90, 93, 114, 179, 180, 189, 197, 215, 216, 241, 274, 281, 282
reverse angle, 136
rhetorical question leads, 148
rhythm, 118
roman numerals, 60, 64, 110

safety, 15, 44, 162, 177
Sandler, Adam, 202, 208
Sandman, Peter, 78-80, 289

scarcity, 162
scene description, 136, 138-141
scene heading, 138, 140, 273, 274
Schrader, Paul, 29
scratch-tracks, 194
scripting visuals, 129-143; formatting issues, 132-141; general considerations, 129-130; single camera layout, 132-136; split-page layout, 132; storyboards, 130-131
secondary pages, 134-135
sender, 9, 12-13, 14, 15, 22
sequence, 25, 35, 51, 67, 90, 101, 104, 107, 149, 150, 165, 181; dramatic sequence, 186, 205, 215; dream sequences, 125; editing, 126-127
sermonic function, 16, 161, 170
setting, 137, 138, 198-200, 201, 209, 273
shared information, 111
sharing, 23, 31, 36, 37, 213, 214, 220
shot-by-shot, 133, 135
significance, 90, 115, 150
single camera layout, 132-141; preliminary page, 134; rules 136-140; secondary pages, 134, 135; terms, 135-136
situation format, 164
slice-of-life documentary, 188-189
slogans, 17, 163, 262, 263, 277
slogos, 163
slug, 117, 130, 138, 140, 141, 142, 154, 225, 227, 231, 247
snob-appeal, 163
social media, 211-220
soft news, 149
SOT, 151, 153, 154, 193, 254, 260
sound, 30, 31, 49, 65, 72, 88, 102, 105, 107, 108, 113, 117-119, 130, 131, 138, 151, 153, 154, 160, 161, 191-195, 233, 247, 253, 254, 260, 262, 270, 273, 275, 281
sound effects, 118, 119, 138, 160, 161, 253, 262, 273,
sound on tape list, 192
special effects, 8, 151, 164
spectacle, 162
split-page layout, 132, 152, 160, 261, 275
spokesperson, 117, 160, 164
sports documentary, 188, 189
spots, 53, 130, 132, 133, 157-165, 277
SS, 153, 255, 260
staccato leads, 93
staff ladder, 179, 182, 183
stage direction, 136, 138
statistics, 47, 60, 62, 65, 70, 72, 177
stories on speeches, 95
story design, 197, 204, 205-206, 209
story events, 205
storyboards, 126, 130-131, 160
straight leads (summary or comprehensive), 69-70, 113, 148
strategic ambiguity, 11, 19, 121
Structural Considerations, 1, 6-7, 9, 21, 72, 102, 109, 111, 113, 114, 119, 121, 145, 147, 157, 163, 170, 189, 206, 210, 218
structural pre-recorded spots, 164
structuration, 77
Strunk and White, 18, 36, 39, 40, 41, 46, 49-53, 58, 60, 65, 88, 116
summary leads, 69, 113
swish-pan, 125
synthesis, 80

talent, 104, 105, 106, 109, 110, 114, 117, 118, 129, 130, 132, 139, 142, 143, 145, 149, 152, 153-155, 161, 164, 253, 255
talking points, 33, 175, 176
Tarantino, Quentin, 12, 133-143, 187, 200, 203, 210, 271, 289
target audience, 13, 14, 68, 159, 161, 162, 165, 170, 236, 253, 263, 273
Taxi Driver, 29
television entertainment, 179-183; proposals, 182; rules, 180-181; staff ladder, 182-183
television news, 1, 8, 10, 51, 90, 109, 110, 132, 145-156, 160, 168, 172, 174, 176, 195, 221, 225, 254, 257-258, 259, 260-261; building blocks, 152-153; ethics, 154-155; leads, 148-149; organization, 149-151; scheduling, 145-146; types, 150-151; writing stories, 147
The Elements of Style, 39, 49, 50, 289; compositional style, 39, 49-52; grammar, 39, 44-48; punctuation, 46-48; vocabulary, 39, 40-44
theoretical consideration, 9-22
thesis, 80
Thompson, Hunter S., 29, 289
three-act structure, 181, 205
throw-away leads, 149
tilt, 124, 125
timbre, 118
timeliness, 69, 90, 108, 113, 115, 116, 147, 150
times, 60, 61, 63, 198
titles of works, 60, 64
titles, 63, 64, 108, 109, 110, 116, 132, 234
Transactional Model of Communication, 10, 14, 220
transitions, 72, 94, 105, 114, 119, 125-126, 130, 131, 136, 140, 225, 262, 275
treatment, 24, 182, 185, 190, 195, 209, 221, 272, 274, 275, 277, 278, 280, 281, 283, 284-287
truck, 125
Twitter, 212, 213-220
two shot, 131, 136, 192, 255

umbrella leads, 148
unity, 6, 21, 22, 54, 72, 102, 109, 111, 114, 121, 147, 155, 157, 170, 189, 206, 219, 281

value-economy, 162
variety, 6, 21, 22, 34, 45, 51, 53, 70, 72, 102, 104, 105, 108, 111, 114, 121, 122, 147, 151, 153, 156, 157, 170. 175. 182, 189, 192, 193, 206, 219, 255, 262, 272, 276, 281
video news releases, 176
VO, 153
VO/SOT, 151, 153, 254, 257-258, 260-261
vocabulary, 39, 40, 41, 44, 48, 58, 87, 103, 105, 114
vocal cues, 105, 114
volume, 118

Walters, Roger L., 16, 186, 194, 289
Weaver, Richard M., 16, 170, 289
web, vii, x, 12, 15, 20, 22, 27, 28, 43, 45, 68, 176, 178, 183, 211-220, 225, 253, 254, 263, 279, 280, 281, 286
White, E. B., see Strunk and White, Elements of Style, 289
wide-shots, 136
will/want, 3, 90, 150, 197, 274, 282
Winfrey, Oprah, 31, 132, 169

wipe, 125, 126, 262
world perspective, 75

YouTube, 98, 168, 212, 270

zoom, 123, 124, 187, 188